STUART McCABE

Queen Margaret Tudor

The story of a courageous but forgotten monarch.

STUART McCABE

Queen Margaret Tudor

The story of a courageous but forgotten monarch

MEREO
Cirencester

Mereo Books

1A The Wool Market Dyer Street Cirencester Gloucestershire GL7 2PR
An imprint of Memoirs Publishing www.mereobooks.com

Queen Margaret Tudor: 978-1-86151-614-5

First published in Great Britain in 2016
by Mereo Books, an imprint of Memoirs Publishing

The address for Memoirs Publishing Group Limited can be found at
www.memoirspublishing.com

The Memoirs Publishing Group Ltd Reg. No. 7834348

The Memoirs Publishing Group supports both The Forest Stewardship Council®
(FSC®) and the PEFC® leading international forest-certification organisations. Our
books carrying both the FSC label and the PEFC® and are printed on FSC®-certified
paper. FSC® is the only forest-certification scheme supported by the leading
environmental organisations including Greenpeace. Our paper procurement policy
can be found at www.memoirspublishing.com/environment

Typeset in 9/13pt century Schoolbook
by Wiltshire Associates Publisher Services Ltd. Printed and bound in Great Britain
by Printondemand-Worldwide, Peterborough PE2 6XD

In memory of my parents, Maud Morgan from
Clee St Margaret, Shropshire and
Peter Flannigan McCabe from Douglasdale.

INTRODUCTION

Queen Margaret II of Scotland (1489-1541) is often misunderstood and underestimated by historians, her actions throughout her life dismissed as irrelevant or as consequences of events out of her control. Her motivations are often judged as foolish, self-seeking, corrupt or treacherous, without taking into context the fog of political and national forces that obscured her life.

The daughter of Henry VII, the victor against Richard III at Bosworth Field, and the brother of Henry VIII, Queen Margaret has been near forgotten in the story of the Tudor Dynasty established by her father. Intended to bring a lasting peace between Scotland and England by marrying the cultured and warlike James IV of Scotland, she had to become more than a symbolic queen after the death of her husband at Flodden in 1513. Alone and vulnerable, she was beset by powerful men who sought to cast her aside and gain political power by possessing her infant son James V. These men were the warring nobles and feudal lords described by the Earl of Rothes as 'bound by ropes of sand', difficult individuals to command by legal or royal authority. And religion provided no sanctuary for reason and negotiation, as leading churchmen donned sharpened weapons to do battle against rival contenders for the vacant benefices. Margaret would also have to contend with intrigues with the popes of Rome and the kings of France, as well as the imperialist intrigues of her brother Henry.

A youthful, inexperienced queen without an army, she had to grow up fast and become a stateswoman. To defend her rights and those of her son, she formed alliances with powerful and dangerous men, whether through love, as with the young Earl of Angus, or out of necessity, with former enemies such as the Duke of Albany, the French aristocrat and cousin to the King of Scotland. Her relationship with her brother Henry VIII was troublesome, and it was his clumsy and inept policies that gave her the most problems. Whether through jealousy or resentment, Henry treated his older sister like his young sister, not as an equal. Yet despite many heartbreaks, multiple deceptions, defeats and victories, Queen Margaret had the determination to win through, and she would display these qualities in many dangerous situations. Throughout she would fight tooth and nail with whatever weapons she had available to free her son from her enemies. Success would come eventually, and through her efforts Scotland would produce in James V a strong, ruthless and independent-minded King.

This book sets out to tell the story of Queen Margaret and her many struggles to ensure the survival and full regal rights of her son. It is an important story, as she would give birth to a son and a daughter whose linages would eventually lead to the Union of the Crowns in 1603 and the establishment of the British state.

CONTENTS

Introduction

Chapter One

HAIL ROSE, BOTH RED AND WHITE: 1503-1515

In 1502, the Treaty of Perpetual Peace was agreed by King James IV (1473-1513) of Scotland and King Henry VII of England, heralding the prospect of a new era of co-operation between two nations who for over two hundred years had been fierce enemies. Henry ratified the treaty on January 24th 1502 at Richmond Palace, with Robert Blacadder, Bishop of Glasgow, Patrick Hepburn, Earl of Bothwell, and Andrew Forman, postulate of Moray, signing on behalf of James. Further to the treaty a marriage was agreed between Henry VII's daughter Margaret and the King of Scotland. Henry pledged a £10,000 dowry and James would gift his bride a payment of £1,000 per year and lands and castles which would provide revenues of £6,000 per year. She would be allowed to bring 24 English servants, and upon James' death she would receive £2,000 per year.

James, the son of James III, had taken the crown of Scotland after the death of his father following the battle of Sauchieburn on June 11th, 1488. Whilst this dynastic dispute was initially the result of nobles aggrieved at being excluded from the Royal councils and the government of James III, the young prince would take responsibility for the death of his father and as an act of penance took to wearing an iron belt around his midriff for the rest of his life. [1]

As a young King, James managed to gradually take control of government and impose royal authority across Scotland, even into the Western Isles and Highlands. By 1495 he would assume personal rule. James IV was a prince with a keen interest in bringing renaissance ideas and styles into Scotland, whether through architecture, art, poetry, science or fashions. There was an encouraging of literary works and ideas, especially Latin and vernacular, and James would encourage and offer patronage to gifted poets, writers and artists such as William Dunbar, Gavin Douglas and others.

James sought to improve education in Scotland; one of his early promotions was that of establishing the University of Aberdeen in support of the Bishop of Aberdeen. He himself could speak French, Latin, Flemish, Spanish, Italian, German and Gaelic. He also enjoying the traditional aristocratic sports of hunting and hawking, tournaments, jousting, cards and dice, boating, golf, staged plays, the antics of comic clowns and listening to musicians, and he could play a range of musical instruments. He would also devote some considerable efforts to crown finance, and employed financial experts to develop a system for proper collection of customs and rents, as well as collecting revenue from feudal lands. Improved finances allowed him to build up Scotland's military capabilities, such as the land and naval forces.

Within Scotland there was a feudal system where the crown owned vast tracts of lands which were leased out to the nobility in return for payment of taxes and military service. Succession was through primogeniture, through the line of eldest son. The next layer of power below the King was the Dukes and Earls, who parcelled out lands to lords, barons, and knights. Below them were farmers, tenants and householders. The rulers also appointed sheriffs, who administered crown-owned regions called sheriffdoms. They were responsible for collecting taxes and rents, and acted as magistrates by trying civil and criminal cases. Overseeing the sheriffs were Justiciars, who were expected to tour the sheriffdoms twice a year. There were other royal positions such as the chancellor, responsible for the great seal and checking all charters, documents and treaties before authorising them with the King's seal. There was also constables, chamberlains, treasurers, comptrollers, justice clerks, clerks of council, advocates, secretaries and others with various important roles to play with the government administration. [2]

The Scottish Parliament would become known as the Three Estates, as it was made up of nobility, cleric and burgesses. The Parliament could be called at different parts of the country, whether Perth in Fife or Edinburgh, Stirling or Linlithgow Palace south of Firth of Forth. In order to introduce legislation the monarch needed the votes of the majority within parliament. However as a parliament would take time to call, the Privy Council, also known as Lords of the Council, would effectively become the government. The Privy Council was a body which existed to assist the King or Queen with advice, and made up of nobles and churchmen. The numbers could range from ten to twenty, depending on circumstances. [3] The priority of this council was to ensure stability in the realm and consider matters of national and international importance. It would act on issues such as treaties, war, peace, trade, criminality, economics, and religion. It would also consider judicial and civil disputes if they were potentially a danger to national security. [4]

Representing the economic arm of Scottish were the burghs, towns built on crown land and confirmed by charter. Exempt from feudal fees, they were allowed to establish their own markets. They produced goods that were traded or sold with other burghs, or exported to other countries. They were virtually autonomous entities and could form police forces, elect magistrates called baillies and form their own assemblies. The burghs developed into powerful mercantile townships and formed strong economic ties and treaties with European townships and trading cartels. [5]

The Scottish Church was another hierarchical power structure. At the top end were the Archbishoprics of St Andrews and of Glasgow, and below them bishops, and then abbots and parish priests. The pope originally had the power to appoint bishops and all church appointments, until Innocent VIII conceded the right of the monarch of Scotland to nominate candidates, for which eight months was granted to allow for consideration. In time the Scottish rulers would effectively pick appointees. The Scottish Church was powerful and wealthy, owning nearly half the land rents. From the agricultural produce of each parish a tenth, or tithe, was granted for the functioning of the parish church. The church also had political influence, in that appointments to church positions could be offered to the members of powerful families in return for protection and promotion. [6]

James had a curiosity about science, especially military science. Scottish kings did not have standing or contracted armies, although they had the power to call a muster if the country was under threat, after approval by council or parliament. Men were obliged to serve free for thirty-forty days, and to bring their own supplies and equipment and outfit themselves depending on status. Each gentleman would be expected to show with helmet, armour, sword, dagger and pike, while those without adequate resources or land could be supplied with equipment by sheriffs and baillies. Yeomen between 16 and 60 years of age were to bring bows and arrows or axes, swords, pike and shields, targes bound with leather or board. The pike was the most important weapon for the infantry, allowing men to stand side by side, shoulder to shoulder, presenting to an enemy a thick array of pikes in a formation called a schiltron.

Training was ordered four times per year at local

wappenshaws, or weapon shows. Drills and manoeuvres were practised, especially dealing with how to effectively form up a troop of archers, a troop of horse or a division of pikes. Parliament also enacted laws requiring that during each holiday, and within each parish, archery was to be practised by the inhabitants at especially-designated archery ranges called "butts". Anyone who did not attend these showings was fined. This led to some limited successes in building up an archery arm, yet the pastimes of golf and football were more popular with the people. The Gaels of the Highlands and Isles used the bow and arrow, a traditional weapon amongst them, and also more suited to their form of warfare, where in battle arrows would be loosed towards an enemy before a charge with sword, spear and targe. The nobility provided troops of horse, yet more often than not the Scots nobles would fight on foot alongside their men during battles. The borderers rode small horses or ponies that gave them the ability to move fast during a campaign, to scout or skirmish or hinder supplies to the enemy. [7]

James IV believed in the value of artillery in modern warfare and would build up an impressive train of ordinance based on European designs and of various sizes. The first cannons were probably exported from France or Flanders, although James financed factories and home-grown production. Government attempts to enact into law the furnishing of carts of war to carry ordinance, the casting of cannon and the training of gunners by the nobility did not lead to the building up of a large land army of artillery. The reluctance was due no doubt to expense and the infrequency of English invasions. The privateers and pirates preying on English and European shipping were more skilled at the use of cannon, which was a vital arm for survival in the seas. In 1506-11 James IV sanctioned the construction of three massive warships, one of which, called the *Michael,* wasa vessel of massive proportions. This ship was measured at 240 feet long and thirty-six wide, with the sides ten feet thick. Pitscottie claims that to construct these vessels, apart from wood from Fife, wood was also exported from Norway at great expense to the treasury. The

Michael had 32 guns as well as a range of smaller artillery such as serpents, falcons, hag buts and crossbows. The ship capacity was 1,000 men including 300 mariners and 120 gunners. [8]

Architecture also interested him, and he sponsored adaptations and modifications to Linlithgow Palace, Edinburgh Castle, Stirling Castle, Holyrood Palace and other buildings, where new English, French and European styles were employed. A printing press was also established at Edinburgh for producing published charters, laws and statutes. James' ambition was to turn Scotland into a modernising nation-state, and he immersed himself in international diplomacy and events. He sought to establish strong rule and stability in Scotland based on strong laws and justice by improving the court systems, which also could provide finance through fines and remissions.

During the 1490s James got the opportunity to test his military capacities against England and Henry VII when on November 1495 he gave support to the pretender to the English throne, Perkin Warbeck, called by his supporters Richard, Duke of York. No major battles occurred, though there was destruction of towers and castles and large-scale plundering raids along the borders. The inconclusive campaigns seriously weakened the finances of both Scotland and England, and a peace treaty was sought and concluded on September 30th 1497, negotiated by the Spanish ambassador at the Scottish court, Pedro de Ayalo, to last for seven years. Henry however wanted something more lasting and would offer the hand of his daughter as a royal bride, the 'dove which was to bring to the island-kingdoms the blessing permanent peace'. [9]

Margaret was the second child and eldest daughter of Henry VII (1457-1508) and Elizabeth of York (1466-1503). Her father had been the Welsh-born founder of the Tudor dynasty, who at Bosworth won the last battle of the War of the Roses. She was born Princess Royal of England within the Painted Chamber of Westminster on November 29th, 1489. The following day, St Andrews Day, November 30th, the bairn was escorted with great royal splendour by Lady Berkeley and the Earls of Arundel and Shrewsbury to Whitehall and to a church near Westminster Abbey dedicated to St Margaret, patron saint of Scotland. Here the Bishop of Ely performed the rites of baptism, using a sacred silver font brought from Canterbury Cathedral. The porch of the church was hung with elaborate tapestries and the ceiling with fine embroidery. The Princess's eldest aunt, the Lady Anne of York, bore the white chrisom, and Lord Wells, the husband of the Princess Cecily of York, carried the salt in a grand gold salt-cellar wax taper, unlighted. The Countess of Richmond gave the Princess her name, Margaret. The Duchess of Norfolk was made godmother, and the Archbishop of Canterbury, Dr Morton, also Chancellor of England, was made godfather.

Princess Margaret spent most of her infancy at the Palace of Sheen on the Thames, brought up with her older brother Arthur and younger brother Henry. Her governess was Lady Guildford, wife of Sir Richard Guildford, one of the knights of the royal household. A Welshwoman called Alice Davy was her main nurse. Anne Mayland and Margaret Troughton were her assistants and would receive each £3 3s. per year.

Margaret Countess of Richmond supervised the upbringing of her granddaughter and goddaughter. As the princess reached early literacy years the Countess of Richmond appointed as tutors the scholars Thomas Linacre, John Colet and William Crocyn, giving Margaret a good grasp of Latin and French. She could dance and play instruments such as the lute and clavichord, and at her brother Arthur's marriage to Catherine of Aragon, she and her brother Henry performed an energetic dance for the entertainment of the audience.

She would also enjoy outdoor activities, and became an accomplished archer. She was very close to her brother Arthur, and they expressed a warm and loving relationship which carried on after Arthur's marriage to Katherine and his relocation to Ludlow Castle in Shropshire, where he would bestow gifts and favours on his sister.

Arthur's death in April 2nd 1501 would be a source of emotional turmoil for her. [10] It would make Margaret heir-apparent to England after her younger brother Henry as long as he remained childless. Henry VII had long favoured the idea of a marriage alliance between the Stewarts of Scotland and the Tudors of England, and the status of Margaret in the succession made the prospect more attractive to the Lord's Council of Scotland. [11]

Once a treaty of marriage and peace had been negotiated, King James, before the High Altar of Glasgow Cathedral on December 10th 1502, would ratify the treaty and give his oath to keep to the terms. The ratification had to be repeated, as during the reading of the Treaty the name of France was accidentally inserted instead of England.

On January 15th 1503 at Richmond Palace a proxy wedding was enacted when Patrick, the Earl of Bothwell, played proxy for the king, wearing a gown of cloth-of-gold. Margaret was proclaimed Queen of Scotland, and this was followed by celebrations, feats, tournaments and dancing, whilst the sound of church bells filled the air and bonfires lit up the parks and streets. The two kings would exchange laminated copies of the ratifications. To further solidify the treaty Henry VII sent envoys to Rome to gain confirmation from Alexander VI, the Borgia pope, who granted this on May 28th 1503, and also proclaimed that whatever King broke the treaty would be subject to excommunication.

The dower of the Queen was negotiated at 31,000 gold nobles, to be paid in three annual instalments. The Queen's dowry was to be £2,000 sterling per year, and to raise the sum she would be granted legal rights over Ettrick Forest, the tower of Newark, the lordship of Dunbar and Cowbrandspath, the castle of Stirling and lordship of the shire, the palace of Linlithgow and lordship of the shire, the earldom of Monteith, the palace and lordship of Methven and the lordship and castle of Down. For personal use Margaret would also be paid £1,000 at Easter and Michaelmas. [12]

Margaret's mother would die in 1503, and her funeral and mourning period afterwards would delay the arrangements for the marriage. After an appropriate time of mourning had passed the thirteen-year-old Queen of Scotland would finally set off from Richmond Palace for Scotland on June 27th. She was granted a large wardrobe of expensive clothes and crimson curtains made of Italian sacrenet emblazoned with the red roses of Lancaster. One of her companions, Lady Catherine Gordon, the daughter of the Earl of Huntley and widow of Perkin Warbeck, was also outfitted with clothing of the highest quality. Margaret was accompanied some of the way by her father before responsibility for leading her convoy was transferred to the Earl of Surrey. In her train were the countess of Surrey, with the Somerset Herald to make an official record of the proceedings. Gentlemen, squires and pages accompanied the ladies, who were pulled on litters or rode on palfreys. Margaret would stop at York, Durham and Newcastle before crossing the border at Berwick-upon-Tweed on August 1st, and she met the Archbishop of Glasgow and a thousand nobles at Lamberton, all attired in 'rich jewels and massy chains'.

Stopping at Newbottle, Margaret, whilst playing cards in her chamber, was visited by James on August 3rd, riding in with a troop of horsemen and dressed in a crimson velvet jacket. They had supper together and later that night James played the lute and clavichord. He would meet her again at Dalkeith a few days later, when she showed her own skills with musical instruments, and James listened attentively on bended knee. On August 7th James rode towards Edinburgh with Margaret riding pillion behind him, with two hundred knights following on. Before entering the town a show of chivalry was performed on the road, a knight capturing a damsel and Sir Patrick Hamilton playing the hero entering into combat with the villain. The entertaining joust continued until James called for 'peace'.

Upon entering Edinburgh Queen Margaret passed by many pageants, one of which represented the union between Scotland and England, with a thistle supported by a greyhound linked by a red rose to a unicorn. [13]

On August 8th at Holyrood chapel the marriage of James and

Margaret was conducted by the Archbishops of Glasgow and York, followed by a nuptial mass and coronation ritual. James wore a gown of white damask with crimson satin sleeves and Margaret wore a gown trimmed in crimson. There were several days of festivities, feasts and dances, with bonfires illuminating the nights. William Dunbar would compose several pieces for Margaret on her arrival in Scotland, one called *The Thistle and the Rose*, where the queen is symbolised as the symbolic joining together of the Houses of York and Lancaster. In this poem birds sing to her in praise, and a lark greets her as the 'rose, both red and white'.

After the celebrations and feasting, which lasted for days, Margaret would tour the country before settling into what would be her main residence at Stirling Castle. Here she would come face to face with the grim realities of royal life, for James had many mistresses and several illegitimate children, all of whom were housed in Stirling Castle, James being an attentive and kind father.

It is not known how Margaret responded to this domestic situation. James' affairs with other women were tolerated by Margaret, although William Dunbar, the poet, criticized him for these distractions, which took him away from his queen. James, when Duke of Rothesay and a young man, had fallen in love with Margaret Drummond, a maiden of his mother and daughter of Lord Drummond of Stobshall, said to be one of the wisest men in Scotland.

It is possible that James married Margaret Drummond, although if so it was not made official or public knowledge. This is believed to have occurred on October 1488 at Linlithgow Palace. The story goes that James had intended to marry Margaret Drummond even though the majority of his council wanted him to marry Margaret Tudor. He sent off to the papacy for a dispensation to marry, since he and Margaret Drummond were related by a few degrees. A dispensation would make the marriage legal and would also legitimise the daughter they had conceived. Before the dispensation was received Lady Drummond, along with two of her sisters, Euphemia, Lady Fleming and Sybella were poisoned in Drummond Castle, possibly in 1501 or 1502. Suspicion was aimed at those nobles and clergy who opposed this wedding, and the Kennedys were named as the agents of these murders, although the members of this family have not been identified. The three sisters were buried at Dunblane, and King James took the little daughter, Margaret Drummond, back to his castle at Stirling, where he raised her as one of his family, Lady Margaret, the King's daughter. [14]

James was very fond of Queen Margaret, and there are many records of his kindness and consideration towards her. Margaret would during her time with James have six children, yet only the future King James V would survive into adulthood during the father's lifetime. Fond though he was of his wife, he could also be deceitful and hypocritical in his affections. When Margaret had a child on February 10th 1506 at Holyrood, her life hung on the balance. Whereas James should have been more supportive, staying by her side, he instead decided to pray for her health by taking a pilgrimage to the Shrine of St Ninians in Whithorn, where he also renewed his friendship with a former mistress, Jane Kennedy, mother of his natural son James Stewart. When Margaret recovered her health, she herself would take a pilgrimage to St Ninians. Her child would die almost a year later at Stirling. [15]

The cultural life of the nobility and aristocrats, after collecting rent and revenues, was play and entertainment. Games, music and dancing were favoured pastimes. Indoor games like tennis, chess, dice and cards were popular. Archery was the royally sanctioned game, although prescribed games like golf and football were more common, even though they diverted from the soldiery skill of bow and arrow. For courtly humour, fools and clowns were employed; the former wearing brightly-coloured green and yellow clothing and spouting witty comments, jokes and performing slapstick. King James would also have tale-tellers who recite stories before his court. Such performances would be passed on by word of mouth to other towns and villages to be told and retold. Music was a major part of courtly life with James IV employing up to 31 minstrels playing fiddles, drums, trumpets, lutes, harps, pipes, bagpipes and flutes. Music would be traditional Scots, and also French, Italian and English.

Spanish and French style dancing was also popular, the former called the 'pavo' or peacock. The dances of the common people were more energetic and would have been similar to Gaelic reels. Whilst courtly dances exhibited a civilised grace, within palaces and stately homes the dancing could become somewhat ruder and lewder. Dunbar writes about a sexually-explicit dance which was performed in the Queen's bedchamber.

Many contemporary poets and satirists, such as William Dunbar and Sir David Lindsay, would comment on the sexual excesses of the Scottish court, where nobles and aristocrats recruited sexual partners and mistresses from their lands and holdings. King James IV would ensure the advancement of his own illegitimate children either through the ranks of the nobility or within the church. This patronage was reflected with the lesser nobility and churchmen, whose illegitimate children became dependents and would be given positions to provide a living. These illegitimate children, if successful in their careers, could become useful allies and assets to the father. Cardinals, bishops, priests, abbots and monks also earned reputations for promiscuous behaviour, and many prominent bishops would have mistresses and illegitimate children. Whilst not all churchmen were hypocrites to their faith, the satirists used artistic licence to describe a clergy they viewed as corrupt and decadent. [16]

James IV had an interest in chivalry, jousting and martial tournaments. He would promote these activities through making proclamations inviting every noble and knight to come to Edinburgh and test their prowess with weapons and horses. These games would attract not only the warrior classes in Scotland but also men from England and across the waters. On one occasion cited by Pitscottie, Sir Patrick Hamilton fought with a Dutch knight, Sir John Cockbewis, below Edinburgh castle whilst King James IV and his entourage watched from the walls. Real live duels would also be fought out before the King and court, in which men who lived through theft and lawlessness were invited to extinguish their lives and lessen the burden of the communities they tyrannised. Sir David Lindsay makes a humorous parody of the whole jousting obsession with his *Jousting betwixt Watson and Barbour* where two royal servants, both medical practitioners and ill-experienced at jousting, make a Laurel and Hardy attempt to injure each other and fail. Martial combat and prowess was very much part of the Scottish psyche, yet so was the ability to deride this practice in order to find humour in it. [17]

This was the nation of which Margaret was Queen, and she was revered wherever she went. In one visit to Aberdeen in 1511 the magistrates at great expense had the dunghills cleared from the streets and alleyways and the swine-sties moved from the city centre. Four young men wrapped in velvet gowns met the Queen outside the city and carried her through the gates on a red pall. At great expense the civic powers had the streets cleaned and washed, and tapestries hung along the streets. Many pageants displayed colourful themes for the Queen's pleasure: the expelling of Adam and Eve from paradise, the Three Wise Men, Robert the Bruce and other stories. Smaller stalls offered plays, music and poetry, and the people dressed in colourful attire and shouted loud greetings as the Queen passed. When she reached the Market Cross, minstrels played music and maidens danced in brightly-coloured clothing. A fountain was set up to spout wine, and Margaret was presented with a gift of a gold cup filled with £200 in coins. [18]

Being a substantial landowner Margaret would learn about the Scottish economy, and that agriculture was not as productive as it should have been. Farmers and tenants were granted short-term leases from the landowners, who did not encourage long-term planning and expansion, and a tenant could be expelled without rights once a lease expired. Tenants largely ensured their survival in the feudalistic society of Scotland by being loyal adherents to their feudal masters and supporting them in their fights and quarrels.

On the borders of Scotland an agricultural economy was practically non-existent due to the nature of life there, where feuds and cross-border raiding often resulted in the burning of crops. The rearing and theft of livestock fuelled the economies of the borders. In the highlands and islands and amongst the Gaelic societies, livestock was an important source of produce and income.

Gaelic soldiers were also valued, and the axe-wielding chain-mail armoured *galloglach* and the more lightly armed *caterans* were mercenaries who largely fought in the wars in Ireland. Fisheries were another important source of revenue for the government through dues and customs, and statutes were passed through offering recommendations for the type and size of fishing vessels that should be constructed. The Scottish free burghs allowed the merchants and burgesses to regulate Scottish trade in line with local needs. The Low Countries were the main markets for Scottish produce and enjoyed a profitable and friendly relationship. The Baltic region, France and England were also important markets. [19]

Margaret's father Henry VII would die in 1509 and the new King Henry VIII would develop a more problematic relationship with James and his own sister Margaret. He would refuse to hand over those possessions formerly belonging to Arthur and bestowed on her at his death. Henry VIII would also marry the widow of his brother Arthur, Katherine of Aragon, which obviously gave England a powerful link with Spain and drew her further into European politics and intrigues. Whilst the treaty between Scotland and England was renewed there were many diplomatic incidents between Scotland and England. Although these were not enough to cause war, they did breed the beginnings of a real antagonism. James saw himself as a European statesman and would try to compose peaceful solutions to conflicts and disagreements between European countries. The rivalry between France and England would be a problem, as France, on the strength of age-old alliances and friendships, would often attempt to draw Scotland away from the treaty with England. [20]

France's fear was that of encirclement. On October 5th 1511 Pope Julius II, the founder of the Papal States, had formed an anti-French coalition called the Holy League comprising Venice, Ferdinand of Aragon and England, and by May 1512 the Emperor Maximilian and the Swiss would join. France was in a dangerous situation and would plead with James IV to enter into an alliance with France, hoping no doubt that this would discourage Henry from travelling with an army to the continent. [21]

Queen Margaret would give birth to a son on April 11th, 1512 at Linlithgow Palace, baptised James and proclaimed Prince of Scotland and the Isles. The infant who would grow up to become James V was born into a time when his father James IV was playing a dangerous game that could affect Scotland badly. James would agree to a renewal of alliance with France in July 1512 in return for 50,000 francs and the equipping and supplying of the Scottish fleet to France. In the event of England attacking either France or Scotland one nation would aid the other, in Scotland's case by declaring war and invading England. [22]

In February 1513, Pope Julius II issued letters proclaiming that if James invaded England then he and his nation would suffer excommunication. After Julius' death shortly afterwards on February 21st his successor Leo X would confirm this proclamation. The Holy League would lose Venice as a member, Venice aligning itself with France. The remaining members, Pope Leo X, Henry VIII, the Emperor Maximilian and Ferdinand of Aragon, would on April 5th 1513 sign the Treaty of Mechlin, and the English were looking to invade France in order to gain territory.

Queen Margaret would oppose her husband's plan to provoke war with England, yet she had her own disputes with her brother. Her late brother Arthur had left a significant fortune to the Scottish Queen, now in the keeping of her brother Henry. In the spring of 1513 Margaret asked the English ambassador, Nicholas West, for Arthur's bequest and also for the plate and jewels left her by her grandmother Lady Margaret Beaufort. West replied that these would only be handed over if James IV remained at peace with England, instead of joining France. Whilst not enough of a reason to justify hostilities, this rejection of Margaret's rights served as yet another insult to James. Further contempt was heaped upon him when a Scottish merchant called Andrew Barton, a favourite of James, was attacked and killed off the English Downs by Thomas Howard, the Admiral of England. He had been returning from Flanders. Whilst this was considered a breach of the treaty by the Scots, Henry VIII would argue that Barton was a pirate and had been preying on the Portuguese, who were allies of England.

Within Scotland there was a build-up of support for war, which reached a pitch in July 1513 when Henry VIII led an army to France. William Elphinstone, Bishop of Aberdeen, spoke out against war, as did Archibald 'Bell-the-Cat' Douglas, Earl of Angus and head of the faction known as the Red Douglases. Queen Margaret also opposed war, obviously despairing to think of her King and Scotland fighting against her brother and the country of her birth. She also feared the fact that James had only one son, and if her husband should be killed then this would put his successor and guardians under severe strain.

However the influence she had with her King was being challenged by Anne of Brittany, the Queen of France, who had been sending correspondence to James pleading with him to invade England and divert English forces from France. She appointed James her knight-errant and sent him an expensive ring from her royal hand as a token of her esteem. Queen Margaret had not only to compete with the wealth of France, she had no answer to those appeals to James' chivalric idealism which were in many ways his Achilles heel. To assist King Louis, James sent a fleet, including the two great warships the *Michael* and the *Margaret*, to France to be commanded by the Earl of Arran. [23]

It was reported that one night Queen Margaret chastised James on why he would prefer to follow the pleadings of the Queen of France and not consider the thoughts and fears of his own wife, who would claim that she had dreams in which she saw him slaughtered. James was determined to invade England, and Margaret proposed that if she was allowed to accompany him the sight of her to her countrymen might give pause and provide an opportunity for peaceful discourse. It was also said that Queen Katherine of Aragon might lead the English army in Henry's absence. The royal couple argued, but James was determined to go to war and had ordered an armed muster for August. He sent a message to Henry calling him to desist from war with France or he would invade England. Henry at the time of receiving the message was commanding the siege of Tournay.

Whilst preparing to march into England James IV was supposed to have been approached by a mysterious figure at Linlithgow's St Michael's church, an elderly man wearing a long robe, who warned the King that the invasion was doomed to fail. Before this man could be questioned he walked into the church crowd and then apparently vanished. This incident was witnessed by Sir David Lindsay, the poet, writer and herald. Pitscottie believed that this approach and disappearance was staged by Queen Margaret and others who were opposed to the war, with the intention of having James believe that divine powers were making an intervention. It was even suggested that the apparition was one of Margaret's servants.

If James needed a more earthly warning of the dangers of invasion it occurred when Alexander Lord Hume, the Lord Chamberlain and warden of the marches, led a large-scale raid into Northumberland, burning and looting villages and communities. On August 13th this incursion became known as the 'ill raid' when his forces fell into an ambush at Milfield engineered by Sir William Bulmer, leaving 500 dead and 400 captured with Hume barely managing to escape. Buchanan would claim that despite the reverse the parties guarding the plundered goods managed to reach Scotland. [24]

This encounter did not fill James with caution, but instead made him determined to continue the course. He would make up with his Queen a few days before beginning the invasion. He made up a will by which, in the event of his death, Margaret was to be appointed regent and have the full authority over her son the King, as long as she remained a widow. She would be helped in this by William Elphinstone, Bishop of Aberdeen. It is also written by chroniclers that James presented her with his hidden treasure, which amounted to 18,000 golden suns or crowns, the remainder of that bribe paid to him by Louis. This along with other valuables was to be used for the upkeep of herself and King James. [25]

Whilst James prepared to invade England, more mystical occurrences were reported. One night at the Market Cross in Edinburgh, whilst the heavy cannon from the castle were being brought down into the town, an unseen entity called 'Platcock', possibly a version of Pluto, God of the underworld, made a proclamation for all to hear in which he read out names of those nobles, gentlemen and burgesses who within forty days would join him in Hades if the Scots invaded England. It was a prophesy of disaster, and the agent making the proclamation was not caught or identified. Some believed that Queen Margaret had conceived of this enterprise, and like the incident in Linlithgow, had employed the actors to perform open-air theatre before unsuspecting audiences. It says much for Margaret's imagination that she was able to transfer her knowledge of theatre into stage-managing such a production. The purpose was not for entertainment but to call halt to a war between her adopted country and the land of her birth. Unfortunately the Scots were determined to go to war. [26]

In late August the Scots, estimated at 30,000, crossed into Northumberland and soon after captured Norham Castle and the strongholds of Wark, Etal and Ford. The surrounding region of Northumberland was wasted, which meant that whilst James resided at Ford, apparently being entertained by the wife of Heron of Ford, a prisoner in Edinburgh, his army was dispersed over a wide area. Many of his advisers wanted to march to Berwick and lay siege to it, and even if they could not capture the city they could at least plunder the countryside. James however seems to have been too distracted by the charms of Lady Heron, who is said to have smuggled details of the Scots army and their composition to Thomas Howard, Earl of Surrey, who had been left in charge of the defence of northern England.

Heralds were sent by Surrey to appoint a time and place for battle, and James' advisers suggested that with the approaching winter weather the Scots should withdraw across the border. The English would also be at an advantage since they were gathering fresh recruits whilst many Scots were returning home with their plunder, and those remaining would be fatigued through storming castles and raids across the region of Northumberland, as well as succumbing to the cold weather and disease. It was argued that the Scots had fulfilled any commitment to the French, since they were attracting an English army north which could not be used for France, and if the Scots returned home the English would have to make the choice of chasing into Scotland or disbanding their forces as the weather became more deplorable and supplies became sparse. It was the French ambassador who pleaded with James to fight and defeat the English in battle, and ignoring the advice of the likes of the veteran warrior Archibald 'Bell-the-cat' Douglas, earl of Angus, he followed that course. [27]

When James learned that the Earl of Surrey with an estimated 26,000 men and the banner of St Cuthbert was marching to meet him, he ordered the Scots to take a strong position on Flodden Hill. On September 9th Surrey outmanoeuvred James by threatening to cut off his northern retreat, forcing him to abandon his advantageous position and bring his men from the higher ground to Branxton. The Scots camp would be set alight and the smoke would drift towards both armies. James would lead the advance. The English were arranged in five divisions; Lord Thomas Dacre commanded a reserve whilst Surrey and the Lord Admiral commanded two central divisions, and Stanley the left and Edmund Howard the right. King James' left was commanded by Lord Hume and Alexander, third Earl of Huntley, and the next division by the Earls Montrose, Errol and Crawford. James commanded the next division and the Earls of Lennox and Argyll commanded the right wing of Highlanders and men of the Isles. The Earl of Bothwell commanded a reserve.

The battle began at 4pm. The English gunners proved more experienced and deadlier than their counterparts, whilst the Scottish foot, struggling over marshy and wet ground and armed with 22-foot pikes, had to contend with English foot armed with 8-foot halberds, also known as 'brown bills', which were used to chop up the pikes. The Scots however would gain a significant opportunity when the left wing commanded by Hume and Huntley swept through the right wing commanded by Surrey's son Edmund Howard. Lord Hume is said to have then led his men to loot the English baggage train, taking horses, goods and prisoners, whilst Lord Dacre and his border horsemen blocked Huntley and stopped him from swinging into the exposed flanks of the English.

Across the battle line the two sides fought savagely. The division of Errol, Crawford and Montrose was routed and the earls killed. Lennox and Argyll were also slain, along with thousands of Gaelic warriors. James' division met with Surrey's and then was assaulted from the flanks by Lord Dacre, the Lord Admiral and Edmund Howard.

Huntley, after his engagement with Dacre, managed to regroup and meet up with Lord Hume, wanting to assist King James. Lord Hume is said to have replied, 'We have fought their vanguards and won the same; let the rest do their part as well as we.' In Lord Hume's opinion his men had fought enough, and it was a decision that would haunt him for years to come. Huntley led his remaining men towards the King just as Stanley led his division into King James' other flank. At 6pm the battle began to peter out when the autumn darkness made it difficult for both sides to continue. The English withdrew from the field in the best order they could, and Surrey made camp nearby. The survivors of the Scots centre kept the field, whilst elsewhere Lord Hume and his borderers, who had managed to regroup, spent the night collecting the plunder of the battlefield. [28]

The following morning in the full light of day, Surrey saw that the Scots still occupied the hill in a large body. He fired ordinance and scattered them. He then sent Lord Dacre with horsemen to survey the field, and in Buchanan's words, found the 'greater part of the dead stripped'. There was a large concentration of slain spearmen, near a body that Dacre would identify as King James, although he could not be fully certain as his face appeared to have been smashed in. It was also said that the body may have been Alexander 1st Lord Elphinstone, an individual who bore a resemblance to the King, and he was one of many that day that had been armoured and attired like the King in order to deceive the English. Surrey would claim the victory, and would even claim that King James had fallen nearly a spear length from the position he had taken on the battlefield. Surrey would take command over the Scottish artillery of around seventeen pieces, although Lord Hume would make a failed attempt to recapture them. The English would naturally downplay the number of their dead as compared to the Scots, with reports claiming 500 English dead and 10,000 Scots. Chroniclers like Buchanan would claim that both sides lost 5,000 dead and wounded. The ambassador to the Duke of Milan would write that both sides lost heavily, whilst the Venetian ambassador would state that the Scots lost their king and 4,000 men. The artillery train of the Scots was captured and taken to Berwick. There was also mention that Frenchmen had been slain during the battle, some by Scots who blamed them for 'being the cause of their destruction'. Despite the differing accounts the English won a great victory at Flodden, or the Battle of Branxton as it is also called. It was also a moral victory as the Scots were the aggressors when James broke the treaty with England. With regard to the structures of power, the Scots lost a king, the Archbishop of St Andrews, the Bishop of the Isles, nine earls and fourteen lords. The victorious leader of the English, the Earl of Surrey, would later be rewarded by Henry by being granted the Dukedom of Norfolk. [29]

The Lord Chamberlain, Alexander Hume negotiated with Lord Dacre for a short truce. This was agreed and both armies would withdraw, the Scots northwards. Surrey would on Sept 14th disband his remaining army of 18,689, which he claimed he was doing in order to save the Crown the expenses of continuing to pay the soldiers until the end of the month, the period until which they were raised. It was quite an early demobilisation considering it was only a few days after the battle. The justification given was not just saving wages; the weather and the lack of appropriate clothing, meat, drink, supplies and transport would make sustaining an army on the field difficult. Lord Hume's thorough looting of the baggage train appears to have weakened Surrey's capacity to continue the campaign. Thomas Ruthall, Bishop of Durham, would note that the English borderers had apparently joined the Scots borderers during the raiding of goods and horses, actions which he believed discouraged the 'capitayns and souldiours' from continuing due to material losses and distrust of the borderers, described as 'falser than Scottes'.[30]

The body identified by Lord Dacre as James was taken to Berwick. The Earl of Surrey would make a request to Henry on what burial arrangements should be made for him. Although no answer is recorded, the excommunicated King of Scots was kept unburied in a lead coffin. Henry's queen Katherine of Aragon would send her husband a segment of the dead King's plaid coat, and exult in the defeat of the invading Scots army. James would be later taken in secret to London, and whilst pope Leo X asked that Henry VIII bury him with full honours in St Paul's cathedral, having received reports that James had prior to the battle sought repentance, the King of England refused this request and had James buried in St Michael's Churchyard, Wood Street. [31]

Chapter One: References.

(1) (ODNB, vol.29, pp. 609-619). (2) (Grant, pp. 150-151. Somerset Fry, pp. 71-72). (3) (RPCS, vol 1, June 5th, 1546, (24). (4) (RPCS, vol 1, x-xii). (5) (Somerset Fry, pp. 70-71). (6) (SHD, 89-90. Somerset-Fry, p.64. Thomson, vol 3, pp. 225-226). (7) (Thomson,

vol.2, pp. 481-483). (8) (Buchanan, pp. 241-242.Thomson, vol.2, pp. 481-483). (9) (Strickland, vol.1, pp. 4-5). (10) (ODNB, vol.36, pp. 648-652. Strickland, vol.1, pp. 4-6). (11) (Strickland, vol.1, pp. 4-6). (12) (Buchanan, pp. 239-240). (13) (Buchanan, pp. 239-241). (14) (Strickland, vol.1, pp. 19-21). (15) (Strickland, vol.1, pp. 64-67). (16) (ODNB, vol.29, pp. 609-619. Thomson, vol.3, pp. 2-13. Thomson, vol.3, pp. 45-50). (17) (Buchanan, pp. 240-241. Thomson, vol.3, pp. 30-31). (18) (Thomson, vol.3, pp. 19-20). (19) (Thomson, vol.3, pp. 14-18). (20) (Buchanan, pp. 243-245. Strickland, vol.1, pp. 67-70). (21) (Buchanan, pp. 242-244. Johnson, pp. 67-71. Norwich, pp. 274-276). (22) (Buchanan, pp. 242-244. Johnson, pp. 67-71. Norwich, pp. 274-276. Strickland, vol.1, pp. 68-69). (23) (Buchanan, pp. 243-248. Johnson, pp. 76-78. Norwich, pp. 276-278). (24) (Buchanan, pp. 248-251). (25) (Strickland, vol.1, pp. 81-83). (26) (Strickland, vol.1, pp. 80-82). (27) (Buchanan, pp. 251-254. ODNB, vol.28, pp. 420-423). (28) (Buchanan, pp. 258-259. ODNB, vol.28, pp. 420-423. SBSH, vol.2, pp. 61-67). (29) (Buchanan, pp. 255-260. LP, Paolo da Laude to the Duke of Milan, Sept 16th, 1513. LP, Spinelly to Cardinal Bainbridge, Sept 20th, 1513. LP, Venice, Oct 12th, 1513. ODNB, vol.28, pp. 420-423. SBSH, vol.2, pp. 61-67. SBSH, vol.2, pp. 77-79. Thomson, pp. 534-537. pp. 88-90). (30) (MSHS, vol.viii, Mackie (ed.) pp. 64-69. ODNB, vol.28, pp. 420-423. SBSH, vol.2, pp. 61-67). (31) (Buchanan, pp. 258-260. LP, Katherine of Aragon to Henry VIII, Sept 16th, 1513.SBSH, vol.2, pp. 61-67).

Chapter Two

A PERNICIOUS DESIGN: 1513-1515

Before the news of Flodden was made official, the burgesses and merchants of Edinburgh reacted to rumours of disaster by sending out orders that the townspeople were to arm themselves. They also threatened to banish any females who were caught weeping and making laments, as this would dishearten those around them. They were ordered to stay indoors, and the more composed were asked to go to the churches and pray for the army of the King. When the news was confirmed that the King and many of his nobles, prelates, citizens and subjects had lost their lives, the streets of nearly every town were filled with widows, orphans, and grieving parents.

Queen Margaret acted decisively. At Stirling on September 19th she called the surviving nobles and prelates together to set plans for Scotland's defence. It was decided that the slain King's son James, although only one year and five months of age, should be crowned King of Scotland and the twenty-three year old Margaret should rule in his name as Regent. The choice of Queen Margaret as Regent had been authorised by James IV in the writing of his will before setting off for England. Her council was to comprise James Beaton, Archbishop of Glasgow, the bishops of Dunblane and Aberdeen, the earls of Morton, Argyll, Lennox, Eglinton, Glencairn, Atholl, Huntley, and the Master of Angus. The Queen and her son were to reside at Edinburgh. [1]

Two individuals who would rise up in political power and influence during the following years were the twenty-five year old Archibald Douglas, heir to the Earldom of Angus, and James Beaton, Archbishop of Glasgow. Archibald Douglas (c.1489–1557) was the son of George Douglas, Master of Angus, and grandson of Archibald 'Bell-the-Cat' Douglas, fifth Earl of Angus. The Master had died at Flodden and the Earl soon after at Tantallon Castle. The Earldom of Angus would give him authority of the strongholds and lands of Douglasdale, Crawford-Douglas, Abernethy, Jedburgh Forest, Selkirk and Tantallon, as well as the lands and barony of Bothwell. Queen Margaret would confirm him in this title within twelve weeks. Angus would form an able partnership with his twenty-three-year-old brother George Douglas of Pittendriech, who besides offering a quality of astute advice beyond his years, would also develop into one of the most able diplomats and statesman of his age, in addition to being an able adherent to the political dark arts. [2]

Another important Douglas, and one of cultural and literary significance, was Gavin, born 1476, the third son of Archibald 'Bell-the-Cat' Douglas, Fifth Earl of Angus. Educated at St Andrews, he was versed in poetry, classical studies and humanism and a friend of such literary figures such as John Mair. Douglas composed works of poetry such as *The Palice of Honour*, written in 1501, which was an examination of the different paths to honour, influenced by Ovid and Chaucer. He also translated Virgil's *Aeneid*, which he termed *Eneados*, and which is considered the first major translation of a classical work into English. This was completed in July 22nd 1513, several weeks before Flodden.

Gavin Douglas became parson of Linton and canon of Dunbar by 1504, but his most important post was provost of St Giles in Edinburgh. After the battle of Flodden he was made a free burgess of Edinburgh. Margaret had a special affection for Gavin, who had proved a close companion in the days following the death of her husband, and would offer guidance and spiritual solace.

Up until the battle of Flodden James Beaton would prove an energetic and able Archbishop of Glasgow. With the death of Andrew Stewart, Archbishop of St Andrews, at Flodden, Beaton was now the strongest representative of ecclesial power in Scotland. In the presence of the nobles and prelates of Scotland, Archbishop Beaton crowned the 18-month-old King James V of Scotland at Stirling on September 21st, 1513. The coronation would become known as the 'Mourning Coronation', and as the crown of Scotland was placed on the head of the infant King, the palace was filled with weeping and lamentations, with the audience powerless to hide their feelings at the heavy losses met at Flodden. Beaton would rise further in influence and responsibility when he was appointed chancellor on September 29th. [3]

As news of the battle passed through the country, thousands of women were faced with the prospect of a life without husbands, or brothers or sons, and 1,000s of children were left without fathers or brothers. Margaret would seek to counter-balance the devastation that would be experienced by the women of the slain of Flodden with an order made on October 3rd at Edinburgh by the Council of Public Affairs threatening treason to anyone who harmed or hurt any widows or daughters. There was an impression that 'evil disposed persons' were targeting undefended women and maidens, to exploit them either sexually or financially. Margaret would have empathized with these women, she was alone and encircled by dangerous men in a nation unaccustomed to being ruled by a female regent. Initially the situation was accepted as there were at that time no any viable alternatives to her rule. However it would not be long before the nobles and prelates began to aggressively reposition themselves in the new order. [4]

At a sitting at Perth on October 22nd the members of the council were chosen, with four councillors to attend the Queen in a mini-council, these being Beaton, Angus, Alexander Gordon, 3rd Earl of Huntley and James Hamilton, 1st Earl of Arran, although the latter was still absent in France. Beaton was appointed Chancellor which gave him possession of the Privy Seal of Scotland. It was suggested that Margaret should oppose this appointment; however there is no record of this at the time, so regrets may have been expressed after both she and Beaton became enemies. (5)

News of the battle brought elation also to the Cardinal of England based in Rome, who along with the ambassadors of Spain and the Emperor burned bonfires in celebration. Henry VIII had different ideas regarding the makeup of the rule of Scotland. Elated by the victory and endeavouring not to let the chance slip, he also instructed Lord Dacre to find means to get the young King James 'placed in the hands of the King of England' but to do so in a way that would not alert the Scottish government so that they did not take James to the Isles or anywhere else out of reach. Henry also suggested that the Queen of England should send a servant to the Queen of Scotland for 'comfort'. It is possible this 'servant' would be a means not just of spying on events but of abducting James. (6)

Henry VIII, during his summer and autumn campaigns of 1513, had gained the towns of Terouenne and Tournay, and it appeared that France would be portioned up between Henry, Maximilian and their allies. He would write to Pope Leo X regarding Flodden claiming it as a victory for the Holy League and proof God was on their side. Henry stated that he would be sailing to England to attend Parliament on November 1st and to finalize this issue with Scotland. He intended returning to the continent with a larger army. Henry was clear in his intention to reap further humiliation on his Northern neighbour, asking that Leo demote the Archbishopric of St Andrews to a bishopric which in turn would be subservient to the Archbishopric of York, and requesting that Leo should not dispense with any Scottish bishoprics until Henry was allowed to offer a preference. Leo however would assign the Archbishopric of St Andrews, which had belonged to Alexander Stewart, illegitimate son of James IV, to Cardinal Cibo. [7]

Louis of France however was not finished, and although apparently outmatched on the military front, France was helped by the fears and jealousies of its enemies. King Ferdinand of Aragon decided to make a secret treaty with the King of France due to concerns about the expansionism of the Empire. He would set out to undermine the agreement between the Emperor Maximilian and Henry VIII. Pope Leo X also made an agreement with France by November, in which he reconciled himself with Louis and the French cardinals in return for French assistance in supporting his brother Giuliano to gain Naples. [8]

There was no follow up on Flodden or invasion of Scotland, because the Earl of Surrey had disbanded the northern army. Whilst Pitscottie would claim that Henry threatened treason if any English invaded the territories of the Queen of Scotland, his sister, and the King his nephew, and sent letters assuring Margaret that he would endeavour to keep the peace, he would contradict this apparent mercy by sending instructions to Lord Dacre commanding him to continue applying pressure on the Scots through raids and incursions across the border, and not to release for ransom any captured Scots.

Teviotdale was invaded by the Duke of Gloucester and the Earl of Northumberland. Whilst Dacre raided the Western and Middle marches, the devastation that the Scots had inflicted on Northumberland during the invasion made it difficult for him to organize raids along the eastern march due to logistical problems and want of supplies and men. He had to settle for men from the Bishopric of Durham. He was assigned 2,000 merks in total, and this allowed him to also recruit men from Berwick, but he complained of men taking wages, then disappearing. The weather was bad, with rain and floods hindering the raiders in their efforts.

With 3,000 horse and 300 infantry, Dacre continued to raid and burn towns and communities until he met with a reverse near Jedburgh. The Kerrs of Ferniehurst, the Sheriff of Teviotdale and the Laird of Bondeworth combined forces to confront the raiders. They were joined by 2,000 horse led by Alexander Hume, the Lord Chamberlain. According to Dacre the whole countryside was alerted to the raids, and beacons lit up the hills and mountains as the English with their plunder and livestock struggled to reach safety. The Scots were obviously reorganising more effectively and Dacre complained that he could leave the middle march unprotected. By the end of November, due to the worsening winter weather and the resistance of the Scots Lord Dacre was finding it difficult to conduct raids into Scotland. [9]

Preparing for defence became a priority, with the Master of Angus instructed on October 29th to fortify many strongholds south of the Forth that were not under the authority of Lord Hume, such as Cumnock, Uchtree and Semple. Angus, the Earl of Morton, Lord Hume and Borthwick were to assist the sheriff of Tweeddale. Whilst the House of Douglas and Hume were rivals in the south of Scotland, they would during this period of national crisis be expected to work with each other. Wappinshaws (weapon shows) were ordered to be mustered in every shire in order to prepare the Scots for further invasions, and to gather together adequate weapons; 'axes, and Jedworth staves, halberds and good two-handed swords'. [10]

Earlier in the previous month French munitions, comprising gunpowder, guns, bullets, pikes and other weaponry had arrived at Dumbarton and the lords of Glasgow, Paisley and Newbottle were requested to bring them to Glasgow, then to Stirling. North of the Forth the breakdown of authority resulted in war bands pillaging and terrorizing the regions. In Atholl a captain called Marcobet Struan leading 800 raiders 'preyed and spoiled' widely. To counter these bandits the Earl of Crawford was commissioned as Justicier of the North. [11]

Besides lawlessness, contagious disease was a threat to

stability. Towards the last few months of the year a pestilence broke out in Edinburgh. This forced the government to temporarily pursue business north of the Firth of Forth. The Edinburgh provost and city magistrates ordered that for fifteen days all windows and doors were to stay shut, and shops were to close. Beggars and homeless people were prohibited from travelling in the dark without a light, so that they could not pass the disease in the dark. All inflicted were taken to barns and buildings in the Boroughmuir, and sailing then to Inchkeith Isle from the Leith beaches was another option. These systems of quarantine were installed until the threat of disease lessened in the early months of 1515. [12]

With Margaret as Regent there would also have been many nobles and prelates who feared her brother Henry VIII, and would be suspicious of any influence the King of England could bear on the Queen of Scotland. She would write to her brother asking for an end to warfare and stating that her son was an infant King within a nation beset by feud and rivalries. She asked that Henry VIII be a supportive uncle to his young nephew. Margaret would receive a letter of condolence from the Queen of England on November 11th, and within it Henry expressed kindness to his sister. Nevertheless despite kind words Henry would be looking for opportunities to impose his will on Scotland, and Lord Dacre would continue to launch large raids across the borders. [13]

At that period soon after the battle, there were too few of the nobility to offer effective opposition to a female becoming regent. However a party within the nobility would propose to send a letter to the French King calling on him to send the Frenchman John Stewart (Stuart in the French style), to Scotland and become tutor to the King as well as become governor of Scotland. John was son of Alexander, the forfeited Duke of Albany and brother of James III. He was also heir-apparent to the crown after James V. This suggestion was opposed by Beaton, who whilst acknowledging the ancestry of John Stewart, reminded the others that he was a Frenchman who would not understand the ways of the Scots.

Beaton suggested either the Earl of Arran or the Earl of Lennox as regents, both being Scots of royal blood. Arran would have been a controversial choice. Prior to Flodden he had commanded the Scottish fleet, and instead of supporting the strategic aims of the land army, he led it on a pointless although profitable raid on Carrickfergus in Ireland. It is highly unlikely that he would have been able to command widespread support or confidence. [14]

Whether in response to this communication to Louis or a result of a French initiative, two ambassadors, Anthony D'Arcy, Sieur de la Baste, known as the White Knight due to the gleam of his armour, and Master James Ogilvy, arrived in Scotland and requested a meeting of the Three Estates. They were to deliver a message from Louis XII. The Estates gathered on November 26th in Perth and the ambassadors, of which Baste had been a favoured friend to James IV, offered two proposals; one to renew the alliance between Scotland and France, and the second for King Louis to send John Stewart if Scotland accepted him as governor of the realm. Arms and money would also be sent. In contemporary correspondence John Stewart would be known as Duke of Albany, despite not having been confirmed in this title by James IV. The Scots agreed to consider these proposals.

James Hamilton, the Earl of Arran, had arrived in Scotland bringing with him the remains of the Scottish fleet. Arran and Lord Fleming, whilst in France, had pressed King Louis to send Albany to Scotland. The reports of this possible development were circulated widely across the continent, and the victory of Flodden was seen by some, such as Robert Stewart, Lord of Aubigny, a Scots soldier of fortune, as of no lasting consequence since the Scots/French alliance would endure and grow stronger whilst Albany schooled the young James V in the laws of kingship. The figure of Albany began to become a significant propaganda asset for the Scots and French, and reports of his movements and intentions became priorities for the English diplomats and their spies overseas. [15]

The Council meeting at Perth on November 26th also set out to appoint candidates for the benefices made vacant by the losses at Flodden. It was proposed that the Bishop of Aberdeen should be nominated to the Archbishopric of St Andrews, and the Bishop of Caithness should take Aberdeen, whilst the Bishopric of Caithness went to a brother of the Earl of Atholl. James Hepburn was chosen for the Abbey of Dunfermline and David Hume, brother of Alexander Hume, for the priory of Coldingham. As the King of Scotland had the right to nominate candidates to the benefices, it can be assumed that the Queen used her royal authority as regent to support these choices, especially as her close friend Gavin Douglas was nominated for the priory of Arbroath, and it was reported that she supported the Bishop of Aberdeen for the Archbishopric of St Andrews.

Yet over the next few months after Flodden there would be disputes over the superiority of royal rights against papal rights to appoint churchmen, and localized rivalries would develop into vicious battles over revenues and legal and judicial privileges. Whilst the Lord Chamberlain's brother David Hume would occupy the Priory of Coldingham, he would still need to be confirmed by the pope or a papal envoy, so his position would remain uncertain. Andrew, Bishop of Caithness, would complain that Master Thomas Kerr had taken over the rights and revenues of Kelso Abbey against the authority of Caithness, and had the backing of his kinsman Dandy Kerr, who used armed force to occupy the abbey. At an international level Henry VIII would ask Pope Leo to demote the Archbishopric of St Andrews to a bishopric under the authority of York, whilst it was reported that Leo had granted St Andrews to his nephew Cardinal Cibo. [16]

Margaret returned to Stirling from Perth during December. She would appoint herself another group of advisers who may have been more akin to a personal bodyguard, comprising Alexander Lindsay, Earl of Crawford, Lord John Drummond of Cargill and Stobhall, Lord Patrick Lindsay of the Byres, and Lord William Ruthven, who were instructed to keep themselves with the Queen, and offer council. Such a body, which could call on a significant number of retainers, would develop into a rival to the parliamentary appointed council, and it is significant that they were allies of the Red Douglases. Lord John Drummond was the maternal grandfather of the Earl of Angus, his daughter Elizabeth having married Angus' father George Douglas.

He was also the father of Lady Margaret Drummond, who was alleged to have secretly married King James. Queen Margaret would show a remarkable kindness and loyalty to the elderly and experienced Lord Drummond, and such bonds would have been strengthened through his granddaughter, Lady Margaret, described as the 'King's daughter' residing in Stirling. She also may have felt some empathy with Drummond, his daughter having supposedly been poisoned to make way for a young Margaret Tudor to come to Scotland and marry James. Stirling Castle was to be assigned the residence of James V, and Queen Margaret was to retain possession of it. To assist her Lord Drummond was assigned custodian of the castle. [17]

By a parliament called at Stirling on December 21st, the Scots nobles and prelates would have been aware that Margaret was now around five months pregnant. She would still take an active part in government, yet by the spring she would be forced to retire from public procedures to care for her unborn child. With such a development the nobles and prelates would have actively sought alternative regents and governors. The Duke of Albany was the one choice who would cement the alliance with France, whilst Margaret ensured that her interests were represented by the Red Douglas faction, which comprised the Earl and Master of Angus, Gavin Douglas, Lord Drummond and their adherents, all of whom sat on the various councils and committees.

For the Lords of Scotland, they were faced with options for who to support during the minority. Margaret had legal right according to the Will of James, whilst the Lords Council would agree to send word to Albany inviting him to become governor of Scotland. There were others who preferred the Earl of Arran, who also had a claim as heir presumptive after Albany. Margaret had the friendship of the Douglases, with the possibility of English support through her brother. If Margaret remained as regent and tutor of James, peace between Scotland and England could be achieved, although there was the risk that Scotland could be become subservient to Henry VIII's ambition to become Lord Paramount. With the Duke of Albany the Scots would have alliance with France, with money, arms and diplomatic support. The danger was war with England, and remembering Flodden, the danger of being used to assist France without that assistance being reciprocated. The choices were difficult and each offered many stark possibilities. (18)

The Scots were also faced with a government with little or no revenue to finance a viable defence beyond the traditional feudal obligations. Crown officers had been tasked with auditing crown finances and found that the treasury was empty. Queen Margaret had been given command of a treasure chest which included the 18,000 gold crowns paid to King James by France. It appears that James used much of that sum in his invasion of England, whilst Margaret would use the remainder as part of her dowry, and for her upkeep and the education of her son.

William Elphinstone, Bishop of Aberdeen, 'deplored the situation of the country' where private armies were engaged in feuds, thefts and oppressions which were harming the poor and defenceless. He blamed the war of James IV for the depletion of the treasury and the lack of funds needed for the upkeep of king and queen. He would support the proposal to make the Duke of Albany governor, and even though he did not believe that the French intervention would stop the bloodshed it would at best introduce a measure of law and order. (19)

Whilst Lord Dacre devastated the Scottish marches, the English King would write to Pope Leo stating his commitment to prosecuting war against France in the New Year. However one of Henry's allies on the continent, King Ferdinand of Aragon, believed that the 'Scotch business' would distract Henry away from warfare against France, because the Scots had no inclination towards peace. He passed his doubts about Henry's ability to continue the war to the Holy Roman Emperor. However these opinions should be seen in the light of Ferdinand's secret agreement with King Louis of France, and as attempts to discourage Maximilian from his alliance with Henry VIII. [20]

Open warfare was still a daily occurrence on the borders, yet despite Flodden the Scots were still able to retaliate, with five towns on the Eastern March being burned and a raiding force drawing within two miles of Berwick. The dominant Scottish power on the Eastern marches were the Humes, and Buchanan gives a description of Lord Alexander, Warden of the Scottish Marches and Lord Chamberlain, as being 'actuated by a criminal ambition' where he acquired power and prestige through the sponsoring of raiding and grand larceny. [21]

On the Eastern March Dunbar and Fast Castle was in need of artillery, supplies and manpower, and the council discussed how to acquire this. The captain of Edinburgh castle also complained that there was scarcity of cannon and Sieur de la Baste, who had recently came over from France with the Earl of Arran, had visited the castle along with Robert Borthwick. Whilst bulwarks and trenches had been established by both, the defences were still inadequate for such a 'principle strength of the realm'. De la Baste also wrote to the King of France stating that the Scots would prosecute war with England and ask for 1,000 Lanziechts and 600 horse, besides money and arms. The captain Patrick Creichton of Granston complained that he had not been paid his pension or received funds for maintaining the castle due to lands assigned to provide revenue being wasted, and his own goods stolen. [22]

By January Dacre was reporting that 30 towns close to the border had come into an agreement with the Warden of Scotland, Lord Hume, 'for want of defence'. This meant they were paying Hume not to attack them. The commander of Berwick or his lieutenants had done little to challenge a growing Scottish ascendancy on the Eastern marches. [23]

In the Western Isles there had also been armed turmoil, and

Donald MacDonald of Lochalsh led an uprising. With the death of Colin Campbell, 2ndEarl of Argyll, at Flodden, his son Archibald became 3rd Earl of Argyll. He was successful in quelling the violence and his military and political talents were recognized when in 1514 he was appointed Justice-General of Scotland. This allowed him to use judicial tools and mechanisms to extend law and order into the Gaelic regions of Scotland as well as furthering his own feudal authority. Alexander Gordon, Earl of Huntley, became the lieutenant of the highland regions north of the Firth of Forth which did not infringe on Argyll's sphere of influence. [24]

By March 1514 there were reports from Dacre that there were Scots who were opposed to the arrival of Albany, although he did not identify them. There were also rumours that the Frenchman would bring an army of French and Danish soldiers, and his Scots supporters were said to be preparing to capture Berwick upon his arrival. There would be obstacles to Albany's journeying to Scotland, more from Louis who hemmed in by the Holy League was striving for better relations with Henry VIII, and as a sign of goodwill and faith he was reluctant to let Albany pass and stir up hostilities between Scotland and England. He would claim to the Scots that Albany was too valuable to be allowed to leave France, yet his Scottish allies could see that despite their sacrifices at Flodden the French King was preparing to leave his allies in the lurch. [25]

Whilst there was uncertainty about whether Albany would arrive in Scotland, it is not clear how much genuine support Queen Margaret had amongst the nobility, yet she appears to have offered effective government despite her pregnancy. She also faced opposition. As the historian Tytler relates, many of the Scottish lords saw the rule of women as an opportunity to expand their own power, and she especially complained in letters to her brother Henry of Alexander Hume, the Lord Chamberlain, who acted as a law to himself. At a parliament in Edinburgh during March it was decided that Patrick Hamilton, Lyon Herald, would travel in April to France to request that Albany come to Scotland and be confirmed as guardian and tutor. Queen Margaret could see that whatever power she had now would be diminished when Albany and the French interests arrived in Scotland. Henry would write to Margaret advising her to oppose the bringing over of Albany, as he would work for the interests of France against those of England. He also warned that her son's life would be in danger since the Duke of Albany was next in line of succession to James, blatantly suggesting that the Duke of Albany might murder the young King for the crown of Scotland. It was malicious scaremongering, but Henry was deeply concerned about the Scots using French resources to threaten the northern border. [26]

Margaret gave birth to another son, Alexander, on April 13th, 1514 at Stirling, eight months after the death of James IV. He was baptized by the Bishop of Caithness and titled Duke of Rothesay. She was afraid that she or her infants could be subject to capture by the more ambitious nobles who would see possession of the young King as a method of acquiring power. Nor was she confident that her brother would be able to protect her. There were also reports that Louis XII sought to marry Margaret, a coupling that worried Henry VIII, as this would raise the possibility of a Frenchman becoming King of Scotland, and his sister becoming Queen of France with some strong hereditary rights to England if Henry died childless. These reports appear to have been French tactics to unsettle the King of England, and to persuade him to seek a peace with France, as the alternative could become very complicated. [27]

Queen Margaret was not holding out for the hope of protection from far-off France and instead would look closer to home. She decided to enter into a friendship with the twenty-five-year-old Archibald Douglas, Earl of Angus, who according to Pitscottie she 'loved and thought most able'. Angus was described as being 'very lusty in the Queen's sight', suggesting that the friendship had developed into an intimacy that was openly displayed. Other chroniclers say he was a handsome and good-hearted individual, and the Douglas name was popular across the nation due to history and legend.

Yet there was a purpose to the Douglases' friendship with Queen Margaret in that it drew them closer to the centre of power. Margaret was young and attractive, with a reputation for having strong 'amorous propensities', as well as strong emotions. Such descriptions would be used by enemies and critics alike to discredit her; however the evidence of her many letters would reveal a strong-willed and intelligent woman, who could be manipulative if need be, although in her defence she was surrounding by manipulative forces. Not only aware of the complexities of Scottish politics, she was more than capable of putting up challenges against the many dangerous obstacles that she would be forced to face. [28]

On the continent Louis continued to seek peace with England, yet he also exploited English fears of Albany as a negotiating tactic. On June 3rd 1514 he apparently agreed to an estimate for sending forces to Scotland, where four months funding of 438,950 livres tournois was to be provided for 8,000 soldiers and sailors. There were also reports that Richard de la Pole, the 'White Rose' and pretender to the throne of England, was to join with Albany. These were not genuine proposals as Louis did not want Albany to leave for Scotland.

He would also offer 25,000 livres tournois to the King of Scots in the event of a peace treaty between France and England. Although this payment was offered to help with royal finances, it was obviously a bribe to ensure the party in power did not provoke war. The Duke of Albany would also explain to the Scottish ambassadors that the Scots needed to be vigilant against English aggression and intrigues, emphasising the importance of Queen and Council staying united.

A Scottish parliament was called for July 12th and the disorders within the kingdom were discussed. It was agreed that two envoys should be sent to England to broker for peace. On July 28th James Ogilvy, Abbot of Dryburgh, and Sir Patrick Hamilton, the Lyon Herald, returned from France with letters from the King of France and the Duke of Albany, in which both explained that armed forces could not at that time travel to Scotland until some kind of peace was agreed between France and England. It was also important for Louis' European strategy to neutralize the threat from England through a meaningful treaty, and he did not want Scotland to upset his political balancing act. Whilst disappointing for the pro-French party, this development would allow Queen Margaret the time to build up an alternative power base. [29]

Lord Drummond would suggest Margaret marry his maternal grandson the Earl of Angus. Allying with a pro-English party would counter Albany and the pro-French party. Realising that she needed a strong figure such as Angus by her side she took the advice, and they married at the church of Kinnoull on August 14th. John Drummond, a nephew of Lord Drummond, and the Parson of Kinnoull and Dean of Dunblane, conducted the ceremony. This marriage caused anger and bitterness amongst many of the nobility, as Douglas power was now propelled into the machinery of government. Angus had already been married, and was now a widower. Young as he was he possessed ambition, as well as an aggressive personality. Other observers were less kind; Gavin, his own uncle, would later call him a 'young unwise fool', although Godscroft would suggest he was a man of 'greater wisdom than he made show of'. He was confident enough to present himself as a suitor to a widowed queen, success in which would bring him immense power.

Whilst it was said that his brother George was the planner, Godscroft believes this was a perception that Angus encouraged, for he often had the mind to make decisions for himself but preferred not to reveal his purposes until the time was right. As for being a fool, Scotland was a dangerous and testing place for nobles, with rapidly changing political events that forced individuals, no matter how wise, to act rashly or reckless. Whatever Angus' true qualities, his marriage to the Queen would undermine her own position as regent, as the will of James IV had stipulated that she would retain the regency only if she remained unmarried and 'kept her widowhood and her body clean from lechery'. [30]

The Red Douglases on their part could envisage power and prestige through the figure of the Queen, if she was allowed to continue to administer the government. With divisions in Scotland, Margaret sought to quell the warring between Scotland and England and would write to her brother requesting that he agree to a truce and cease waging war against a country with a child-king. Henry, whilst replying that he would seek a peace if peace was forthcoming, and expressing a desire for peaceful coexistence, would contradict these sentiments by ordering Dacre to continue waging war against the Scots. The Queen and nobility appeared powerless to stop the constant bloodletting on the borders, and the rivalry that was developing between the powerful became a priority more important than the misery of the common folk. [31]

Louis would enter into a peace treaty with England in August 1514, and Scotland would be comprehended into the peace but on harsh conditions. The treaty was to be concluded on September 15th, but if in the period leading to that date the Scots invaded England then the comprehension would be voided. As the Scots had entered the war with England in 'defence of the King of France's quarrel', Lesley had a good right to claim the treaty brought 'dishonour' to Louis. The Scots for their part refused to accept the terms of the treaty, stating they would await the arrival of Albany before negotiating, although as yet there was no definite date for that to happen. Part of the treaty provided that Louis would also marry Marie, Henry VIII's sister, and this took place on October 7th at Abbeyville. Marie was a fifteen-year-old who had been betrothed to Charles, the grandson of Maximilian, whilst Louis was a widower of fifty-two years of age. [32]

Margaret, seeking to pass crown power to her new husband, demanded that Beaton, the Archbishop of Glasgow, should hand over the Great Seal and resign the chancellorship. This he refused to do and retired to Fife. Margaret and Angus pursued him. Angus managed to arrest Beaton in Perth and violently deprived him of the Great Seal at the reported instigation of Queen Margaret. The Great Seal was then apparently handed over to Gavin Dunbar,

Dean of Moray. Gavin Douglas also gained the keys to the Seal.
The Archbishop of Glasgow would later manage to free himself
from Angus' hold.

Between August 9th 1514 and June 28th 1515, it is recorded
that Beaton hired a garrison of 200 men to defend his castle,
Falkland, against the Queen and 'her violent and unjust actions',
words that reflected this period of civil strife and uncertainty. The
nobility and clergy were incensed at this tyrannical contempt by
Angus and the Queen against the laws and traditions. Across the
land there were more and more people prepared to challenge the
Queen's party. (33)

At an Edinburgh assembly on August 26th Margaret reiterated
the granting of the Great Seal to Gavin Dunbar, Dean of Moray.
Arran, incensed at the actions against Beaton, opposed this,
demanding that the Great Seal be re-granted to Beaton. There was
a great danger of civil warfare breaking out, with Queen Margaret
at a disadvantage. To offset war, and to broker much needed time
to build up sufficient forces, the Queen and her spouse the Earl of
Angus, along with Gavin Douglas, postulate of Arbroath, Lords
Drummond and Ogilvy, the bishop of Argyll, the Abbot of
Holyroodhouse and the Dean of Moray, agreed to send for Albany
and for her to discontinue using the power of the crown from Sept
7th 1514. Sir Andrew Wood of Largo was authorised to travel to
France and invite Albany to become Governor of Scotland. The
Earl of Arran asked that on Sept 7th the Great Seal should be
passed to the Bishop of Glasgow. Margaret however had no
intention of honouring these agreements, and would seek out an
excuse to reject them at the first opportunity. The presence of
James Beaton amongst the opposing party would provide such an
excuse. (34)

Beaton on September 18th would come out of hiding, and
attend a council meeting at Dunfermline, joining Elphinstone,
Huntley, Arran and Hume in renewing the invitation to the Duke
of Albany, and also requesting that the King of France should
comprehend Scotland into the peace between France and England.

41

Margaret sent Gavin Douglas as her commissioner to this council meeting, and he made it clear that on Margaret's behalf he would not recognise the authority of those lords or prelates that Margaret considered 'being suspect to us'. He declined a request by Beaton to present the Queen's mandate to the council, stating that 'he should not sit as judge'. (35)

On September 21st the Lords of Council sitting at Dunfermline sent Lord Erskine, the Bishop of Argyll, the Abbot of Quitthern and the laird of Balvery to Stirling to meet with lords that were part of the Queen's party. They sought to debate matters regarding the 'public well of the realm', whilst reminding them that since September 7th the Queen no longer possessed the power to administer in the King's name. Gavin Douglas and Gavin Dunbar were sent letters from the council demanding that they respectively hand over the keys of the Great Seal to James Beaton, Archbishop of Glasgow, who was also designated chancellor. Douglas and Dunbar would refuse. A parliament was called to be held at Edinburgh for November 17th. (36)

Alexander Hume, the Lord Chamberlain, is quoted as saying that the council had:

'...shown heretofore our willingness to honour the Queen contrary to the ancient custom of custom of this kingdom; we suffered and obeyed her authority the whiles she herself kept her right by keeping her widowhood. Now she has quit it by marrying, why should we not choose another to succeed in the place she has voluntarily left? Our old laws do not permit that a woman would govern in the most peaceable times, far less now when such evils do threaten as can scarcely be resisted by the wisest and most sufficient men.'

Hume was one of the most vocal supporters of the Duke of Albany becoming governor, possibly to curb the power of his border rivals the Douglases, who were regaining influence in Annandale and Liddlesdale, areas that were traditional strongholds of the Douglases before become lordships of the Humes. He was also blamed by his enemies for committing treason during the battle of

Flodden, in which he failed to assist King James at a crucial period in the battle. There were also stories that King James had survived the battle of Flodden and fled by horse across the Tweed and to Kelso, where he was said to have been killed by followers of Lord Hume, in response perhaps to the threat of royal blame falling on the powerful border lord. Possibly fearing the power of these rumours, Lord Hume made a calculated decision to ally himself with Albany. He also calculated that since Albany would be claiming the Earldom of Dunbar when he arrived in Scotland, Alexander Hume would be an indispensable ally due to his power and influence in the south-eastern and border regions. [37]

The Lord of Council also sent the Lord Lyon, Sir William Cumming, to the presence of the Queen to demand that Angus make himself available for examination by the Lords and demand his reasoning for marrying the Queen without their approval. Upon approaching the Earl of Angus to give the summons, Lord Drummond is said to have hit the Lord Lyon. Margaret would write to her brother and downplay the assault, although she would defend Lord Drummond in that the Lord Lyon's attitude was provocative. According to the Queen there had been a demand in the name of the Lord's Council that she surrender her rights to her two children and hand them over to appointed guardians. [38]

The Queen's party decided to retire from Stirling and travel to Perth, where they would attempt to appeal to those powers north of the Firth of Forth. The opposing Lords of Council established their power in Edinburgh. The Edinburgh parliament of October 24th would decree that Queen Margaret cease using the authority of the King and stop acting as tutor. She was also blocked from lifting rents and revenues from the crown lands, and not allowed to profit from the King's possessions, including jewels and treasure. The Lords Council also determined to create a new seal, although there is no record that this happened. Queen Margaret however would report that her enemies had the Great Seal and were acting 'as if they were kings'. Whether the Lord Council had somehow gained possession of the Great Seal from Dunbar or made another one is unclear. To add to the confusion Gavin Douglas from November began to act as chancellor, which suggests he still had possession of the Great Seal, and the following year James Beaton on January 5th, 1515, was styled Chancellor. [(39)]

In the parliament and royal councils the prelates had begun to gain a significant political voice in respect of the political void created by the slaughter of many of the nobility at Flodden. The issue of dispensing benefices after the slaying of several prelates at Flodden would cause many of the prelates to fall out. Queen Margaret and the Lords of Council had wanted William Elphinstone, Bishop of Aberdeen, to replace the slain Alexander Stewart as Archbishop of St Andrews, through a letter sent in James V's name and addressed to Pope Leo X, dated August 5th, 1514. However when Elphinstone after a bout of serious illness died on October 25th, other competitors would arise. In Ephinstone Scotland had lost an able adviser, who was also a constant supporter of peaceful solutions and conciliation, and would have acted as a counterbalance to more the aggressive and warlike policies of the nobles and prelates. [(40)]

One candidate for the post of Archbishop of St Andrews who enjoyed the support of the papacy was Andrew Forman, bishop of Moray. He was opposed by John Hepburn, the prior of St Andrews, who had the backing of the monks of Fife, who followed ancient tradition where an Abbot was successor to the Archbishop. Queen Margaret in November stepped in and nominated Gavin Douglas as Archbishop of St Andrews. She would later recruit the support of her brother Henry VIII, who would write to Pope Leo X in glowing terms regarding the virtues of Gavin Douglas, his 'extraordinary learning conjoined with prudence, modesty, probity and a great zeal for the public good'. The Red Douglases took over the castle of St Andrews. John Hepburn was not going to accept this invasion. The monks elected him as Archbishop.

As proctor, John Hepburn was able to collect the revenues of St Andrews, and during November 1514 he was reportedly in Edinburgh, possibly to recruit and finance professional soldiers.

Hepburn would also profit from the support of the Lord Chamberlain and the Humes with their vast resources of manpower. Adding this force to that of local levies, Hepburn was able to lay siege to St Andrews. By November 23rd, Margaret would write to her brother calling on him to help raise the siege by sending a fleet of ships stationed near Berwick. She also sent Angus with 600 horsemen to St Andrews. Her chief enemy, she asserted, was the Lord Chamberlain. Fearing that the Lords of Council would also attempt a siege of Stirling, she asked her brother to send a land army and at least distract Hume to the borders. She claimed to be paying £1,000 in wages per day, and funds were shrinking. If it is true that Margaret had gained possession of her late husband's treasure, then this civil strife was steadily depleting her fortune.

As Angus advanced towards St Andrews to assist his uncle, he could do little, as Hepburn was too difficult to dislodge, and Lord Hume and the Earl of Arran used Angus' absence to advance on Stirling and compel Queen Margaret to accompany them to Edinburgh and attend the council. This forced Angus to divert away from St Andrews and he rode south to rescue his wife and take her back to Stirling, although no details are given on how this was achieved. With Angus distracted and with no relief eminent, Hepburn managed to storm St Andrews and expel the garrison. In commenting on these proceedings, Lord Dacre on November 27th stated that Scotland was beset by 'robbery, spoiling and vengeance', which 'I pray Lord God to continue'. [41]

The Vatican-sponsored competitor for the see of St Andrews, Andrew Forman, Bishop of Moray, was commendator of Dryburgh, Pittenween, and of Nottingham in England. He was also Bishop of Bourges by right of Louis XII, King of France. On November 13th 1514 Leo X translated him as Archbishop of St Andrews, as well as having confirmed him in the abbacies of Dunfermline and Arbroath. He was also conferred as papal legate by Leo X.

Forman had a rich and varied church career behind him, and he was not universally popular in Scotland. Born in 1465, a son of Nicholas of Hatton in Berwickshire, he graduated at St Andrews in 1483. Employed briefly by the fifth Earl of Angus, he settled into a career with the state, becoming by 1490 James IV's procurator in Rome and being promoted to apostolic promontory. He, along with the poet William Dunbar, was an ambassador in negotiating the Treaty of Perpetual Peace between Scotland and England, resulting in the marriage of James IV to Margaret Tudor. In 1510, in support of James IV's plan for organising a European crusade, he tried to broker peace between France and the Pope, and in 1511 between France and Venice. Louis of France also sent Forman to Scotland to stop James IV joining a Holy League against France.

Despite his part in the Treaty between Scotland and England, Forman would become notorious for changing direction and supposedly persuading James IV to renew the alliance with France and break with England. To win his support and loyalty, King Louis granted Forman the Archbishopric of Bourges. When considering who to grant the Archbishopric of St Andrews, Pope Leo, although initially promoting Cardinal Cibo, decided after Scottish opposition to appoint Forman, requesting that he resign Bourges in favour of Cibo. Leo had written to the Duke of Albany on April 11th 1514, recognising him as Governor and Regent of Scotland and informing him that Forman was his choice as Archbishop of St Andrews . Forman was also compelled by the French to give up the Abbacy of Arbroath to James Stewart, Earl of Moray and illegitimate son of James IV, who was residing in France, a request he opposed.

A letter was sent to the Lords of Council in November resulting in the transfer of Dunbar Castle from Robert Forman, Dean of Glasgow, and brother of Andrew, to Sieur de la Baste, the Duke of Albany's representative in Scotland. Dunbar was one of the most strategically important castles on the east coast, with a seaport which would allow supplies from France into Scotland, as well as giving Albany a significant foothold on the marches. Albany was also claiming it as part of his birthright through his father's forfeited Dukedom of Albany, which included the Earldom of March. [(42)]

Margaret was now regretting having supported the August assembly to invite Albany to come to Scotland and become Governor, although her support had been insincere and meant to buy time. Possibly she was hoping and expecting support from her brother, which was not forthcoming. Her authority was becoming steadily more challenged by the opposing party, and she now viewed the arrival of the Duke of Albany as an ultimate threat to her own authority unless she could get her brother to intervene.

The Duke of Albany's crossing over to Scotland would be dependent on gaining permission from Louis, and the French King had on October 7th married Henry's other sister Mary Tudor at Abbeyville. Albany was present as a guest. There was no indication from Louis that he would allow Albany to leave, yet Margaret would continue to raise this possibility and wrote from Stirling pleading with Henry to use the English navy to block any French fleets. Henry meanwhile was calling himself Protector of Scotland, a fact that caused an angry Lords of Council to write to Pope Leo on November 14th stating that this title was nonexistent and conjured out of Henry's imagination.

The Queen and Gavin Douglas also entered into a correspondence with Adam Williamson, a Scottish cleric employed on the borders by Lord Dacre, and a trusted agent of Henry VIII. Writing from November into January 1515, Williamson was promoting a scheme where Margaret and her sons should seek refuge in England, and the Earl of Angus was offered a base at Penrith or Carlisle. Williamson assured Gavin Douglas that Angus would be supplied with 'money or men, Scots or English, or both, to subdue the rebel Lords of Scotland'. It was also conveyed that Englishmen would in large numbers support Margaret against her enemies, and that her son James would be recognised as heir-apparent to the crown of England if Henry died without issue. There is no evidence that Margaret thought self-exile would have been a good idea, and Angus rejected the idea despite being offered a safe conduct and a wealth of promises. [43]

Margaret also had to contend with a letter of December 8th 1514 from Pope Leo informing her that he had translated Andrew Forman as Archbishop and had also made him papal legate, or *a latere,* for Scotland. On December 11th he was commissioned to serve in Scotland for life. Gavin Douglas, by a consistorial act, was to resign the Arbroath abbacy to Forman, and James Hepburn, nephew of John Hepburn, was to surrender the Abbacy of Dunfermline. Meanwhile the English Navy was on alert to prevent Albany or Forman from arriving in Scotland. With the aid of a French vessel, Forman's clerk, Master John Sauchie, managed to avoid the English ships and landed at Leith on January 16th 1515. [(44)]

The death of Louis on January 5th 1515 brought his cousin, the 21-year-old Francis of Angoulême, to the throne. His mother was Louise of Savoy, who would encourage the aggressive statesmanship of her 'Caesar'. Francis I was minded to strengthening the alliance between Scotland and France, and sent ambassadors Vaire and Vilesbresmc with a message from the Council of State asking the Scots to accept comprehension into the treaty between France and England. He would also intend to send Albany to Scotland, not to provoke war but to discourage England from invading France. Francis had ambitions to the east with plans to invade Italy. [(45)]

Towards the end of 1514, Arran, the Earl of Glencairn, and John Stewart, Earl of Lennox and nephew of Arran, would enter into an alliance against Angus. On January 12th 1515, Lennox and Glencairn would take Dumbarton Castle for the Duke of Albany, expelling the governor Lord Erskine. The Earl of Angus would rendezvous with Lennox so as to discuss the present situation. After the meeting he travelled to Glasgow, and along the route the Earl of Arran positioned 600 men and artillery to set upon the young Earl as he passed by. The trap however failed, and Angus survived unscathed. [(46)]

Master John Sauchie had the papal bulls published at the Edinburgh High Church and Abbey Church on January 16th and 17th 1515, respectively. No one however was prepared to proclaim the bulls because of opposition from the Humes. Similarly nobody would proclaim in St Andrews through fear of Hepburn and his followers. Hepburn would occupy St Andrews with a strong garrison. After the papal proclamations in January 1515, Hepburn organised an assembly at St Andrews Cathedral, which Forman would claim was a usurpation of royal authority. Those present were temporal; lords and supporters of Hepburn. Andrew Forman and his friends and allies were proclaimed exiles and there was a plan to attack Spynie Castle in Moray and waste the lands and properties of Forman's tenants and adherents. On January 25th 1515 Hepburn appeared before the Lords of Council on the business of having received the nomination for Dunfermline, but also to accuse Andrew Forman of going against the royal privilege and of benefiting from the slaughter of Flodden by buying up the vacant benefices. Forman's brother Robert, Dean of Glasgow and promoter of his interests in Scotland, made the defence that any benefices bought up were done to stop Italian speculators from doing the same. The Council, after listening to all arguments, did not judge the arguments of either side, but decided to write to the Duke of Albany asking him to uphold the king's privilege to nominate benefices, to oppose anyone seeking to circumnavigate this right and take advantage of vacant benefices during the King's minority. (47)

Another important vacancy would be contested when George Brown, Bishop of Dunkeld, died, and whilst the Queen was in Perth with her supporters on the Council she forwarded Gavin Douglas as candidate. The members present were the Earls of Angus, Crawford, Errol, Huntley and Glencairn, the new Bishop of Aberdeen, Lords Drummond, Ogilvy, Innermeitht and Hay. Queen Margaret had already written to Leo X in June 1514 regarding another church position for Gavin Douglas, the Abbacy of Aberbrothock or Arbroath, one of the wealthiest abbeys. The letter stated that since Gavin was controller of the revenues of the monastery he was the only practical candidate for the abbacy. Margaret also included a warning in that 'his family' would not 'permit him to be deprived of the office', and he could only be expelled by 'superior force'.

Douglas also wrote to Adam Williamson, asking him to use his influence in promoting his candidacy, and sent money to help this endeavour. Williamson was still promoting the idea of Margaret and her children fleeing to England, which would have gained Henry VIII a diplomatic advantage in possessing the person of the King of Scotland. Gavin Douglas, writing on the 21st January 1515 to Williamson, stated that there would be difficulties for the Queen and her sons in travelling to England, and instead proposed that Henry VIII should lead an army into Scotland, and that the majority of Scots would support him so that in Douglas' words Henry could free the people so 'oppressed for lack of justice, by thieves, robbery and other extortions that they would be glad to live under the great Turk to have justice'. [48]

Douglas had one significant rival for Dunkeld, in Andrew Stewart, brother of John, 2nd Earl of Atholl. When Bishop Brown died Atholl arrived at Dunkeld with a large force and compelled the canons to select his brother as bishop, even though he was only a sub deacon. After Brown's funeral a chaptor of canons was assembled and Andrew Stewart was postulated. Letters would be sent to the Duke of Albany in France but he would not make a decision on the granting of benefices until he had reached Scotland. On February 18th, 1515, at the request of Margaret, Henry VIII wrote a letter to Pope Leo favouring Gavin Douglas as Bishop of Dunkeld. [49]

The subject of Forman's appointment as Archbishop of St Andrews would briefly bring antagonists around the table and seemingly unite them under a common purpose. Queen Margaret even believed that if Albany sided with Forman the Lords would oppose the Frenchman. A meeting was held in Hepburn's St Andrew's chamber, dated precisely on the minutes as 5pm on March 5th, and although not technically a Lords of Council meeting it was listed in the register, since several prominent lords were present. Errol, Huntley, Crawford, Arran and James Beaton were in attendance, as was Gavin Douglas, acting on behalf of the Queen.

The King's advocate, James Wishart, raised an act to denounce the Papal Bulls which favoured Forman. The Lords however decided that they could not make a decision on this as they were few in attendance. Letters written on March 3rd at St Andrews, in the name of James V to Leo X, made a range of accusations against Andrew Forman. The letters repeated the accusation that Forman, whilst resident in France, had been a major promoter of war between Scotland and England instead of a supporter of peace, and once more Forman was accused of buying up all the vacant benefices made available by the slaughter of churchmen at Flodden, and using letters from the King of France and Albany to add credence of these enterprises. There is obviously a great deal of opposition to Forman, and Angus himself was present at this meeting. The letters, under the name of James V and stamped with the Great Seal, ask that Leo should reverse Forman's appointment. James Beaton was still recognised as Chancellor, although it is unclear who, whether Beaton or Gavin Douglas, possessed the Great Seal. Beaton's opposition to signing the denouncement against the papal bull may have been down to not wanting to directly oppose the Pope, whilst signing the letter requesting Forman's withdrawal as Archbishop was merely a request for consideration of the proposal. [50]

To dislodge the Lord Chamberlain from supporting Hepburn, Forman, possibly through his brother Robert, used an associate called Fraser, who was on good terms with Hume, to visit Lord Hume at his stronghold in the Merse. He offered the incentive of confirming his brother David Hume as prior of Coldingham. Whilst the Lords Council had nominated Hume for the priory of Coldingham, opposition from the Lord Chamberlain to the Queen and Angus would have not made this a guarantee. The Lord Chamberlain was ambitious and aimed to gain the abbacy of Holyrood for his brother; however Coldingham was rich pickings, and the offer was accepted.

The Humes now placed their support behind Forman. Hepburn was betrayed and deserted by his Hume allies, but he would not give up so easily. The Humes gathered together a considerable force, led by William Hume, brother of the Lord Chamberlain. They rode into Edinburgh and proclaimed the papal bull in favour of Forman. Adopting the authority of the King, Hepburn and all his supporters were declared rebels and put to the horn. The Humes, with Robert Forman representing his brother's cause, then advanced towards St Andrews, seeking to intimidate Hepburn into surrendering the benefice. Hepburn gathered his forces from amongst the gentlemen of Fife and elsewhere. He fortified the town, and artillery was placed in the cathedral, castle, and on the town walls to discourage the Humes from mounting an assault. [51]

Even with the support of the Humes, Forman could see that force alone would not achieve his ambition. He would eventually settle into making a deal with his rival Hepburn, who had a reputation for secret cunning, as opposed to Forman's supposedly more forthright approach. Forman employed the tactic of winning favour by distributing money and gifts, which appealed more to the commoners and was less violent. Through his brother Robert it was proposed that in return for Hepburn surrendering the Archbishopric of St Andrews Forman would forgive him the revenues he had already collected as proctor, and pay him 3,000 French crowns annually from the ecclesiastical revenues. Forman would also surrender the Bishopric of Moray and grant it to Hepburn's nephew James Hepburn. The offer was accepted, although John Hepburn would continue to hold St Andrews until Forman was in a position to claim it and pay what he promised. They would both need to wait until Albany finally reached Scotland in the spring of 1515 and went about settling the troubles within the country. Hepburn however would not forget how the Humes had betrayed him and set out by whatever means to destroy them. [52]

Whilst during the winter and spring the movements of Albany

and Andrew Forman on the continent were reported on by English spies, Forman would receive a commission from the Pope to travel to Scotland. Despite opposition from the Scottish nobles, Leo continued to retain Forman as papal legate. Forman also sought to ingratiate himself with Henry VIII in order to gain a safe passage through England, but also because Pope Leo was trying to convince Henry to join his Holy League, and was opposed to Albany crossing over to Scotland and diverting English attention. Leo was also a supporter of Gavin Douglas as Bishop of Dunkeld; part of that support might have something to do with Douglas' intention to pay for important friends in high places. On June 29th his proctor would pay out 450 gold florins in Rome. Forman would even try to win over the Douglas faction by using his influence to support the claims of Gavin Douglas. However, remembering that Forman was chief instigator of the recent war, and presently of no use to him, Henry denied him passage. [53]

After the embassy led by Sir Andrew Wood of Largo arrived in France, King Francis I decided to allow Albany to travel to Scotland and take over the governorship, furnishing him with arms and money. As Francis was preparing to embark on further warfare in Italy he wanted Albany to divert English attention, a strategy that seemingly worked as Henry VIII became more and more concerned about his arrival in Scotland.

Chapter Two: References

(1) (SBSH, vol.2, pp. 61-67. Thomson, vol.2, pp. 538-539). (2) (Fraser, pp. 178-180). (3) (ODNB, vol.4, pp. 554-557). (4) (ALCPA, xxvi, f.8. pp. 3-4, Edinburgh, Oct 3rd, 1513. Tytler, pp. 147-149). (5) (ALCPA, xxvi.f.3.pp. 1-2. ODNB, vol.4, pp. 554-556). (6) (LP, Instructions to Lord Dacre, Oct, 1513). (7) (Johnson, pp. 76-78. LP, Henry VIII to Leo X, Oct 12th, 1513. LP, From Vettor Lippomano, Oct 12th, 1513). (8) (Johnson, pp. 76-78). (9) (LP, Dacre to Ruthal, Oct 20th, 1513. LP, Dacres to Henry VIII, Oct 22nd, 1513. LP, Thos, Lord Dacre to (Ruthal, BP of Durham), Oct?, 1513. LP. Dacre to Henry VIII, November 13th, 1513. LP, Thomas Lord Dacre to Wolsey, November 23rd, 1513. Pitscottie, pp. 280-282. Thomson, vol.2, pp. 539-540. Tytler, pp. 147-149). (10)

(ALCPA, Perth Oct. 29. 1513, xxvi, f.11. [15] pp. 4-5). (11) (ALCPA, xxvi, f.6. pp. 2-3. Edinburgh, Sept 29th, 1513. Tytler, pp. 147-149). (12) (Thomson, vol.3, pp. 22). (13) (Buchanan, pp. 264-265. CSPS, Nov.11. 1513. Perth. p.2). (14) (ODNB, vol.4, pp. 554-556. Pitscottie, pp. 280-281. ODNB, vol.24, pp. 823-826). (15) (Holinshed, pp. 464-466. LP, Spinnelly to Henry VIII, November 15th, 1513. ODNB, vol.4, pp. 554-556. RPS, Perth, November 26th, 1513. Thomson, vol.2, pp. 540-541.Tytler, pp. 148-149. (16) (ALCPA, Edinburgh, Jan 10th 1514, xxvi, f.30. pp. 7-8. LP, Henry VIII to Leo X, October 12th 1513. LP, Venice, 15th October, 1513. LP, Dacre to Henry VIII, November 13th, 1513). (17) (ALCPA, Dec 1st, 1513, xxvi, f.26, [17] pp. 6-7. Exc rolls, vol. 14, pp. lviii-lix. Holinshed, pp. 463-464. SP. vol.4, pp. 257-259. SP, vol.7, pp. 40-45. Strickland, vol.1, pp. 90-91). (18) (ODNB, vol.29, pp. 619-627. ODNB, vol.36, pp. 648-652). (19) (Buchanan, pp. 264-266. Strickland, vol.1, pp. 91-92). (20) (Johnson, pp. 77-78). (21) (Buchanan, pp. 262-264. LP, Ferdinand King of Aragon to Quintana, January 1st, 1514). (22) (ALCPA, Edinburgh, Jan 10th 1514, xxvi, f.30. pp. 7-8). (23) (LP, Thomas Lord Dacre to Wolsey, January 15th 1514). (24) (Buchanan, pp. 262-263. ODNB, vol.9, pp. 748-749. SP, vol.4, pp. 531-533). (25) (Holinshed, pp. 465-467. Pitscottie, 280-281. Tytler, pp. 149-150). (26) (Holinshed, pp. 465-467. Pitscottie, 280-281. Tytler, pp. 149-150). (27) (Fraser, pp. 178-180. Pitscottie, 280-281. Strickland, vol.1, pp. 92-93. Tytler, pp. 149-150). (28) (Fraser, pp. 178-180. Pitscottie, 280-281. Tytler, pp. 149-150). (29) (Holinshed, pp. 465-467.ODNB, vol.52, pp. 709-715. Thomson, vol.2, pp. 540-541). (30) (Buchanan, pp. 264-265. Godscroft, vol.1, pp. 125-126. ODNB, vol.4, pp. 554-556. Pitscottie, pp. 280-281. Small, pp. x-xii. SP, vol.7, pp. 40-42.Thomson, vol.2, pp. 540-541). (31) (ODNB, vol.4, pp. 554-556). (32) (Johnson, pp. 77-78. Lesley, pp. 100-101. Tytler, pp. 149-151). (33) (Strickland, vol.1, pp. 98-99). (34) (ALCPA, Edinburgh, Aug. 26, 1514. xxvi. f.159. pp. 19-20. Buchanan, pp. 265-267. Exc rolls, vol. 14, pp. lxi-lxiii. ODNB, vol.4, pp. 554-556). (35) (ALCPA, September 18th, 1514, xxvi, f.160. ALCPA, September 18th, 1514, xxvi, f.162). (36) (ALCPA, September 18th, 1514, xxvi, f.162. ODNB, vol.4, pp. 554-556). (37) (Buchanan, pp. 258-260. Strickland, vol.1, pp. 97-98. Strickland, vol.1, pp. 105-106). (38) (ALCPA, October 24th,1514, xxvi, f.168, pp. 23-24. ALCPA, October 24th,1514, xxvi, f.117, pp. 24-25. Exc rolls, vol. 14, pp. lxi-lxiii. ODNB, vol.16, pp. 943-945. Strickland, vol.1, pp. 98-100). (39) (ALCPA, October 24th,1514, xxvi, f.168, pp. 23-24. ALCPA, October 24th,1514, xxvi, f.117, pp. 24-25. Exc rolls, vol. 14, pp. lxi-lxiii. ODNB, vol.16, pp. 643-647). (40) (ALCPA, October 24th,1514, xxvi, f.168, pp. 23-24. ALCPA, October 24th,1514, xxvi, f.117, pp. 24-25. Dowden, pp. 129-13. Exc rolls, vol. 14, pp. lxi-lxiii. ODNB, vol.16, pp. 643-647). (41) (Buchanan, pp. 263-264. Exc rolls, vol. 14, pp. lxi-lxiii. Fraser, pp. 180-182.ODNB, vol.20, pp. 369-

370. LP, Margaret of Scotland to Henry VIII, November 23rd, 1514. Small, pp. xxx-xxxi. Strickland, vol.1, pp. 100-102. Thomson, vol.2, pp. 542-543). (42) (ALCPA, November 20th, 1514, xxvi, f.175, pp. 27-28. Dowden, pp. 38-40. 165-167. LP, Dacre to the Council, November 27th, 1514. ODNB, vol.20, pp. 369-370). (43) (Fraser, pp. 180-182. Small, pp. xx-xxviii. Thomson, vol.2, pp. 538-539). (44) (Exc rolls, vol. 14, pp. lxi-lxiii. ODNB, vol.20, pp. 554-556. Small, pp. xxxii-xxxiii). (45) (Johnson, pp. 78-79. Tytler, pp. 150-151). (46) (Hume-Brown, vol.1, p.285. Lesley, pp. 101-102. Thomson, vol.2, pp. 543-544. Tytler, pp. 150-152). (47) (ALCPA, January 25th, 1515, xxvi, f.179, pp. 29-30. Herkess & Hannay, vol.2, pp. 110-120). (48) (ODNB, vol.16, pp. 643-648. Small, pp. x-xii). (49) (Dowden, pp. 82-86. Small, pp. xxxii-xxxiii. pp. xxxix-xli. p.lxiv). (50) (ALCPA, January 26th,1515, xxvi, f.190, p.30. Herkless & Hannay, vol.2, pp. 112-119. Herkless & Hannay, vol. 3, pp. 52-58. Small, pp. xxxii-xxxiii). (51) (Buchanan, pp. 263-264. Cunningham, vol.1, pp. 216-218. Herkless & Hannay, vol.2, pp. 112-119. Pitscottie, pp. 286-287). (52) (Buchanan, pp. 267-269. Dowden, pp. 169-170. Dowden, pp. 38. Exc rolls, vol. 14, pp. lxi-lxiii. Herkless & Hannay, vol 2. ODNB, vol.20, pp. 369-370. Small). (53) (Dowden, pp. 82-83. Herkless & Hannay, vol.2, pp. 126-129).

Chapter Three

TWO FACES UNDER ONE HOOD: 1515-1517

John Stewart was born in Auvergne, France, in 1482, the only son of Alexander, 2nd Duke of Albany and Anne de la Tour, Alexander's second wife. Alexander was the second son of James II, and had been banished out of Scotland and his titles forfeited in July 8th 1483 for a treasonous alliance with England against his brother James III. He was killed in Paris in November 1485 during a joust, and buried in the Celestine church.

In 1487-88 John's mother would marry Louis the Viscount of Maurienne, a member of a wealthy Savoyard family. From 1494 John would be brought up in the court of King Charles VIII. John's early career was devoted to military affairs, especially under Charles' successor, Louis XII. John was one of the nobles who accompanied Charles in 1499 when he invaded Lombardy with

20,000 troops, capturing Genoa. During a crusade in 1501 he received a minor wound during an attack on the Aegean Island of Mytilene, whilst receiving credit for his part in the campaign. Setting off to return to France in December, his ship was wrecked off an inhospitable coast and his party was rescued by a Venetian ship. Being appointed a captain of 100 lances and stationed at Bordeaux, he was soon sent to Italy in 1503, where during these wars the French were practically driven out of Italy. In 1505 Louis arranged for John to marry a cousin, Anne de la Tour of Boulogne, an heiress to the Comte d'Auvergne. He would acquire through marriage the county of Lauragaic and Seigneuries of Douzenac. During 1507 he was in the company of the King when Italy was once more invaded and Genoa was again captured on April 28th.

On December 5th 1512, Louis requested that James IV should restore John to the forfeited dukedom of Albany, a request that received no answer. Whilst John was a French aristocrat, he was also aware of his Scottish ancestry. There were Scots in French service, such as Robert Stewart, fourth son of the 1st Earl of Lennox, who distinguished himself in the Italian wars, and on October 4th 1512 would be appointed captain of the King's Scots Guards. Albany would attend the wedding of Louis to Marie Tudor in October 9th 1514, as well as the coronation of Francois I on January 25th 1515.

He would also associate himself with another famous Frenchman of Scots descent, Berault Stewart (Stuart in the French spelling) son of Sir John Stewart of Darnley. Dying in 1508 whilst on pilgrimage to St Ninians in Scotland, Berault, who was chamberlain to the King, had made himself famous in the Italian wars, and during the latter part of the English Wars of the Roses, when leading 1,000 Scots and French soldiers, he helped Henry Tudor defeat Richard III at Bosworth. Such links and contacts would have inspired John to rediscover his Scottish roots. [1]

The Rev Thomas Thomson, in his well-researched histories of Scotland, is dismissive of the Governor's character, questioning his courage, intelligence and temperament. Having been brought up a Frenchman in the refined courts of France and indulged in the finest luxury, he believed Albany would have been overwhelmed by the poverty and coarse habits of the Scots. Yet he was a veteran soldier of campaigns in Italy and the Mediterranean, where hardship and poverty would have been common. Comforts did not seem to be his main consideration, although he would enjoy choice wines and foods and the trappings of luxury when available. Lord Dacre would report that he would hurl his bonnet into the fire whenever he was angry, and jokingly mention that he had so far lost 30 bonnets. It was a piece of zany correspondence meant to amuse the reader, although it does suggest that Albany was passionate and could be hot-headed. Events would show that he was politically astute, ruthless and ever willing to go to war if need be, and Dacre would also describe him as a man that 'uses two faces under one hood', emphasising the fear and distrust the English authorities had of the French aristocrat's policies whilst he remained in Scotland. [2]

Albany would command eight ships well furnished with supplies, such as six field pieces, six cannons, and other artillery. There were ammunitions, powder, harquebusier, crossbows and a range of other weapons. Whilst this small fleet hurriedly took to sail and made for Scotland, English ships set out to intercept, but as the ships were well furnished with cannon and well manned with fighting men, they could see no way of winning an encounter, so they allowed Albany to pass to Scotland. He stopped at Ayr on May 16th, and then arrived at Dumbarton on May 20th 1515.

Lord Hume was said to have met him there at Dumbarton with a large following of his border riders. He was attired in Kendal green velvet and possessed the attitude of a proud and indispensable lord of Scotland. It could be argued that Lord Hume came out well from the Battle of Flodden, having routed one wing and then plundered the English baggage train and battlefield to the profit of himself and his followers. He had also continued to defend the borders against the raids of the English warden and his raiders. Sieur de la Baste was also present with the Duke of

Albany, and painted a different view of Hume, claiming that he was widely blamed for the defeat at Flodden and was responsible for the death of King James. Sieur de la Baste's vitriol against Lord Hume may have been a result of his being a rival to him on the eastern march, where he was governor of Dunbar. Albany was not impressed by Lord Hume's large following, or his lavish attire, which he thought not appropriate for a person he believed of the meanest type.

The meeting between the two was said to have been cold and unproductive. The Duke of Albany was in Glasgow on May 22nd and was well received by the people, who were hoping for peace and justice after years of war and feud. Reaching Edinburgh on May 26th, he was met not only by throngs of people but by the burgesses, prelates and lords of Scotland, who put on pageants, plays and processions in honour of his arrival.

The Queen also paid a visit from her castle of Edinburgh to greet the Duke of Albany. She would later write to her brother that in her initial meeting with Albany he had 'made pleasant semblance to her at his first coming'. Obviously Albany was finding his way around Scotland, and would need to learn who he could trust or rely on. With Queen Margaret being sister to the King of England this made her a significant obstacle to Albany's agenda to wrest power in Scotland. He would also need to gain as much support as possible before challenging the powerful Angus and Drummond factions.

At a Council meeting on May 30th in Edinburgh the Frenchman was offered the government of Scotland, and accepted. He also arranged to have a full parliament convened for July 12th. Albany was given the residence of Holyrood, and would be granted the use of many other castles and palaces throughout Scotland. Whilst Queen Margaret had her stronghold in Edinburgh Castle, Albany would already be using Holyrood as an alternative centre of power, and would make it an attractive place for guests to visit by stocking up the cellars with the finest imported French wines. [3]

Before the Duke of Albany set foot on Scottish soil, Scotland had been offered to comprehend itself into the peace treaty between France and England on April 5th 1515 and given three months to decide. It is believed by Dacre that the comprehension would be hard to keep since there was 'great disorder' on the east and middle marches and money and men were requested to defend Berwick from possible attack. [4]

John Hepburn, still in possession of St Andrews, would draw himself close to the Duke of Albany by spreading money and favours amongst his associates. He began to use this opportunity to gain the Frenchman's confidence, or as Buchanan describes, 'the entire possession of his ear'. Hepburn would also intrigue against his former allies the Humes. In this he had a willing co-conspirator in Sieur de la Baste, Governor of Dunbar Castle. Albany would entrust Hepburn to travel across Scotland and report on the state of the nation in regard to the feuds and disputes and give accounts of these affairs so that he could at least gain an insight.

Whilst these accounts may have been presented honestly, in matters of the Humes and his prejudice against them he employed informers to report on their criminality and oppressions. According to Pitscottie, Hepburn constructed 'secrets and inventions' so as to embellish the facts and further blacken the name of his hated rivals. Albany would also have been aware of his own father's past troubles with the Hume family; Hepburn reminded him that they had conspired against his own father, Alexander, Duke of Albany, to get him banished from Scotland.

The Humes are also said to have stood back during Flodden when King James IV was most in need of assistance. There were even darker rumours, whereby the Humes were accused of playing a part in James IV's death, with stories circulating that he had initially survived the battle before being murdered by adherents of the Humes when he encountered them at Kelso on the Scottish side of the Tweed. The Lord Chamberlain would also be accused of being corrupted by the English and not hampering the rebuilding of the strategically important Norham Castle. Stories such as this would have somewhat demonised the Humes, even in public opinion.

Hepburn also advised that whilst there were many nobles guilty of tyranny, attacking one may force former enemies to join together, for royal justice was the thing all the nobles feared most. Examples should be made, but in a fashion subtle and measured. He said Albany should bring in more French troops into Scotland to ensure a loyal following if he was needing to face down powerful Scots. [5]

Hepburn suggested three men to be made examples of; Lord Hume, the Earl of Angus and Andrew Forman. Although the latter was not a dangerous warrior like Angus and Hume, Hepburn feared he could use his wealth to support one side or the other. Forman however appeared to be liberal with any revenue or monies he acquired, dispensing it widely so that few except Hepburn could wish him harm.

Hepburn however got his way and the Lords of Council held a debate regarding the accusations that Forman had bought up benefices in opposition to royal privileges. Despite fierce argument from Andrew's brother Robert, it was decided that when Andrew Forman landed in Scotland he would be put under house arrest and ordered not to leave the place. When Forman landed at Pittenween, having left the continent in early June, he was met by a representative of the Lord Advocate and informed actions would be made against him and also that he was not permitted to attend court or council. He was detained in the priory until the end of the year. Despite this setback his appointment as Archbishop of St Andrews was recognised in the July Parliament, although he would still be denied access to the temporalities of the see. [6]

Gavin Douglas was to receive papal bulls confirming him as Bishop of Dunkeld dated May 25th 1515. He was summoned to attend the parliament at Edinburgh in July, and also elected as a member of the Lords of Council. However Albany was suspicious of Douglas' past dealings with Henry VIII and decided that letters, including Papal Bulls, passing through England to Scotland and sent via Lord Dacre, were to be intercepted. On July 4th a batch of letters was taken from an English messenger at Moffat and passed to the Lord Chamberlain, Alexander Hume, and from there to Albany. A letter to the Queen was left unopened and passed on to her. One letter opened revealed that Pope Leo was supportive of revoking the tradition whereby the Archbishop of St Andrews becomes guardian to a young king during minority rule, and that instead he should support Gavin Douglas, Bishop of Dunkeld, to that position. The letters reveal that Queen Margaret and Henry VIII petitioned Leo X for this. Douglas was summoned to a meeting of the Lords of Council for July 6th. Before that he met with Albany and was accused of being promoted to the Bishopric of Dunkeld through use of the services of Henry VIII and Cardinal Medici without permission or licence from the King or Council. Douglas denied all knowledge of this and was then taken before the Lords of Council.

Albany stated that he 'would be well content' if Douglas would speak 'honestly and well of such matters'. Douglas made a vigorous defence and replied that if he was found guilty then he would 'be content that my said lord should cut off my head'. Albany had given Douglas an opportunity to admit his intrigues and possibly gain a pardon, but the evidence was strong against him and he was found guilty on July 9th of 'purchasing places at the court of Rome without the King's license'. He was warded in Edinburgh Castle, and later placed in the sea tower of St Andrew's Castle under the custody of John Hepburn, who still held this important stronghold. Pope Leo would later that year send a strongly worded letter to the Duke of Albany for imprisoning Douglas and conferred ecclesial punishments on him and his helpers which would pass onto the next generations. [7]

At a Council meeting on July 11th, the day before the full parliamentary sessions, Lord Drummond was accused of treasonably assaulting William Cumming of Inverallochy, the Lyon King-at-Arms. He was also accused of treasonably corresponding with England, and suggesting that Henry VIII should be elevated to Protector of Scotland and gain possession of the person of King James. He was ordered to appear before the

Lords of Parliament on July 26th, and until then Lord Drummond was to ward himself at Leith under James Logan. On July 12th, 1515 before the Queen Margaret and Three Estates, it was declared that by marrying the Earl of Angus, the Queen had forfeited the terms of James IV's will, and that she no longer had the right to the guardianship of her children. She would be expected to surrender the children into the custody of the new government; Albany was appointed Governor of Scotland and confirmed as Duke of Albany. The sword of State was borne by the Earl of Arran, whilst the Earls of Angus and Argyll set the coronet on Albany's head. [8]

Albany made an oath to be true and obedient to the King and to defend the Commonwealth and administration of justice during the King's minority until he reached the age of eighteen. He was restored to his father's estates within the Earldom of March, granting him the stronghold of Dunbar recently occupied by Sieur de la Baste. Albany also invited James Stewart, Earl of Moray, half-brother to the King to court.

One of Albany's first public acts was to implement laws whereby nobles and lords would be responsible for bringing lawbreakers to justice. He showed a firm hand in tackling the lawlessness of the realm, and an example was made of one Peter Moffat, a notorious lawbreaker accused of committing 'many cruel and nefarious acts'. Being invited to court, he was apprehended near the assembly. He was tried and executed, and according to Buchanan this swift action by the Governor served to send a message to other killers and thieves that they were not above the law. [9]

At the Parliament of July 26th Lord Drummond was found guilty of treason and it was only through the intervention of Queen Margaret that he too was not executed. She would come down from Edinburgh Castle and visit Albany at Holyrood Palace, imploring him with tears and on bended knee that he release her husband's relatives. This plea saved Drummond's life. Albany had Drummond imprisoned in Blackness Castle and his possessions and estates confiscated. This breakdown of relations between Albany and Queen Margaret was discussed in a Venetian ambassadorial report where previously Albany had been described as an 'amiable nobleman' who was once on good terms with Margaret and had spent much time in her company. Queen Margaret was now experiencing the true agenda of Albany, which was to steadily carve away at her own authority and 'vex and trouble her and her friends'. [10]

Albany would write to Pope Leo X in July making a vigorous defence of royal rights regarding the granting of benefices against the perceived undermining of these rights by the papacy. These rights he attested had been granted to Scottish monarchs since Pope Alexander VI, and he asserted that despite the youth of the present King of Scots these rights were to be upheld. The dispute between royal rights and papal rights had been the main source of dissention between the nobles, prelates and commoners within the realm. He cited the example of St Andrews being granted to Andrew Forman despite initial opposition by the Scots. They were also aware that for this papal support the pope's nephew gained the Archbishopric of Bourges when Forman resigned that position.

Albany also accused the Pope of intending to dispose of the bishoprics of Aberdeen and the monasteries of Dunfermline, Inchfrey and Coldingham when they became vacant, and would make claim to the monastery of Arbroath and the priory of Whithorn. Albany, using royal privilege, put forward his own nominations, such as Alexander Stewart for the bishopric of Caithness. The abbeys of Arbroath were to go to Gavin Douglas, this decision was made before Douglas was found guilty of treasonous dealings. James Hepburn was to get the abbey of Dunfermline. James V would also write to Pope Leo confirming that Albany was governor of the realm in the name of King and Parliament, and asking Leo to continue to acknowledge the rights and privileges of Scotland's monarchs. He also informed the Pope that whatever representations Henry VIII made regarding nominating for Scottish bishoprics, or supposedly acting as Scotland's protector, he had no such rights. [11]

Hepburn's stirring against the Lord Chamberlain seemed to have also worked, as the relationship between Albany and Hume would steadily deteriorate. The Governor's grant of the Earldom of Dunbar in the Eastern March effectively set a challenge for Lord Hume, who had possessed these estates since the forfeiture of Albany's father. He had also fortified Fast Castle without permission. He was also subject to the influences of Lord Dacre, who was becoming aware of tensions between Albany and Lord Hume and began to encourage him to join the Queen's party.

Hume was obviously concerned with the growth in power of Albany, and his own diminishing influence in council due to the malice of James Hepburn and the French. The rumours and reports spread against him in respect to his actions at Flodden and afterwards had the potential of further undermining his position. Hume decided that for self-preservation he should ally himself with Queen Margaret and the Earl of Angus. Their initial meeting to discuss common grievances and an alliance is not recorded by chroniclers or otherwise, although it must have occurred after July 4th when Hume performed his last task for Albany in passing on the captured correspondence of Gavin Douglas. It may have been initiated during the July 11th and 12th parliaments, where Margaret was to lose the guardianship of her children and Hume was losing power in the eastern march. Edinburgh Castle would likely be the place where discussions would begin, as Margaret was custodian and Hume was also Provost of the town.

Given the growing prominence of Sir George Douglas of Pittendriech in intrigue and conspiracies, it is possibly that he was the broker for talks between the Queen and Hume. The prospect of alliance would initially have been a difficult process due to Hume's prior aggression against the Queen, and the dark rumours regarding Flodden and the fate of the King. The Queen however needed an ally, and who better than one who had a proven record in warfare and politics, besides commanding a large following on the borders. Lord Hume could use Queen Margaret and her links with England as a powerful buffer against the hostile intentions of Albany, and make it difficult for him to establish himself on the eastern march.

Once the alliance was settled, Lord Hume got to work and began to spread poisonous rumours against Albany, stating that Scotland was now in dangerous times with the Governor having the potential to take possession to two royal sons. Hume reminded his new allies how Albany had been brought up in a foreign nation as a result of his father Alexander having conspired to win the throne from his own brother, James III. It was implied that the son of Alexander would be planning the same usurpation of royal power. If a tragedy occurred involving the sons, then Albany would be next in line to the throne. Hume apparently suggested that Margaret should take her sons and escape to England to gain the protection of her brother. By this time she was once more pregnant, and expecting a child around October. [12]

Albany, through spies or informers, discovered this plan of Hume's to spirit James out of Scotland. He ordered that the Parliament appoint eight lords to the guardianship of the King and his brother, and that they should be taken out of the custody of the Queen. Four of the eight were chosen by lot and sent to Edinburgh Castle. Of these four the Queen would be allowed to pick three to be guardians. They were also tasked to take custody of the King and his brother.

Their approach and mission became publicly known, and a large crowd followed them up to the gates of Edinburgh Castle. The Queen met them at the gates with the infant King holding her hand and a nurse cradling her other son. The crowd that followed was loud and noisy in support of Queen Margaret, yet they became silent to allow the Queen to ask the business of the four. They declared that they were to take possession of the two royal brothers. Margaret had the portcullis lowered and addressed them through the grating. She answered, 'This castle Edinburgh is part of my infeoffment! By the late King my husband, I was made sole governess of it, nor to any mortal shall I yield command. But I require, out of respect for parliament and to the nation, six days to consider their mandate. For my charge is infinite in import, and alas my councillors be few!'. [13]

Angus, who was present, was concerned that this resistance could lead to his forfeiture and accusations of treasons, and demanded that his Queen hand over the children. Margaret refused. The four, impressed by her resolute spirit, returned to parliament to convey her reply. Angus, to protect himself from forfeiture, would later arrange for instruments to be produced proving that he had requested that the Queen give up the children. He also promised Albany that he would act on the Queen to persuade her to surrender the King and Duke of Rothesay. Such an action may have been kept secret from the Queen and raises obvious questions about Angus' commitment and loyalty.

Over the next few days Margaret would seek to negotiate an agreement. She still demanded full access to her sons, but she did offer a compromise in which if 'the lords had any suspicion of her', she would permit four lords, three of her choosing, to act as guardians, of which the Earl Marshal, Angus, Lord Hume and Robert Lauder of the Bass were favoured. She also asked to be allowed to see her children whenever she wished. [14]

Albany refused this proposal and Queen Margaret decided to exit Edinburgh and travel with her children to the refuge of her other castle, Stirling. The Duke of Albany, when he learned of her escape decided that the next course was force and prepared to raise an army. At Stirling Angus suggested that in the event of a siege Margaret should put James on the battlements with sceptre in hand and crown on head so that the opposing army would know they were waging war against the King of Scotland. Angus however was not intending to stay for the fight and fled to his lands in Forfarshire. His uncle Archibald of Kilspindie held Douglas Castle, whilst his brother George was in Edinburgh.

The Duke of Albany, in order to apply pressure on the conspirators, ordered the Lord Chamberlain Hume, who was also provost of Edinburgh, to arrest George Douglas. The charge is not given, although it strongly suggests that Albany was aware of the growing influence of Douglas in the latest intrigues. Hume refused to make the arrest on the technicality that it had not been ordered by parliament, allowing Douglas the time and opportunity to flee to Bonkill Castle near Berwick, whilst Hume would ride to Newark. Albany then ordered that all within Stirling Castle should surrender under threat of treason. He also sent for Angus, ordering him to go to Stirling under threat of treason and to impede supplies and victuals from getting inside the castle.

Angus refused to do this and Lord Dacre offered to support him and the Lord Chamberlain by supplying 60 horsemen as part of a plan to help the Queen and sons escape to England. With the promise of English help, although small, Angus returned to the vicinity of Stirling and joined with the Lord Chamberlain, who made the long journey from Newark. Their daring plan to take Queen Margaret and her children to England was hindered by the appearance of the Earls of Lennox and Gilbert Kennedy, 2nd Earl of Cassillis, who arrived at Stirling with the Lords Borthwick and Revan. Before they could tighten the siege George Douglas managed to smuggle himself into the castle, but Margaret refused to consider sending herself or her children to England. Outside the walls a skirmish ensued between the two parties, in which Angus and Hume lost sixteen men. [15]

Albany set out to raise an army and besiege Stirling. He sent letters to sheriffs across the land ordering them to bring men and enough victuals for twenty days. With the approach of the Duke's army Douglas decided that he was of little use against such power and made his escape from Stirling. An estimated 7,000 men were said to have marched to Stirling to surround the castle. Behind the heavy walls of Stirling, assuming the Queen had enough victuals, the defenders could have held out, especially as compulsory military service for common soldiery was thirty days. However the Duke brought with him several guns from Edinburgh Castle carried by 18 carts including *Mons Megs*, the mighty 8½ ton cannon estimated to be able to fire a 549-pound stone shot 2,887 yards, or a 1,124 pound iron shot 1,408 yards at an elevation of 45 degrees. Such a weapon would have caused massive destruction to the town and castle, and inflicted terrible casualties amongst the population.

On August 3rd, faced with the possibility of such carnage, and aware that there was little hope of relief from husband or allies, or from her brother, Queen Margaret decided to surrender. At the gates she handed the massive keys of the castle to her young son, who in turn handed them to Albany. The Governor knelt before the King whilst accepting the keys and swore allegiance. Queen Margaret was treated with kindness and Albany assured that she would have access to her sons whenever she wished, although both would be housed in Stirling. The Queen was then escorted to Edinburgh Castle, where she would endure a form of house arrest.

By an Act of Parliament the Duke of Albany appointed four nobles, Lord Fleming, the Earl Marshal, Lord Borthwick and Lord John Erskine, the new governor of Stirling, to defend and protect the King and his brother and supervise their education. James was allocated a guard of 700 men. Albany would make proposals to Margaret whereby he would support her and her husband in legal claims to lands and possessions, and ensure she was supported by the state according to her high position as Queen Mother. He asked in return that she cease all treasonous correspondence with her brother. Arguably these could be considered reasonable terms, yet she would refuse them, and even pass details of the proposals to Lord Dacre. (16)

It seems that Queen Margaret had serious concerns about the safety of her sons, and whilst she would protest against her fall from grace she had no choice but to submit to the power of Albany and his supporters. Yet in secret she set out to find another way to free her sons from Stirling Castle and take them to England. Lord Hume and his brother William, because of their aims to bring Margaret and the princes to England 'by craft and subtlety', and place them under Henry VIII's power to 'their perpetual subjugation and utter destruction', were charged with treason and ordered to attend parliament on August 9th. Both would flee to

England, and the Earl of Arran and the Earl of Lennox were tasked with entering the Hume lands and capturing the strongholds. In one incident a troop of men entered Hume Castle, but a trap was set and gunpowder was lit by the fleeing occupants, resulting in explosions which caused deaths and casualties. In a letter of August 7th to the Council, Lord Dacre took credit for inducing Hume to join with the Queen and Angus. In fact his instructions had been to cause dissention between Albany and Hume, and between Albany and Angus, and drive the Governor out of Scotland.

Hepburn however should take some credit for his own contribution in turning Albany against Hume. His importance with the court of Albany can be confirmed in that Hepburn and his nephew James, postulate of Dunfermline, were frequent witnesses of charters from June to November, with James employed as Lord Treasurer between June 25th 1515 and January 1516. [17]

Albany sent envoys to England and would communicate to Henry VIII that he meant Margaret or her companions no harm, explaining that he would not instigate procedures to deprive Margaret, the Douglases or Humes of their lands and possessions. From England Hume organised raids and incursions into the middle and east marches, destroying towns and villages and ensuring no truce could be kept between Scotland and England. Albany, recognising the danger of allowing Hume to rampage from England, sent word to him and Douglas inviting them with good faith to return. Obviously Albany could see the danger of English support of the Scottish exiles and sought to defuse the situation. However Albany needed a show of force and would order a muster at Boroughmuir with the intention of advancing to the borders. [18]

Albany wrote to Dacre requesting that he ensure stability on the borders, and informed him that Hume had been deprived of the March wardenship and he was appointing Lord Maxwell to the West Marches and the Laird of Cessford to the middle marches. Dacre was supportive of his choice of Maxwell but not of Cessford, who was untrustworthy due to his father having been killed by the

English and might seek revenge. He also passed to the English Council reports on the mustering of Scottish forces at Boroughmuir with 16 pieces of ordinance, which although claimed to be in pursuit of Hume were feared to be intended for capturing Berwick. However Albany assured Dacre that the forces were raised against Alexander Hume. Fast Castle was also held for Hume by the Lady of Fast Castle. [19]

Albany led a reported 40,000 men to the borders. Hume Castle was taken and Blacadder Castle secured. The army got within five miles of Berwick. Whilst Albany asserted to Dacre by letter that he would raise as many forces in respect to the King's pleasure, the hostilities were halted when Hume's forces melted away, and he agreed to surrender his strongholds and castles, such as Fast Castle, under the supervision of Lord Fleming. Hume was also invited to meet with Albany, with four lords offered in security. However it appeared that at that period Hume stayed away from the Duke and his adherents.

Albany also heard a report that Dacre's brother Christopher was supporting Hume with 300 horsemen, a report that Dacre denied. Dacre decided that now was a good time to offer a goodwill gesture. He proposed to Albany a meeting of commissioners for 31st August at Coldstream or Cornhill to address any wrongs. [20]

Queen Margaret by this time was heavily pregnant, and expecting to give birth by October. Shortly after writing a letter to her brother from Edinburgh dated August 20th, she moved to Linlithgow Palace, which she believed with its fresh air and open spaces would be more a healthy and appropriate place to give birth, away from the public eye. It would also lessen the constraints of private scrutiny as she would be served by staff who were in the majority female, whether lady chamberlains, lady ushers, serving girls or others. Access for males was limited, and this gave her more freedom to make plans to free her children from Stirling. She would complain of severe sickness and as a ploy asked that her husband should visit her. This he did, and with a party of several companions he helped her to escape during the night. They had travelled only a few miles outside Linlithgow before they were met by Lord Hume and a troop of horsemen. Lord Hume suggested a plan in which he would take the royal brothers out of Stirling Castle through burning a nearby town and drawing out the garrison. This attempt did not work, as the King's guard remained by the side of James. Margaret was instead escorted along with Angus to Tantallon Castle on the North Berwickshire coast, a journey that for her physical and mental condition must have been arduous. [21]

On September 17th the Duke of Albany sent out 146 letters to all the lords and prelates ordering them to muster at Edinburgh for the end of September. Letters were also sent out to the Sheriff of Edinburgh and constables of Haddington and Lauder requesting them to set up combustible bales on top of high hills so as to warn of an advancing army. Albany wrote to Dacre assuring him that this army was not intended to invade England but to 'seek the thieves, traitors and rebels of the realm'.

Bothwell castle was captured for the crown, although the circumstances are not recorded. Dacre suggested that Margaret should escape to Blacadder Castle, which had been recaptured by Hume's men, and from there he could arrange to escort her to the borders. This was arranged, and she left Tantallon Castle by September 23rd with a party of forty of Lord Hume's men to take her to Blacadder Castle. Albany sent John Adamson with a letter for Margaret at Blacadder, and the same messenger was to deliver a letter to David Kerr of Ferniehurst. Possibly the latter was being employed to spy on the Queen and keep Albany informed.

From Blackadder Queen Margaret travelled to Coldstream Nunnery. She was also visited and tended by Lady Hume, the mother of Lord Hume, who was a source of kindness and comfort during the sixteen days that Margaret resided at Coldstream. Queen Margaret sent word to her brother and asked for exile into England. When a reply finally arrived she was offered sanctuary in Morpeth, which would be fully furnished to await her needs. Angus would meet with her at the nunnery, and both would travel towards Morpeth, the family residence of Lord Dacre. [22]

Queen Margaret's escape from Tantallon had been fortunate, for soon afterwards ships commanded by Robin Barton were ordered to Angus' stronghold of Tantallon in order to cut the coastal castle off from victuals from the sea. David Falconer would command an artillery train to later force the capture of Tantallon. Supplies were sent by land and sea to Dunbar, Fast Castle and Dunglass. [23]

During the journey from Coldstream Nunnery to Morpeth, Queen Margaret became desperately ill and was forced to divert off the route and seek refuge in Harbottle, a grim citadel deep in the Northumberland countryside and beset by Scots raiders and English outlaws. Lord Dacre was commanding Harbottle in person. Margaret and her group managed to reach the gates unharmed. Dacre raised the portcullis but refused entry for any other Scots, including the Earl of Angus, who would only be allowed access under certain conditions, which Angus at that time was not prepared to accept. The conditions were for Angus to make a pledge of loyalty to Henry VIII. It is assumed that Angus retreated to ponder his next move and consider where his future lay.

Margaret was allowed into the castle on October 5th, without any of her Scottish female attendants. During the next 48 hours Queen Margaret endured pain and discomfort until she finally gave birth to a girl, helped by a 'fair young lady' whom Dacre managed to find within the castle confines. [24]

Lord Dacre had a difficult time tending to the needs of the Queen and Princess in respect to the meagre comforts that were available within the castle of Harbottle. Dacre managed to ensure that the Queen's daughter, who would also be named Margaret, was baptised. He also had to endure the added pressure of protecting a wailing child, the niece of his King, whilst defending against bands of raiders who were increasing the frequency of their attacks once it became known that the Queen of Scots was inside the walls. Queen Margaret also sent out correspondence, which would have been a dangerous mission for the deliverers.

A few days after the birth Dacre negotiated with the Earl of

Angus on the conditions to allow him access to Harbottle Castle. Dacre continued to drive a hard bargain and Angus conceded; he and his cohorts would sign an agreement promising loyalty to Henry VIII.

Once allowed to see his daughter, Angus was reported to have held her proudly and lovingly. The birth of Margaret Douglas would link Angus more strongly in friendship with the powerful King of England, the uncle of his daughter. He obviously perceived the dynastic possibilities, since a lass with Douglas blood was in line to the throne of England through his wife Margaret. Cardinal Wolsey would agree to act as godfather to the princess, which also gave Angus some influence in the English court. [25]

Pitscottie mentions that Albany would visit different districts of Scotland conducting Justice Ayres. A Justice Ayre was a special court in which a king or his deputy would arrive at a locality or town and order that all alleged crimes should be investigated. All the chief lords and chiefs were ordered to be there and give oaths, and possibly pledges or hostages. These were to offer financial pledges, which they would forfeit if they failed to bring forward accused malefactors based within their district. Only employees of the crown officers and royal household were to carry weapons to these Ayres, and anyone disobeying would have their weapons taken from them. The Signet, Privy Seal and Great Seal were important instruments in that any remissions needed to be authorised relied on an official stamp to be valid.

Albany visited Jedburgh, Kelso and Melrose with this army, imposing his authority over that of the Humes, Douglases and other border clans. He next travelled to Dumfries and north to Ayr before going further north, then returning back to Edinburgh. [26]

During these campaigns word would have reached Albany of the great victory of Marignano on September 13th - 14th, when Francis had crossed the Alps and destroyed the forces of the Holy League during a march on Milan. Prior to this engagement, Francis had continued the peace treaty with Henry VIII, made peace with Venice and entered into an agreement with King

Ferdinand of Aragon and with Charles, governor of the Netherlands and grandson of the Emperor Maximilian. Raging against the French were Pope Leo X, the Duke of Milan, Florence and the Swiss. After the defeat Leo X decided to travel to Bologna and make his peace with the French King, which resulted in a truce being agreed between the two. The papacy granted France control of Parma and Piacenza, and Maximilian Sforza abdicated the Duchy of Milan in favour of France in return for a pension.

Albany's role in ensuring open warfare did not break out between Scotland and England allowed Francis to concentrate on his grand strategy of acquiring territory in Italy without distractions from across the English Channel. The presence of Albany close to the borders would have caused Henry VIII to pause for thought if he ever considered breaking the truce with France and leading an army to the continent. (27)

The fact that Queen Margaret left Scotland to seek refuge with her brother Henry was seen as something of a diplomatic failure for Albany. On the continent it was reported to the Doge of Milan that Albany had seized the children of the queen, and chasing her he had captured all her goods, 'leaving her nothing but the garments she had on'. Margaret would later complain that her jewels and other possessions were taken at Tantallon and other places. As she could not claim the revenues from her dowry lands, she would become destitute and reliant on loans and goodwill. (28)

The victory of Marignano was celebrated across Scotland with bonfires. Whilst Albany resided in Edinburgh during the month of October he would receive a letter from Queen Margaret, composed at Harbottle on October 10th three days after the birth of her daughter Margaret. She asked to be restored as tutor to her sons, and to retain the regency of Scotland. She also set out her grievances against Albany, such as the treatment of Lord Drummond and of Gavin Douglas, and the appointment of guardians to look over her sons. She received two answers, which apparently contradicted each other. One from the Lord's Council stated that the governorship of the realm had passed to Parliament after the death of James IV, and that she had forfeited the right to tutor the young King when she had married Angus. Albany would send his diplomat James Hay with other letters asking Margaret to return to Scotland. He also offered to release Gavin Douglas, and the queen would receive control of all benefices within her dowry and be restored as tutor to her children. The offer was the opposite of that of the Lord's Council, and Margaret made note of this and advised Albany to discuss it further with her brother Henry VIII. [29]

Whilst Albany had attempted to appease Queen Margaret and bring her back to Scotland, the French ambassador, John de Planis, would attempt more treacherous methods to lay hands on Alexander Hume. A letter was sent offering to broker a meeting with Albany at Douglas Castle in Douglasdale. Lord Fleming visited Hume with a letter and a pardon and conveyed him to Douglas to meet Albany. As Hume drew closer to the place of the meeting he grew suspicious and passed word to his brothers in the Merse to remain there. Indeed Hume was captured and imprisoned in the castle. He was then taken to Edinburgh Castle and put under the charge of the Earl of Arran, who was threatened with treason if Hume escaped. This capture ruined the plans of Dacre's brother Christopher to muster a large force from both sides of the borders to support Hume in his war against Albany. A proposal was made that if Hume's two brothers would act as sureties then he could be released on parole.

However Arran had taken as his first wife Elizabeth Hume, the sister of Alexander. Although he had divorced her it appears he felt some friendship towards her brothers. Having learned that William, Master of Hume, and George Hume were riding towards Edinburgh and there was a plot to seize them, Arran gave warning and both escaped. The French ambassador John de Planis may have considered these treacherous methods to capture the two Hume brothers justifiable in the context of his own low opinion of Hume's character, and he explained to Cardinal Wolsey his interpretation of events leading to the Queen fleeing to England.

He would blame Hume for planning to capture the royal sons and take them to Henry VIII, an act of treason. He also stated that Hume had corrupted Angus, whom he described as 'young and good natured', and through him persuaded the Queen to become part of his conspiracy. Planis also pointed a finger at English intrigues, especially involving Lord Dacre, whose actions with Hume and the Queen were designed to dislodge Scotland's comprehension in the peace treaty between France and England. [30]

Having warned the brothers, Arran committed himself to an alliance with Lord Hume against the Governor. With Arran being an heir apparent of the crown after Albany, Hume would argue that Arran was in a better position to rule as Governor than a man born outside Scotland.

On October 12th Arran and Hume left Edinburgh castle and began a rebellion. Joining with Angus at Wooler in Northumberland and witnessed by Lord Dacre, they swore to uphold the rights of Queen Margaret and entered into a mutual bond whereby they would commit themselves to freeing the royal brothers from the custody of Albany, and promise not to make peace without the agreement of the others. They reiterated this agreement at Coldstream on October 15th.

A parliament in Edinburgh on October 16th summoned Arran to answer charges of treason and deprive him of the sheriffdom of Clydesdale. It was ordered that anyone who assisted Arran would be guilty of treason and be in danger of losing his life, land and possessions. This was proclaimed on the market crosses of Lanark, Linlithgow and Rutherglen. A parliament of October 24th would once more forfeit Lord Hume and his brothers William and David.

The Governor mustered forces and marched towards Hamilton Castle, which surrendered within two days after enduring a battering from Albany's artillery. In retaliation Hume rampaged along the eastern march and burned the town of Dunbar. John Stewart, Earl of Lennox, who for his support at the siege of Stirling received at the October parliament the crown lands of Dundonald in Ayrshire, decided to join Arran, his uncle, in rebellion against

Albany. He raised a large army of retainers and captured Glasgow Castle. [31]

Three ships from France arrived in Scotland at that time, with money, arms and ammunition. Pitscottie mentions that it landed on the west of Scotland, which could have been Ayr. He also claims that the lords opposed to Albany gathered together 12,000 men, although this must be an exaggeration. Hearing about the shipment they set out to intercept it, successfully capturing some carts of supplies and ammunition and bringing them to Glasgow.

The Governor quickly raised an army in Edinburgh with the purpose of engaging the lords in battle or chasing them out of Glasgow. He was accompanied by Andrew Forman, who Albany had brought in from the cold so that he could make use of his conciliatory skills.

The churchman entered Glasgow to speak to the lords and ask why they had rebelled. Many replied that they did not recognise him as Governor, or whether he was loyal to Scotland or France, a 'Scotsman's son' or 'Frenchman's son', and depending on his loyalty whether they were obliged to grant him authority. Forman reminded them that the parliament of Scotland had invited Albany to Scotland to act as Governor, and they had elected him at the parliament in Edinburgh and given an oath to serve him. He asked them to remember their obedience, but if they did not Albany was resolved to fight them if he had to. He suggested that they should leave Glasgow, then return to obedience to the Governor. Many of the rebel lords after consultation agreed to this only if they could be granted a pardon, which was agreed. [32]

With the rebel force weakened, Albany quickly entered Glasgow and took the castle. The rebellion had broken down quickly with only a few deaths, including a French gunner who had defected. The Earl of Lennox also made his peace, although Arran and Hume escaped. Albany had employed Andrew Forman to compel a mass surrender followed by the promised pardons.

Within a few days Arran had made his peace and given fidelity and loyalty to the regent. He had withdrawn to Hamilton Castle, to which Albany intended laying siege for the second time in a short period. Arran was helped to extract himself from another difficult situation through the assistance of his mother, a daughter of James II, grandfather of the Duke of Albany. She made submission to the Duke on behalf of her son, and Albany accepted this gesture from a kinswoman. The Bishop of Glasgow accompanied Arran to Edinburgh, where on November 12th he publicly submitted to Albany. Hume also won a pardon, but the condition was set that if he strayed one more time all his prior crimes would be brought against him. He joined Queen Margaret and Angus in England. [33]

The following November Queen Margaret became gravely ill, and Lord Dacre thought it best to move both her and her daughter to Morpeth, which would offer more civilised comforts. The illness, which was possibly typhus, was so bad that she was carried in a litter. She was accompanied by the Earl of Angus. He however did not stay at Morpeth, and whilst he would take opportunities to visit wife and daughter he made his home the forests and hills on the borders. [34]

If Albany expected quiet after Arran's rebellion then he was mistaken, as the Earl of Moray started fighting with the Earl of Huntley in Edinburgh. Albany quickly acted and arrested Moray, Huntley, William Hay, Earl of Errol and others, warding them in the castle. After some investigation he learned that the fight had been instigated by James Hay, one of Moray's adherents, and as already noted a diplomat employed by the Governor. Albany had Hay exiled to France until further notice and the earls and lords were released from the castle. [35]

Having put down yet another rising, Albany travelled to Falkland, where he remained for a few months. On December 18th Alexander, the child Duke of Rothesay, died at Stirling. Accusations were attached to Albany, one of the worst claiming that he had engineered the death of the child. Because of her severe illness, whilst languishing in Morpeth, Queen Margaret was not told about the death until she had recovered some strength.

She spent Christmas in Morpeth Castle, in the company of her husband Angus, Lord Hume and Lady Bothwell. Once she heard of her son's death, Margaret pointed the finger of accusation at Albany, and with written word she broadcasted wide and far her hatred for the Governor of Scotland, comparing him to her father's nemesis Richard III of England, said to have murdered his two royal nephews.

It seems likely in fact that Alexander died through a natural illness. It would have served no purpose for Albany, or the Lord's Council to murder the child as they needed the princes alive to continue the royal succession, and two royal sons were better than one. Nevertheless Albany's enemies and those within Margaret's camp including English allies would often repeat the accusation that Alexander had been deliberately slain.

Margaret now became more determined to regain custody of James. She had suffered the deaths of several children during her marriage to James IV. Possibly she would have been hardened to such horrors, but she would have without doubt suffered severe emotional distress at not having been at Alexander's side when he died. [36]

Little is recorded of King James' infancy before Albany arrived in Scotland. After being taken into possession by the Governor the three-year-old's safety was ensured by his 'keepers', Lord Fleming, the Earl Marshal, Lord Borthwick and Lord John Erskine, who were responsible for protection whenever the King resided at either Edinburgh Castle, Stirling Castle or Craigmiller. Albany would organise James' wellbeing and education, and the master-usher, playwright and poet Sir David Lindsay of the Mount was described as 'keeper of the King's grace', and paid £40 annually. He was responsible for recruiting domestic servants such as his governess Elizabeth Douglas, as well as providing entertainment. Sir James Haswell, the master-almoner, provided the chaplains to bring religion and spirituality to James. Musical entertainment and plays were provided by professionals, such as Italian and French minstrels.

As James got older he would learn to use different musical instruments and take an interest in poetry. Sir David Lindsay claimed that he taught James games, stories, dancing and music. It would be reported that in his later life he was not good with writing or reading Latin or French, although this opinion should be challenged, as it is unlikely that Albany did not ensure adequate teaching in these two important international languages, and James would learn to write many letters in them. His bodyguard would have introduced the child-king to martial activities such as riding, archery, tennis, golf and swordplay, although wooden swords would have been appropriate. He would not have able to avoid the martial attitude amongst the Scots nobility and at a young age he would have witnessed from the castle ramparts armies being assembled in his name. Lavish presents would be presented to him from kings of France and England, as well as earls, lords and prelates. With the cheering crowds it is difficult to perceive how this would shape and educate an infant. The absence of his mother would also have had an effect, although we can only speculate on the emotional impact. [37]

In the New Year another rebellion broke out, with James Hamilton, Earl of Arran, John Stewart, Earl of Lennox, Cuthbert Cunningham, Earl of Glencairn and Hugh Montgomery, Earl of Eglinton capturing Glasgow and Dumbarton. The bone of their dissention was the distribution of benefices, and how they were benefiting some lords over others.

They were however too weak to resist and surrendered to Albany. Lennox was briefly warded in Edinburgh Castle until he ordered his adherents to surrender Dumbarton. Albany decided he would need to be pragmatic and attempt to appease the lords in this issue. As Forman and Hepburn were at odds, Albany invited the two to Edinburgh in January/February 1516. Forman was asked to resign all rights to dispense vacant benefices to the Governor, 'so he can dispose at his pleasure'. Andrew Forman was confirmed as Archbishop of St Andrews and of the Abbey of Dunfermline with full right to the temporalities of the see.

Forman's Bishopric of Moray was finally granted to James Hepburn, nephew of John, and the latter was granted a 1,000 merk pension for his services to this part of the agreement. The Abbey of Dryburgh was granted to Master James Ogilvy, brother of Lord William Ogilvy, who was appointed Lord High Treasurer in place of James Hepburn. The Bishopric of Aberdeen went to Alexander Gordon, brother of the Earl of Huntley. The Abbey of Arbroath went to the Archbishop of Glasgow, and from the revenues it was agreed that James Hepburn, the new Bishop of Moray, would receive a pension. A brother of the Earl of Arran received the Abbey of Kilwinning, and Sir George Dundas became Abbot of Perth. Other benefices were distributed in such a manner and contributed to pacifying the jealousies and feuds that had been tearing through Scottish society. [38]

It appears that Scots raiders were causing devastation in northern England. Dacre, in a written complaint against Albany, provided a long list of raids and burnings and noted how troops of Scottish raiders, each of more than 300 men, had been making invasions into England. This breach would cause Scotland's comprehension into the May 15th Anglo-French treaty to be voided, although there was no mention of English sheltering and support of Angus and Hume. The borders were in a state of war, although no official crown declaration had been made by either side. The Lords of Council insisted to Albany that it would be more pragmatic to have Angus and Hume back on their side. [39]

Albany sent more letters to Queen Margaret during the month of January, part of a negotiation to get her to return to Scotland. Dacre reported to Henry VIII that his sister was still sick and could barely move without great discomfort. He requested that a physician be sent to tend to her illness. On January 14th the French ambassador John de Planis, who already knew Margaret, visited her at Morpeth. Although no accounts of their meetings are recorded the Frenchman would no doubt have been attempting to persuade Margaret, Angus and Hume to make peace. However, whilst those three resided in Morpeth, stories of Hume's intrigues reached Albany's ears. The Lyon King-at-Arms had been sent to England with letters for King and Council, and Alexander Hume had captured him at Coldstream and imprisoned him. In Hume's defence Queen Margaret would mention in her complaints against Albany how during her escape to the nunnery of Coldstream, and while heavily pregnant, she was attended by the elderly mother of Lord Hume. When Albany marched to the border in September 1515, one of his French retainers, Sieur de Barody, had captured Hume's elderly mother, forced her to Dunbar Castle and placed her under the custody of the governor, Sieur de la Baste. For six weeks she was reportedly fed on bread and water and under serious distress. Although there is no record of any such trade-off, we can assume that an agreement of some kind was concluded and that the Lyon King-at-Arms was released in exchange for Hume's mother. Despite this the Sieur de la Baste would not be forgiven by the Humes for his actions, and they would wait patiently for an opportunity to enact revenge. [40]

On 28th March, John de Planis, French ambassador, James, Archbishop of Glasgow, Chancellor of Scotland, and Gavin Dunbar, Dean of Moray, as commissioners from Albany, concluded a truce with England at Coldingham. In addition they were instructed to make terms with Angus. Meeting the Earl at Stanetoun, they offered remission for him, friends, family and adherents and servants. Charges of treason were to be dropped, and he and the Queen would be restored of all castles, properties and possessions, with captured charters also restored. Actions for treason were to be dismissed. This agreement was signed by Angus, with the commissioners representing Albany. [41]

This agreement appears to have been signed without Margaret's approval or knowledge. Although initially favourable to offers which would have restored her as Queen with full rights and access to the King, she was persuaded otherwise by the English priest Dr Magnus and Lord Dacre, fearing that a rapport between Margaret and Albany would endanger English interests north of the border. Dr Magnus would play at being a friend of

Margaret, and would express concern over her state of mind considering the death of a son. She was also still recovering from the bout of typhus. Magnus suggested to Henry VIII that he should invite the sister to London. There she could be given further advice and be able to discuss options.

In early April a rich and colourful convoy arrived from London to Morpeth, with a message inviting Queen Margaret and the Earl of Angus to attend Henry at his royal court. Angus initially accepted and was prepared to escort Margaret to London. As they prepared to leave Angus left Morpeth without word to the Queen or anyone else. Whether Angus was distrustful of the English is unclear. He had already agreed to make peace with Albany, a fact that Margaret was unaware of, although if he had travelled to London his enemies in Scotland may well have informed Henry VIII of this double-dealing, and put his life and liberty at risk. [42]

Queen Margaret was soon informed that Angus and Lord Hume had accepted an offer to attend a parliament at Edinburgh on April 6th 1516. In return for allegiance to Scotland the forfeitures of them and their kin, friends and adherents would be reversed. This seemingly was a diplomatic and political victory for Albany, and the favourable terms offered were indicative of a pragmatic approach to bring some peace and quiet to the borders, now that two of his most dangerous opponents had been tempted away from the English. Having attended the parliament in April, both Angus and Lord Hume would be restored to their lands and titles, on May 5th, 1516. Lord Drummond would also have his titles, rights and estates restored to him. [43]

Margaret would have felt confusion and betrayal at this desertion. She would have found difficulty in fully trusting her husband afterwards, especially as she had attracted so much Scottish hostility through her association and subsequent marriage to the young earl. She had also been struck down with typhus when he left her side to return to Scotland. According to Lord Dacre, who also criticized Angus and Hume for betraying the terms of the bond, Margaret was 'in much heaviness at their conduct'.

On her travel southwards on May 3rd, after spending three days at Enfield, Queen Margaret and her daughter, accompanied by a royal escort, were met at Tottenham Cross by her brother leading a procession of nobles and knights dressed up in the finest chivalric regalia. Queen Margaret, with daughter in hand, knelt and awaited her brother. The festivities and entertainments in honour of Queen Margaret and her daughter lasted for near a month. Henry was very proud of his niece, and throughout her early years he would treat her with the utmost love and care. Henry would also have been impressed by the strength and courage of his sister in managing to survive an escape across the border whilst heavily pregnant. When he found out that Angus had deserted the Queen, he exclaimed 'Done as a Scot'. Margaret was housed in the ancient residence of Scotland Yard, and her daughter was taken to the royal nurseries at Greenwich Palace, where she would come in contact with Henry's daughter Mary Tudor, who had been born in February and would become a lifelong friend. [44]

A truce was agreed between Scotland and England, to last from June until November. Henry VIII would use it to write a letter to the Estates of Scotland dated June 1st, asking that for the sake of peace between Scotland and England they remove Albany from Scotland and from the presence of the King. There was a suggestion that since Albany was by blood close to the crown of Scotland, then he was a potential threat to the King. The Estates replied to this by thanking Henry for his concern for the wellbeing of his nephew, but reiterated that Albany had been chosen by the Estates and it was the custom of the laws of Scotland that those closest to royal blood outside that of the direct heir were chosen as Governors. They reminded Henry that through this custom the Estates had chosen Albany to be Governor. They also stated that the King's person was guarded and guided by four members of Scotland's oldest families and Albany had no direct access to the King except through them. Albany would be subject to many such accusations and innuendos regarding his royal ambitions, fanned by English propaganda. [45]

Events on the continent were steadily beginning to politically isolate Henry VIII and England. The death of Ferdinand, King of Aragon on January 23rd 1516 had made his grandson Charles ruler of the Netherlands, King of Spain, King of Naples, the King of Sicily, and the virtual ruler of the New World of the Spanish Americas. Henry's political adviser Cardinal Wolsey sought an alliance with Charles, Pope Leo X, the Swiss and the Emperor Maximilian against Francis. Charles was not ready to go to war with Francis and instead sought a political solution to any grievance through the Peace of Noyon, agreed on August 13th, 1516. Charles was to be betrothed to Louise, the child-princess of Francis. France in return would keep possession of Milan and concede Naples. England tried to form an alliance with the Emperor Maximilian, Venice and the Swiss but by the end of the year Venice would buy Brescia and Verona off the Emperor, and at Friburg the French bought with gold a 'perpetual peace' with the Swiss. (46)

During the summer and autumn Hume renewed his treacherous alliance with Dacre, and the latter would brag that he paid 400 Scots to daily raid and pillage in Scotland. Whilst Dacre might be pleased with his dark methods of stirring up the borders, his efforts did little to disturb the political powers in Edinburgh. The Governor however endeavoured to deal with this problem of Hume. He called him to Edinburgh to attend a parliament for October 12th, along with his brother William and Kerr of Ferniehurst. Hume was advised against this by friends, and told that if he did go he should keep William back, as he was known as a resourceful and brave individual, and Albany might resist taking measures against Alexander if William was still free and able to command the power of the Humes. (47)

Alexander went to Edinburgh, and in an apparently amicable meeting Albany offered him the post of ambassador to England, as he knew the politics and intrigues of the English better than most. Lord Hume decided to take up this offer. Albany however wanted his brother William to play some part in diplomatic duties and persuaded Hume to allow the ring on his finger to be sent to the brother as a sign of faith and trust.

At this gesture William and Andrew Kerr of Ferniehurst travelled to Edinburgh. When he was brought to the Greyfriars Abbey where his brother was waiting, Frenchmen shut the doors and exits and captured and imprisoned the brothers. Both, along with Andrew Kerr, were charged with treason, although Kerr would manage to escape from Edinburgh Castle. At the trial several other charges were made against Hume. James, Earl of Moray, apparently accused him of being guilty of the death of his father. The charge was that James IV had escaped the battle at Flodden and a substitute dressed as the King had died in his place. He was reported to have crossed the Tweed and then been slain at Kelso by the Humes, who may have feared retribution after being accused of failing to support the King at a crucial time during the Battle of Flodden. When Albany first chased after the Humes Gilbert Galbrath apparently confessed to being one of six men who had killed the King. Because the charge lacked evidence, it was discounted. [48]

Hume was also charged with not fully participating in the battle of Flodden, in such a manner that his lack of action was interpreted as treachery. The allegation no doubt related to his initial success in routing the right wing of the English, yet failing to follow up by either attacking the centre or supporting the King. There is no record of Hume offering any defence. There was also a charge of treasonably assisting the English by failing to hinder the strengthening of Norham Castle, and he was accused of being the ringleader of the recent intrigues and treasons against the governor, and corresponding with the English against the authority of the King. Another crime was presented to the judges by Albany, but this crime was considered so 'gross and heinous, that it was on that account concealed from the public'. There is no record of what this crime could have been. [49]

Hume and his brother were found guilty and both were beheaded, respectively on October 11th and October 12th, 1516, and their heads spiked on the Tolbooth. The Hume estates were forfeited to the crown. Whilst many were glad of the verdict, the fact that he was tried for the crimes he had been previously pardoned for may have raised questions about the manner of justice Albany was prepared to dispense. However the previous pardons were under the condition that if Hume committed treason once more his prior crimes and accusations would be held against him. It was believed that Hepburn had been the prime motivator in calling on Hume's destruction, and with Albany planning to travel to France he would have been concerned about leaving behind such a powerful noble as Hume with his dangerous links to England.

The remaining brothers would also later experience misfortune. George was charged with murder and exiled to England. John, Abbot of Jedburgh, was exiled to beyond the Tay, and David, Abbot of Coldingham, was lured to a conference and killed. Albany followed up by mustering a large force to march to Jedburgh and impose law and order on the border districts. After installing officers and reliable chiefs to administer justice, he returned to Edinburgh to continue parliamentary business. [50]

Meanwhile Albany attempted a more amicable relationship with England through offering constructive correspondence with Cardinal Wolsey. He would allow Lord Dacre safe conduct to send an envoy, the Master of Greystock College, north to collect Queen Margaret's jewels, plates and other movable possessions that had been captured at Tantallon. Albany also offered to have the Rothesay Herald accompany officers to her dower lands and collect the rents and revenues, which would then be sent to her in England. Whilst there is no concrete evidence that Margaret received the revenues and rents, an inventory exists which outlines the jewels, clothes, baggage and other valuables that she received from the Scottish commissioners during October 1516. A letter to Margaret, in answer to her request for goods in her son's possession, advised her that to claim rights over them she should come to Scotland and act as executor. There is a suggestion that she already possessed goods belonging to the King, and that his debts had been left unpaid, which would have been her responsibility to clear during the time she was regent and tutor.

Queen Margaret would often complain about her abject poverty in letters to her brother and his leading advisers, yet there are many allegations that she squandered any money she had, and one of the most damning accusations, if true, is that the treasure chest left by James IV was exhausted while in her charge. She would later confess in a letter to her brother dated June 3rd, 1517 that her husband had given her permission to take charge of the 18,000 crowns granted by the French King prior to Flodden. This had been done without the authority of the Lords of Council, and one of her fears was that they would seek restitution of that amount. It also begs the question that another reason why the Scots supported the arrival of Albany and the ousting of Queen Margaret as regent was her irresponsibility with state funds, the King's estate, as well as her own dowry revenues and rents. In all fairness it should be remembered that she was but a twenty-three-year-old, who prior to Flodden had been brought up and pampered in the courts of England and Scotland and definitely had no experience of governance during a time of war. Then her husband led Scotland to a terrible slaughter, and Queen Margaret was left alone and expected to defend the rights of her son, whilst all around were nobles and prelates competing for power and position.

Possibly she did squander money, but there are no precise records of how it was spent and on what. We have her mention in a letter to her brother in late 1514 having to spend £1,000 per day in the civil conflicts, and whilst that seems to be an exaggeration, it appears likely that large amounts of funds would have been spent on furnishing military forces and financial incentives during the period 1514-1515. [51]

A parliament of November 13th 1516 would debate the claim that Albany was second person of the realm after James V. Alexander, the elder brother of Albany, was present at the reading of this ruling and protested that his father had married Katherine

Sinclair, the Earl of Orkney's daughter, making him the legitimate second person. The parliament ruled that Alexander and Katherine Sinclair were not legally married in compliance to the laws and customs, and therefore Alexander, the Commendator of Inchfray, was considered illegitimate and a bastard and had no right to the throne of Scotland.

After some debate Alexander gave his consent to the proceedings and outcome. Albany was declared second person of the realm. Arran also considered his position as heir apparent after Albany, and as he had no legitimate heir, he married Janet Beaton, daughter of David Beaton of Criech and niece of James Beaton, Archbishop of Glasgow, in November 1516. There would however be questions over the legitimacy of the divorce of his first wife which would question the legitimacy of any offspring from the second marriage. [52]

A truce known as an 'abstinence of war' was negotiated and agreed during the autumn between Albany and Cardinal Wolsey, Henry's representative. It was to begin on St Andrews Day, November 30th, 1516, and last until the following St Andrews Day, 1517. The Three Estates would also consider a letter from the King of France, in response to a recent visit from the Bishop of Ross at his palace at Lyons, and delivered by Francis de Bordeaux. The King enquired about the health of the young King of Scotland, and thanked Albany for his hard work in ensuring there would be no war in Scotland. In response to a request to ratify the treaty agreed between Scotland and France, he said he would not as it might prejudice the treaty France had with England, yet he assured the Scots that in the event of England waging war against Scotland, France would side with Scotland, and 'paper and parchment' would not be needed to prove this, only the 'friendship' which 'is so ancient'. [53]

Albany and the Scots would have been concerned that Francis' recent response to a signed treaty had been vague and somewhat abstract. In December Albany brought the King from Stirling to Edinburgh and asked the parliament to allow him to go to France.

He wanted to speak with Francis I and to visit his wife, who was ill. There was reluctance by the majority to let him go. With Albany being granted the governorship and having installed some order into the kingdom, the prospect of him leaving and Scotland once more becoming victim of lawlessness and the intrigues of enemies filled the Three Estates with apprehension. They wanted him to fulfil his duties and responsibilities until James reached the age of eighteen and assumed the kingship. They also argued that once returning to France he might have difficulty returning. The Duke re-emphasised his concern for the illness of his wife and his longing to see her, especially if she was close to death. After further debate the Scots finally gave in to his demands. He was allowed to leave in the summer if he promised to return within a few months. He would travel along with the master of Glencairn and the Bishop of Dunkeld as ambassadors, so as to renew the alliance with France. [54]

Albany entered into correspondence with Henry VIII in order to pass through England and be granted an interview. He hoped to be allowed unhindered passage to France. Whilst the English were keen to meet Albany, the Scots were not so keen, obviously not trusting Henry. Albany wrote letters asking for terms and sureties by which he could enter England, although it seems unlikely that Albany was serious about crossing the border and risking his life and freedom. By offering himself as bait he was diverting attention from his true purpose, to secure a safe passage to France by another route.

Albany spent January in Perth conducting Justice Ayres. During early 1517 Albany would also seek a solution for the destabilizing long-lasting feud between the Earl of Glencairn's family, the Cunninghams and the Earl of Eglinton's family, the Montgomerys, which was over the Baillie of Cunningham, and swept through Ayrshire and the west. Albany would negotiate for the master of Glencairn's heir to marry a Montgomery on May 22nd 1517, although this would have little impact on the actual fighting, which would rage for many decades. [55]

In February Gavin Dunbar, nephew of his namesake Gavin
Dunbar, Dean of Moray, would be appointed tutor to the four-year-
old King, a post where he would responsible for educating James
in politics, culture, mathematics, languages and literature. Sir
David Lindsay was still described as master of the household, as
well as usher. A figure of importance in Scottish literary history,
he would introduce James at an early age to poetry, plays and
court pageantry. Sir William Dunbar had been court poet during
the reign of James IV, and may have continued to play some role
at court, although after 1515 there are no records of pension
payments. Nevertheless in 1517 he would compose a poem *Quhen
the Governour Past in France*, dedicated to the governor Albany
leaving for France. The pursuits of hunting, hawking, archery,
horseracing and martial activities such as jousting, swordplay and
weapons would have been taught by Albany's adherents, the Lord
Borthwick, Alan Stewart and Andrew Towers. Albany himself was
a keen sportsman, and especially enjoyed hawking. He would buy
falcons and pay falconers for their expertise. If James had any
youthful companions, it may have been half-brothers and half-
sisters, as well as siblings and relatives of his guardians and
tutors. [56]

A French ambassador would also pass to Scotland, where
Albany was to be awarded the *colar of cokkyllzeis*. The ambassador
is not identified and the actual title of the award is not certain. Sir
James Balfour Paul, the editor of the ALHTS, forwards two
possibilities, whereby cockles were motives for both the collars of
The Order of the Ship, and *Order of St Michael*. On March 22nd,
1517 letters were sent out to the lords of the west, north and south
to be present at Edinburgh to attend the ceremony in which Albany
is invested with this honour. [57]

Albany invited Queen Margaret to return. He had received
letters asking to be allowed without hindrance to resettle in
Scotland and to be restored to her dowry and full rights. She also
expressed a wish to reunite with Angus. Whether this was genuine
or subterfuge is difficult to guess; she had after all had been left in

England by her husband whilst suffering from typhoid. Her brother supported a reunion, so possibly she was playing a game in order to gain access to her son. Albany's motives were the threat of Margaret remaining in England in exile and the possibility in the future of an English army escorting her to Scotland with hostile intent. Nevertheless he agreed to 'oblige her to the best of his power'. He also wrote to Henry VIII stating that safe conducts would be forthcoming and that Queen Margaret would be welcomed by all the lords.

When the safe conduct was finally published in the name of King James seeking to see 'his mother's face, and so she can provide him with solace', it allowed her the security to pass with 24 English men and women, and as many foreign individuals and Scots as she wished as long as they were not enemies of Scotland. She was also to be provided funds to live in accommodation suited to her station and allowed all revenue and proceeds from her dowry, as well as full access to her jewellery and valued possessions. The Lords of Council however would not grant her the right to form part of the administration of government.

One concern that Margaret had was that there could be a demand for restitution of funds that she had spent without authority, especially the remainder of the 18,000 crowns paid to her late husband James IV by Louis of France. Demands for restitution would depend on how strongly they felt, yet she believed that in Albany's absence and with the support of her brother they would hesitate to follow such a path. However there was a danger that they could make it difficult for her to claim rents and revenues within her dowry lands. [58]

Chapter Three: References

(1) (ODNB, vol.52, pp. 708-715. ODNB, vol.52, pp. 743-744. SP, vol.1, pp. 154-155). (2) (LP, Dacre to Lord (Lords of Scotland?), April 30th, 1524. Thomson, vol.2, pp. 544-545). (3) (Exchequer Rolls, vol.14, pp. lxvii-lxviii. Holinshed, pp. 485-487. Lesley, pp. 107-108. Pitscottie, pp. 288-289. Strickland, vol.1, pp. 104-105). (4) (LP, Scotland and

Denmark, 16th June, 1515. LP, Scotland and the Marches, July 6th 1515. LP, Complaints against the Duke of Albany, 27th March 1516). (5) (Buchanan, pp. 268-270. Pitscottie, pp. 290-291. Strickland, vol.1, pp. 104-105). (6) (LP, Spinelly to Henry VIII, June 17th, 1515. ODNB, vol.20, pp. 369-370). (7) (ALCPA, July 6th,1515, xxvii, pp. 40-41. ALCPA, July 9th, xxvii, f30-f38, pp. 42-50. Herkless & Hannay, vol.2, pp. 132-137. Small, xlix-lix, lix). (8) (Exchequer Rolls, vol.14, pp. lviii-lxi. LP, Dacre to the Lords of the Council, August 1st, 1515). (9) (ALCPA, July 11th, 1515, xxvii, f41, pp. 50-51.Buchanan, pp. 268-273. Fraser, pp. 181-183. Pitscottie, 289-290.RPS, July 12th1515, Edinburgh. RPS, November 22nd, 1516, Edinburgh. Small, pp. lxv-lxvi. SP. vol.4, 609-611.SP. vol.7, pp. 40-42). (10) (ALCPA, July 11th, 1515, xxvii, f41, pp. 50-51.Fraser, pp. 181-183. CSPV, Andrea Badoer and Sebastian Giustinian to the State, August 5th 1515 Pitscottie, 289-290.RPS, July 12th1515, Edinburgh. RPS, November 22nd, 1516, Edinburgh. Small, pp. lxv-lxvi. SP. vol.4, 609-611.SP. vol.7, pp. 40-42. Strickland, vol.1, pp. 106-107). (11) (LP, Albany to the Pope, July 1515. LP, Albany to Leo X, August 1st, 1515). (12) (Buchanan, pp. 270-271. Strickland, vol.1, pp. 105-106). (13) (Strickland, vol.1, pp. 107-108). (14) (Fraser, pp. 182-184. LP, Dacre to the Lords of Council, August 1st, 1515. Thomson, vol.2, pp. 545-546. Strickland, vol.1, pp. 108-109. Tytler, pp. 152-154). (15) (Fraser, pp. 182-184. LP, Dacre to the Lords of Council, August 1st, 1515. LP, Dacre to the Council, August 4th, 1515. ODNB, Cassillis. Strickland, vol.1, pp. 109-110). (16) (ALHTS, vol.5, pp. 27-30. Fraser, pp. 182-184. SBSH, vol.1, pp. 78-79. Strickland, vol.1, pp. 109-110. Tytler, pp. 153-155). (17) (ALCPA, August 6th, 1515, xxvii, f.49, pp. 52-53. Buchanan, pp. 271-273. Herkless & Hannay, vol.2, pp. 37-138. Holinshed, pp. 487-489. LP, Dacre to the Lords of the Council, Augusts 1st, 1515. LP, Dacre to the Council, August 7th, 1515. SP, vol.2, p.144). (18) (ALCPA, August 11th, 1515, xxvii, f.51, pp. 53-54. Lesley, pp. 108-110). (19) (LP, Ughtred to Dacre, August 11th,12th,14th 1515). (20) (ALCPA, August 10th, 1515, xxvii, f.51, p.53. CSPS, August 10th, August 12th, August. 13th, August 14th, 1515, p.3. LP, Ughtred to Dacre, August 17th, 1515. LP, Dacre to Ughtred, August 18th, 1515. LP, Albany to Dacre, 20th August, 24th August. Tytler, pp. 154-156). (21) (Strickland, vol.1, pp. 110-112). (22) (ALHT, vol.5, p.39. LP, Dacre to Margaret, Sept 1st 1515. LP, Seb. Giusinian to the Doge, Sept 20th, 1515. Smith, pp. lxxv-lxxvii. LP, Complaints against the Duke of Albany, 27th March 1516). (23) (ALCPA, September 28th, 1515, xxvii, f.72, pp. 57-58. ALHTS, pp. 38-42, pp. xxx.vi-xxxvii. Fraser, pp. 182-184. Pitscottie, pp. 291-292. Thomson, vol.3, pp. 24-25). (24) (Strickland, vol.1, pp. 113-115). (25) (Strickland,, vol.1, pp. 115-117. Strickland, vol.2, pp. 246-248). (26) (ALCPA, September 28th, 1515, xxvii, f.72, pp. 57-58. ALHTS, pp. 38-42, pp. xxx.vi-xxxvii.

Fraser, pp. 182-184. Pitscottie, pp. 291-292. Thomson, vol.3, pp. 24-25). (27) (Johnson, pp. 78-81. Norwich, pp. 279-282. ODNB, vol.52, pp. 709-715. Thomson, vol.2, pp. 547-548). (28) (ALHT, vol.5, p.39. LP, Dacre to Margaret, Sept 1st 1515. LP, Seb. Giusinian to the Doge, Sept 20th, 1515. Smith, pp. lxxv-lxxvii. LP, Complaints against the Duke of Albany, 27th March 1516. Strickland, vol.1, pp. 112-114). (29) (LP, Scotland, Oct 10th, 1515. LP, Answer of the Council, Oct 13th, 1515. LP, Albany to Margaret, October 18th, 1515. ODNB, vol.36, pp. 648-649. Strickland, vol.1, pp. 114-115. Tytler, pp. 155-156). (30) (LP, Jean de Planis to Wolsey, 1515). (31) (ALCPA, October 16th, 1515, xxvii, ff.74,77, pp. 58-59. Buchanan, pp. 272-273. Fraser, pp. 182-184. Holinshed, pp. 485-487. Hume-Brown, vol.1, p.287. LP, Albany to Margaret, October 18th, 1515. LP, Dacre and Magnus to Henry VIII, October 18th, 1515). (32) (Buchanan, pp. 272-273. Pitscottie, pp. 293-296). (33) (Buchanan, pp. 272-273. Holinshed, pp. 486-487. Lesley, pp. 104-106). (34) (Strickland, vol,1, pp. 117-118. trickland, vol.2, pp. 248-249). (35) (Holinshed, pp. 486-487. Lesley, pp. 104-106). (36) (CSPS, vol.1, December 12th, 1515, pp. 4. Fraser, pp. 184-186. ODNB, vol.36, pp. 648-649. Strickland, vol.1, pp. 118-119. Thomson, vol.2, pp. 547-548). (37) (ALHTS, vol.5, p.37, p.44, pp. 53-54, p.146. ODNB, vol.29, pp. 619-627). (38) (Holinshed, pp. 487-488. Hume, pp. 287-288. Lesley, pp. 106-108. SP. vol.2, pp. 3-4). (39) (LP, Complaints against the Duke of Albany, 27th March 1516). (40) (ALHTS, vol.5, p.66, p.68. CSPS, vol.1, January 6th, 1516, pp. 5. Holinshed, pp. 486-488. Lesley, pp. 105-107.LP, Complaints against the Duke of Albany, 27th March 1516. Strickland, vol.1, pp. 112-114. Strickland, vol.1, pp. 118-119. Thomson, vol.2, pp. 548-549). (41) (Fraser, pp. 185-187). (42) (ALCPA, April 7th, 1516, xxvii, f.223, p.66. Holinshed, pp. 487-489. Hume, pp. 287-288. Lesley, pp. 107-108. Small, pp?? SP. vol.7, pp. 40-42. Strickland, vol.1, pp. 119-120. Strickland, vol.2, pp. 248-250. Tytler, pp. 157-158). (43) (ALCPA, April 7th, 1516, xxvii, f.223, p.66. Holinshed, pp. 487-489. Hume, pp. 287-288. Lesley, pp. 107-108. Small, pp?? SP. vol.7, pp. 40-42. Strickland, vol.1, pp. 119-120. Tytler, pp. 157-158). (44) (ALCPA, April 7th, 1516, xxvii, f.223, p.66. Holinshed, pp. 487-489. Hume, pp. 287-288. Lesley, pp. 107-108. Small, pp?? SP. vol.7, pp. 40-42. Strickland, vol.1, pp. 119-122. Strickland, vol.2, pp. 248-250. Tytler, pp. 157-158). (45) (Holinshed, pp. 488-489. RPS, July 4th, 1515). (46) (Johnson, pp. 82-84). (47) (Buchanan, pp. 273-276. Lesley, pp. 104-106). (48) (Buchanan, pp. 258-260. pp. 273-275. Calderwood, vol.1, pp. 58-60. Tytler, pp. 158-159). (49) (Buchanan, pp. 273-275. Calderwood, vol.1, pp. 58-60. Thomson, vol.2, pp. 548-549. Tytler, pp. 158-159). (50) (Buchanan, pp. 274-276. Calderwood, vol.1, pp. 58-60. Thomson, vol.2, pp. 548-549. Tytler, pp. 158-159). (51) (CSPS, Cardinal Wolsey to Queen Margaret, vol.1, Oct, 1516, p.5. Strickland, vol.1, pp. 123-127. Strickland, vol.1, pp. 134-135). (52) (RPS, November 13th 1516). (53) (CSPS, vol.1, Dacre to Wolsey, Dec 1st, 1516, p.5. LP, France and Scotland, November 3rd, 1516. RPS, October 7th, 1517. Thomson, vol.2,pp. 548-549). (54) (Buchanan, pp. 276-277. Lesley, pp. 108-110.Thomson, vol.2,pp. 548-549. Strickland, vol.1, pp. 131-133. Tytler, pp. 157-159). (55) (Lesley, pp. 108-110. ODNB, vol.29, pp. 619-627. ODNB, vol.38, pp. 848-849. SP, vol.3, pp. 433-437. Strickland, vol.1, pp. 131-133. Thomson, vol.2, pp. 548-549. Tytler, pp. 157-159). (56) (Exchequer Rolls, vol. 14, pp. lxvii-lxviii. Lesley, pp. 108-110. ODNB, vol.29, pp. 619-627. Tytler, pp. 157-159). (57) (ALHTS, vol.5, pp. xlvi-xlvii, p.114). (58) (ALCPA, March 30th, 1516, xxix, f.179, pp. 82-83. LP, Albany to Queen Margaret, March 6th, 1517 LP, Clarencieux to Wolsey, March 17th, 1517P, Seb. Guistinian to the Doge, April 15th, 1517.LP, Albany to Henry VIII, April 16th, 1517. RPS, 1516. Strickland, vol.1, pp. 134-136).

Chapter Four

I PERCEIVE YOUR CONSCIENCE
CLATTERS: 1517-1521

Albany took ship at Dumbarton and left for France on June 7th 1517. His first period as Governor was a political success, especially for France, since he had ensured under difficult circumstances that no war broke out between Scotland and England. He had also showed himself very capable in imposing law and order on very independently-minded and feud-addicted nobles, prelates and lords. The execution of the Hume brothers showed how far he was prepared to go to punish treason, even against the most powerful nobles. He also understood how to apply military strength as a negotiating tactic, and his mustering of forces close to the English border, although not intended to invade, was enough to intimidate. Yet he could also be conciliatory; his inviting Margaret back into Scotland was obviously to keep her in check, and also to try and seduce her away from the influence of her brother. He also realised that Margaret was a determined individual, prepared to match her capabilities against anyone who threatened the rights of her son. In future Albany would attempt to build a better relationship with the Queen of Scotland.

Before leaving for France Albany had James moved from Stirling to Edinburgh and placed under the guardianship of the Earl-Marshal, Lord Erskine, Lord Ruthven and Lord William Borthwick, two of whom were ordered to stay with the King at all times. The regency would be held under the earls of Angus, Arran, Argyll and Huntley, the Archbishops of St Andrews and Glasgow, and Sieur de la Baste. Lord Fleming was appointed Lord Chamberlain. Angus, having made peace with Albany and having his lands and possessions restored, was invited onto the council. Each was allocated authority of a province. The Earl of Argyll had arguably the largest and most difficulty area to administer, being appointed the Lieutenant of the Western Isles and Highlands, a commitment that would often take him away from court and the centre of power. De la Baste was appointed president of the council, and made governor of Dunbar and warden of the eastern March with authority over Lothian and the Earldom of March. Frenchmen were also placed as captains of Dumbarton and Inchgarve. To ensure some kind of hold over Scotland during his departure, Albany took to France sons and relatives of the more powerful families. Gavin Douglas would go with him to France, in an attempt to bring the Douglases away from English influence and closer to the French.

The Earl of Lennox, who had been reconciled with Albany in late 1516, would also travel to France. Possibly because Lennox was designated heir to the crown of Scotland after Arran, he was invited so to ensure that Arran behaved himself. If Arran were to rebel once more then Albany would have ample opportunities to question Arran's legitimate claims whilst promoting the claims of Lennox.

Arran's firstborn illegitimate son, Sir James Hamilton of

Finnart, would also travel to France, and although a hostage he would use the experience of travelling to and from the French and Scottish courts to later become an ambassador. The seventeen-year-old James Stewart Earl of Moray and illegitimate son of James IV may also have gone to France. It would be a logical choice, as Moray had travelled to the continent when eight years of age to study with Raphael Regius and Erasmus at Padua. Erasmus stated that as a student Moray showed 'great promise'. The purpose of this great entourage was not just the keeping of noble hostages but also a means of using the nation of France as a means of seducing the companions of Albany, through its culture, art, politics, society and wealth. [1]

Queen Margaret with her eighteen-month-old daughter Margaret would pass through Durham and Northumberland, then enter Scotland on June 15th 1517, several days after Albany had left for France. She was met at Lamberton Kirk by her husband Angus and the Earl of Morton. How she responded to her husband is unrecorded; possibly she kept her feelings hidden, as she considered the loyalty of a man who had deserted her in England whilst she had suffered from typhus. The new warden, de la Baste, was present also with 300 men. De la Baste was known as the White Knight because of the gleam of his armour.

Upon arriving in Edinburgh Margaret was not allowed to enter and see her son because plague was rife. King James, who was resident in the castle, was taken to Craigmiller, where he met his mother. According to Lesley there were still suspicions that Margaret might attempt to steal James away to England, and soon after the meeting James was returned to Edinburgh Castle. This appears a misjudgement as Margaret had learned the hard way that her brother was lax in supporting her interests, and therefore she would need to find an accommodation with whoever in Scotland held power. Her primary motivation from now on was the preservation of the rights and welfare of her son and herself. She would write to her brother and confirm that James was well and healthy. [2]

Whilst this appeared an amicable diplomatic development to allow Margaret to return to her son, Dacre and Wolsey were still financing the surviving Humes to raid and pillage Scotland from their base at Cawhills in the district of Berwick. Wolsey would pay 100 liberates for these services. The Humes in turn were being harassed by the garrisons at Wedderburn, Blacadder and Coldingham and the bands from the Merse. Dacre also offered to supply the Humes with ordinance, and intended to support the 'evil-disposed' Armstrongs without the crown being directly involved, no doubt because their deprivations were of a nature that King Henry should not be associated with, although clearly he was. Whilst Dacre conspired with the Humes, he complained to Lord Maxwell about Scottish raids into the debatable lands on the borders and sought redress by first writing to Maxwell then to the Lords of Council, and also to the Lord Chancellor. [3]

Albany would not forget his commitments to Scotland, and on August 20th 1517 after negotiations with the Duke of Alençon he signed the Treaty of Rouen in that city. It was a treaty of friendship and alliance, and ensured that in the event of either being attacked by England the other would give military and financial aid, as well as military diversions against English interests. France would supply Scotland with 2,200 troops and 100,000 crowns, and in the event of England attacking France, Scotland would supply 6,000 soldiers. Albany would also be rewarded by Francis with 10,000 livres tournois for his services to France during the past few years. Through the treaty Scotland now had a partner which would support and strengthen its foreign policy. This was also a threat to Henry's continental ambitions, making him more determined to politically interfere in Scotland. [4]

Albany would soon lose his trusted companion Sieur de la Baste when he was lured into a fatal trap. De la Baste had based himself at Dunbar and is reported to have been an able and competent warden of the east March, 'chiefly in restraining robberies' and 'through displaying 'great justice and wisdom'. Being foreign, he was also impartial in respect of administering justice. However he is said to have written to the Council of France stating that there was no need for Albany to return as he was administrating to a level that he believed would be 'to their contentment'. In other words he was forwarding himself as a possible replacement for Albany. His success also made him an enemy of the Humes, who wanted revenge for Albany's execution of Alexander and William Hume, and for the humiliation of imprisoning the late Lord Chamberlain's mother.

In September 1517 he was driven to intervene in a dispute involving William Cockburn, who took command of his young nephew the Lord of Langton's castle by expelling the tutors. The castle was then besieged by David Hume, Laird of Wedderburn. The occupation and siege of Langton appears to have been part of a ploy to lure de la Baste into a trap. Cockburn, who was kin to Hume, having married his sister, pretended to hold the castle for the king, and Wedderburn laid siege to it to claim it for himself. This compelled de la Baste to leave the safety of Dunbar so as to raise enough men to break the siege of Langton. Out in the open de la Baste was intercepted by the Humes, who proceeded to bring up the issue of the execution of Alexander Hume and his brother. De la Baste, who may have felt that his men, apart from the few French knights in his company, were not reliable, decided to ride away towards Dunbar. He was hotly pursued by Hume. His horse collapsed under him and became bogged down in marshland. He was overcome and slain by John and Patrick Hume, brothers of the Laird of Wedderburn. His head was sliced off and affixed to the Market Cross of the town of Duns. The Frenchmen occupying Hume Castle were expelled.

De la Baste's death occurred on September 17th 1517. The murder caused such an upheaval that from September 20th, 128 letters were sent across Scotland to all the prelates, lords, barons and burgesses to attend a parliament at Edinburgh as soon as possible. [5]

George Douglas was suspected of having a hand in the murder as he was known to be a close associate of David Hume. Hume had married Alison, the sister of Angus and Sir George Douglas, so there were justifiable suspicions that the brothers were involved. Angus however was deemed too powerful to challenge directly. When the council was called, the Earl of Arran was appointed Warden of the Eastern March in place of de la Baste, with authority over Lothian and the Merse. He was also made deputy governor and provost of Edinburgh, appointments that angered Angus and the Douglas fraternity. The provost was a powerful position that allowed regulation of trade through the town council and the mustering of civic militias in the event of invasion or riot. Not only was Arran infringing on the eastern march, he was intruding into Edinburgh, where there was a significant Douglas presence with popular support.

Arran had George Douglas and Mark Kerr arrested and placed in Edinburgh Castle, under suspicion that they had favoured the actions of Hume and his helpers. Douglas was then moved to Dalkeith under the wardship of the Earl of Morton, and then transferred to Blackness. The Humes retired to the castles of Hume and Langton. Word was also sent to France calling for Albany to return. [6]

The Lords of Council also sent letters to the Earl of Angus requesting that as he was one of the regents he should come to Edinburgh. Several times during October and November he refused. A letter of November 21st was a last warning to Angus that if he did not attend council or fulfil his duties as one of the regents he would be considered an individual 'not assisting the common well' and not suitable to 'exercise the office the which he had accepted and sworn to'. A parliament was ordered to be conveyed for February 15th, 1518. Letters were also sent out to David Hume and his alleged accomplices for the murder of de la Baste on December 26th, and for the siege of Langton, the spiking of de la Baste's head at the market cross at Duns, and for treasonous dealings with the English authorities. [7]

The divisions were indicators of the potential violence that could erupt between Angus and Arran, but presently it was a proxy war with each side testing the strength of the other. Some respite to this violence may have been gained when Lennox, Gavin Douglas, and possibly Arran's son Hamilton of Finnart and some Frenchmen, returned from France with the new Treaty of Rouen. The terms strengthened the military ties between Scotland and France and there was a firm commitment on France's part to provide arms, men and money in the event of England waging war on Scotland. [8]

Pitscottie writes that when Albany heard of the slaying of de la Baste he had an audience with the King of France. Louis would criticize Albany for placing a Frenchmen over Scots, which would inspire the latter's jealousy. However he would 'support and maintain (Albany's) vow to revenge that matter as you well desire'. He also promised to grant him ships and supplies to allow him to pass through the seas to Scotland. Nevertheless, whilst Albany was advised by his captains to pass quickly into Scotland before his enemies gather further strength, it would be a few more years before he left the continent. Despite his offers of support, for the sake of better relations with England, Francis would keep Albany away from Scotland. Henry VIII would insist on that condition in any treaty. Francis would task Albany with French duties, such as attending the baptism of the King's two-month-old son in April 1518 at Amboise. The dauphin's godfather was Pope Leo X, and at the baptism Leo was represented at the ceremony by his nephew Lorenzo de Medici. Albany's sister-in-law Madeleine de La Tour was to marry Lorenzo under agreement with Francis I. This arrangement would lure Albany deeper into papal and Italian politics, but he would also continue to work for Scotland on the continent. In an effort to strengthen the mercantile classes and bring some economic prosperity he persuaded Francis to grant special privileges through patented letters to Scottish merchants at Amboise in May 1518. Albany was also reported to be planning a return to Scotland alongside Richard de la Pole, the so-called 'White Rose' and pretender to the English throne. [9]

Francis did send to Scotland a French soldier, Morise, who had the authority to act as captain of Dunbar on behalf of Albany. He would fill Dunbar Castle with men and supplies, as well as bringing in masons and craftsmen to strengthen the walls and build a blockhouse which was filled with artillery, ammunition and powder. Dunbar would become a significant power on the Eastern March as well as important link with the sea. To keep Queen Margaret content, the revenues due to her from Dunbar were delivered by order of the Lords of Council. [10]

The business of governing the nation of Scotland would continue. During the parliament held at Edinburgh on February 19th, 1518 the participants debated what action to take against the Humes, as the accused were not showing evidence of attending parliament to answer the charges made against them. The French King had written to the Council in Scotland, in a letter dated November 1517, lamenting the death of de la Baste and criticizing the Scots for not dealing appropriately with the murderers. Arran, as regent closest in blood after Albany to the King, was voted deputy governor and tasked with marching against the Humes. He was to kill, capture or expel the rebels and traitors and take their homes and possessions. Angus was angered at this promotion of Arran, and concerned also, for he wrote to the Lords of Counsel offering to support the King and asking guidance on what role they would have him play in the upcoming campaign against the Humes and others. The Lords thanked him for the offer of support but asked him to remain north of the Forth and not to join Arran. This speaks of the distrust that the lords of Council had for Angus. Whilst not wanting him to join they could at least encourage his neutrality. [11]

In March letters of reply were sent, possibly taken by Sir James Hamilton of Finnart, informing Francis that his father Arran had raised an army and with the King's artillery advanced to the borders. Oxen were gathered to pull the artillery carriages, and an order was sent out, the same as that proclaimed before Flodden, stating that in the event of any death, the heirs of the deceased would enjoy special privileges. The Humes and their followers, seeing that they could not withstand this army, fled across the border to seek refuge in England. This sheltering of Scottish rebels was a clear violation of the truce and comprehension. The army was supplied by Robert Glenn, a burgess of Edinburgh, with fifty pieces of artillery called culverin. Robert Glenn also acted as a captain of footmen in the army. There appear to have been two advances into the Merse. The first entailed a muster at Lauder on March 21st, where the keys of Hume castle were handed to Arran. A nine-day raid then followed, resulting in the strongholds of Wedderburn and Langton being given up. The French King was asked to write to Henry VIII asking him to surrender the Scottish rebels, as no reply had been received after requests by the Scots. [12]

An act of brutal revenge was then enacted against David Hume, the Abbot of Coldingham and brother of the executed Alexander and William. Appointed Abbot through the deal made between Andrew Forman and Alexander Lord Hume, he had been forced to flee to England in 1517 with his other brothers when the government pursued them as traitors and rebels. He returned later under the protection of the Earl of Angus. Hume was described as an 'enterprising genius' with a 'friendly and virtuous disposition' which made him well liked by the commoners, who called him 'David the Innocent'. He nevertheless had a healthy respect for his own safety, being watchful when travelling and attending meetings, and surrounding himself with valued friends and advisers. The Humes had many enemies, and whilst John Hepburn had instigated through Albany a great deal of trouble upon this family, Godscroft claims that one James Hepburn had married David's sister and apparently both were friends, as well as brothers-in-law.

Hepburn invited David Hume to a friendly social meeting, and trusting his sister's husband, Hume travelled to this meeting with no protection. He was reportedly slain by Chirnside of Nisbit and William Cockburn. This Cockburn may be the same that was involved in the ambush of de la Baste; if so then he no longer hired his sword to the Humes and had now changed sides. Cockburn would be subject to a legal action by the Humes in 1532/33 accused of this murder.

Whilst Pitscottie and Lesley mention the Master of Hailes as being involved, and Lesley adds that Arran had apprehended him for the murder, the court action of 1532/1533 does not mention any Hepburn. However Patrick Hepburn, sheriff of Haddington and Admiral-depute, had designated himself 'the Master of Hailes' in 1515, he being tutor to Patrick Hepburn the next Lord Hailes and future Earl of Bothwell. He had married as his first wife Lady Herries, daughter of Alexander 2nd Lord Hume and brother of David Hume. It appears that Godscroft confused Patrick with James, and that possibly this Hepburn organised the murder of Hume. In Pitscottie's words it was done 'thinking to do the Duke of Albany pleasure'. The murder though does not seem to have been sanctioned by the government or the adherents of Albany, as during the hunt for the Humes the Master of Hailes was sought after for his part in the slaying. [13]

Later, in May, the other David Hume, the fugitive laird of Wedderburn, would capture a French ambassador called Poillot and take him prisoner. Poillot was travelling under safe conduct through England, intending to pass into Scotland. Hume's aim seems to have been try to gain a pardon and return to Scotland. The Earl of Arran and the Lord Treasurer Campbell occupied the stronghold of Wedderburn and were intending to draw closer to the borders and meet Dacre at Coldstream or Cornhill, obviously to compel the English to use their influence on Hume and broker Poillot's release. Dacre wanted Hume to allow the Frenchmen free passage, but asked Hume to stay and England would attempt to broker a pardon from the Scots. Dacre wanted Hume to remain in the borders so as to harass the Scots whilst England tried to claim he was acting alone. Hume was based in Cawmill. In respect of the forthcoming meeting with Arran, Dacre asked Wolsey to authorise the loan of cannon from Newcastle so as to fire off cannonballs during the meeting and play psychological games with the Scots. [14]

On the continent a treaty of mutual defence called the 'General League' was agreed by the Pope, Emperor, France, England and Spain, with Scotland and the Swiss to be comprehended if they wished. On October 1518 France and England agreed to the Treaty of London, which allowed Francis to buy back the recently-captured fortress of Tournai for 600,000 crowns, a profit for Henry and security for Francis. Henry's daughter, two-year-old Mary, was betrothed to the one-year-old dauphin of France. King Henry threw in a condition by which King Francis was not to allow Albany to return to Scotland, or gain the government of Scotland, which was to be restored to Margaret. The Scots would reject comprehension into this treaty on a number of grounds, notwithstanding the denial of the Scottish right to choose their governors, but there was also a condition under which none of the parties would give refuge to rebels. As England was clearly giving aid and protection to the Humes then this condition had already been voided, and Wolsey, one of the signatories of this treaty, was also seeking to gain some political advantage from Hume's capture of the French ambassador Poillot.

The Scots sent critical letters to Francis and to Albany regarding their treatment in the treaty, and also wrote to the Pope accusing the English of breaching the terms of the treaty through supporting rebels and encouraging raids. They requested that the Pope should ask the French King to send Albany to Scotland. [15]

One important character in the grand and clumsily-executed strategies of Wolsey and Dacre was the Earl of Angus, the one Scot who was capable of challenging the power of the present Scottish government whilst Albany was abroad. Henry's grand schemers missed their opportunity and failed to supply Angus with the resources he would need to overcome Henry's enemies. Henry would fail to give his sister, Queen Margaret, any meaningful support, despite the fact that as mother of the King she was a prime asset in any endeavours to influence Scotland. Since returning to Scotland Margaret had not enjoyed a good relationship with the Earl of Angus, and sought a divorce. She claimed in writing that they had not cohabited as man and wife for nearly half a year. (16)

Henry wanted Queen Margaret and her husband to be reconciled, as it would make it easier for England to exert meaningful influence. However Angus made matters even more difficult when he acted in a manner that alienated and insulted his wife. In August whilst residing in Edinburgh, Margaret had learned that he had acquired a mistress called Lady Janet Stewart, daughter of Lord Traquair, which he had taken to Douglasdale. Lady Janet had been a former prospective bride of Angus, and from this new relationship she would give birth to a daughter Janet. This would cause Margaret to develop an intense hatred for Angus and seek a divorce. By some accounts a momentous quarrel resulted, after which the Earl of Angus snatched his three-year-old daughter Lady Margaret Douglas from the Queen's arms and took her to Tantallon Castle.

Obviously there was a dynastic advantage in Angus possessing his daughter, who was also the niece of Henry VIII, and whatever recriminations Margaret made, the husband would not surrender custody. Once housed in Tantallon, the Lady Margaret Douglas would be brought up by Angus' relatives and kin, who ensured she was brought up as a royal princess. Elizabeth, wife of Sir George Douglas and the wife of Archibald Douglas of Kilspindie, would administer the wellbeing and education of the royal daughter, and it is also recorded that the garrison schooled her in the countryside pursuits of riding, hunting and hawking.

The Queen decided to separate from her husband and left Holyrood Abbey to travel to her stronghold at Stirling Castle. She also complained to Henry that since Gavin Douglas' return from France, the Douglases had been attempting to get Margaret to break the bond she had made with Angus, witnessed by Dacre, by which Angus would not be allowed to enjoy any of her dowry and landed possessions without her permission.

So far Angus had occupied the house at Newark, taken the rents from Ettrick and Methven Forest and deprived Margaret of revenues worth 4,000 marks per year. It was her intention to sue for divorce that troubled Henry, as he considered Angus the head of a faction sympathetic to English interests. Many nobles also saw the advantages in having Douglas power diminished and also encouraged the Queen to follow the course of legal separation. The Lords of Council, possibly acting on Margaret's complaints, commanded Angus to appear before them and hand Newark into their keeping. [17]

Queen Margaret was in a dire situation, with limited access to her son, and now her daughter Margaret taken into possession by the Earl of Angus. With limited financial resources all she could rely on were a few friends and her willpower. She would write to Henry often complaining that she was destitute and not getting full rights in respect to her dowry. Not only was Angus depriving her, but she was not receiving sufficient rents or revenues from the other parts of her dowry. She would claim that she had to sell her jewellery and other possessions in order to gain food and sustenance, and she pleaded with Henry to use his influence to uphold her rights. [18]

Whilst Margaret moved to Stirling, King James remained at Edinburgh Castle under the protection of Lord Ruthven. There were serious policing issues in respect of Edinburgh Town, where openly-armed men and violence were common. On December 13th 1518, the Lords of Council passed an act ordering that only crown-appointed officials could carry weapons in the town, and anyone found with weapons would be ordered to return to their lodging, or else get arrested. [19]

Better security in Edinburgh was an important measure, as French ambassadors would visit the parliament and the King of Scots on February 1519 requesting that the Scots comprehend into the General League. The Scots refused once more, as Albany had not put his written agreement to it, and the terms were unfair in that the comprehension would be voided if the Scots raided across the border. Yet the English did not suffer the same conditions, despite supporting the Laird of Wedderburn and his Hume faction.

The name of the Humes continued to spread fear and loathing across southern Scotland as they used murder to further gain position and profit. Robert Blacadder, the Priory of Coldingham, was slain whilst out hunting with several of his companions near the village of Lamberton on January 19th 1519. David Hume, Laird of Wedderburn, led the cutthroats who sacrilegiously ended the abbot's life, and William Douglas, illegitimate brother of Angus, was installed as Abbot. [20]

On the continent the death of Maximilian in January 1519 had created a contest to win the title of Emperor. Despite interest by Francis, and a bid by Henry that was less seriously considered, it was Charles who won the election and was chosen as head of the Holy Roman Empire in June 1519. The House of Habsburg was now presiding over one of the most powerful empires in European history, comprising Spain, the Netherlands, Austria, Germany, Naples and a vast slice of the New World, and the riches and resources that ensued. Europe now had two powerful rivals with several serious territorial differences. Francis had spent millions of gold crowns in war and court extravagance and was not in an immediate position to go to war. Charles on the other hand would need English help in the event of war, and Henry and Cardinal Wolsey began to exploit this position in order to gain political influence over the powers, and to keep them to a balance that would benefit England.

Whilst Henry and Wolsey played European politics, it was the intrigues and violence of the Earl of Angus and his allies and the ensuing internal dissentions that successfully ensured that the government of Scotland could not significantly distract England from ambitions across the Channel. [21]

One concern for Henry was the prospect of his sister Margaret being granted a divorce from Angus, which would allow her to remarry. Angus was also deeply concerned about the possibility of a divorce, and having been ordered to attend the Lords of Council he handed over Newark on February 15th, 1519. He also needed to get more involved in government so as to help broker his brother

William's rights to Coldingham, despite the bloody promotion. Angus would rejoin the Lords of Council on February 26th 1519. He immediately sought ecclesiastical support in regard to stopping the divorce proceedings of Margaret. In this he found sympathy with Andrew Forman, Archbishop of St Andrews. Angus petitioned him as papal legate to compel Queen Margaret to live with him as his wife or give reasons why she refused to be by his side. Regarding his brother William's appointment as Prior of Coldingham he would meet opposition, especially as there was a rival to the post in Patrick Blackadder, cousin of the slain abbot. Angus would now seek to build up an alliance within the council that would be strong enough to challenge Arran, and he also sought to gain supporters within Edinburgh where Arran was provost. [22]

Margaret began to toy with the idea of forming an alliance with Albany. Later correspondence from Lord Dacre would mention Henry's concerns that she herself had written to Albany whilst he was in France. She admitted this, although it is clear that with Angus robbing her of revenue and Henry not offering her any meaningful support, she perceived that she will 'get nothing but fair words from any quarter.' [23]

A plague took Edinburgh during the autumn and the King was moved to Dalkeith whilst several of his household died from it. [24] During this period Queen Margaret reported divisions between Angus and many of the Lords of Council led by the Earl of Arran, with the latter bent on the earls' 'destruction'. Arran based himself at Dalkeith with the King, and in September he approached Edinburgh expecting to be re-elected provost. The Douglas and 'other great men' organised a body of citizens to stop Arran and his people from entering the town, which caused an outbreak of violence from both sides, with the forces of Arran being driven off. Blocked from the city, Arran was defeated in the election and Archibald Douglas of Kilspindie, Angus' uncle, was voted provost.

The Lords of Council requested that the people remove Douglas from office and choose someone else who might be neutral in respect to divisions between Arran and Angus. The citizens replied that they chose their provost by the 'form of their old privileges' and would protect their choice, as this would be the same as protecting their rights. One of the leaders of the citizens, a carpenter called Gavin, would be later slain by James Hamilton of Finnart, who would steadily gain an infamous reputation as he carved out a bloody career of murders and mutilations.

Besides the Humes, Angus had drawn together a powerful coalition comprising the Earl of Errol and Crawford, the Lord Glamis, the Archbishop of St Andrews, the bishops of Orkney and Dunblane, and a number of nobles and abbots. He appears to have also brought into his camp Gavin Dunbar, newly consecrated as Bishop of Aberdeen on February 20th, 1519. On the opposite side Arran drew together the Archbishop of Glasgow, the Abbot of Paisley, the earls of Argyll, Lennox, Cassilis, the Lords Ross, Sempill, Maxwell, Fleming and others. [25]

It appears that during this period there were determined efforts made to get Margaret to reconcile herself with Angus. Queen Katherine of Aragon had sent Father Bonaventura to visit Queen Margaret whilst she was in Perth during October. On behalf of Katherine he was to implore Margaret to endure the marriage without following the course of petitioning for a divorce, which would bring public scrutiny to the whole matter. The father was unsuccessful in promoting this idea.

Henry, Wolsey and Dacre needed the support of their strongest Scottish ally in Angus, and realised how damaging a divorce would be to their efforts to intervene in Scottish affairs. Margaret was lacking funds and was being obstructed and frustrated in her attempts to access full rights to her dowry. Besides that, she had little authority over her son and was regulated stringently in her rights to visit him. A friar called Chatsworth of the Observatine order had been sent by Henry to meet Queen Margaret when she arrived in Stirling to protest against her intention to seek divorce, which he termed a 'damnable delusion', and even accused of Margaret of behaving in a manner of 'suspicious living' that her enemies could use to accuse her of adultery. Andrew Forman, the

Archbishop of St Andrews, was also on the side of Angus, and his request sought Margaret to make her peace with her husband. Forman's siding with Angus was purely political as he and Beaton were rivals. Although the exact reason is unclear, Beaton would describe Forman as a 'mischievous fellow', but the rivalry may have had much to do with primacy, with Forman superseding Beaton as papal legate. [26]

Margaret wrote that she had tried to intermediate between the factions of Angus and Arran, but with no success. Arran, the Earl of Lennox, Lords Fleming, Maxwell and Semple, the Archbishop of Glasgow and the bishops of Galloway and Argyll met with her at her castle of Stirling. She had tried to find favour with Arran and the Lords of Council. She would inform them that she had written to Albany in France, and she would admit this to Lord Dacre. She would claim that she received letters stating that he would support her in her rights to govern Scotland as Queen as well as gain access to her son. This claim did not appear to satisfy the faction of Arran and Beaton, and many of the Lords made clear their opposition to her gaining the government. Albany may have been genuine; the peace between England and France was secure, and making overtures to Margaret was meant to help heal divisions within Scotland. [27]

Margaret was under pressure from her brother, the Archbishop of St Andrews, and those followers of her husband to reconcile her differences. And with the Lords of Council around Arran expressing hostility to her claims and rights she decided to concede and returned to the side of her husband on October 15th, being met outside Edinburgh with Angus and 400 horsemen.

The other consideration would be her daughter Margaret, under the custody of her husband and if reports are correct, used as a weapon by the Earl of Angus to torment and emotionally blackmail Margaret. Her position was complex. Although she had apparent support from Albany, she found she was getting none from the Lords of Council. They controlled her rights of access to her son residing in Edinburgh Castle, protected by guardians appointed by Albany. Her husband apparently held rival power in Edinburgh town, with her daughter Lady Margaret living at Tantallon Castle. Her children were being used as levers against her, and perhaps she saw no other option but to return to her husband. At least she would be allowed to visit James, and possibly through reconciliation with Angus she could gain some access to Margaret.

As Queen Margaret entered Edinburgh, there was a loud celebration of cannon exploding and music playing. She was met by the party of Angus, comprising the Archbishop of St Andrews, Gavin Douglas, bishop of Dunkeld, the bishops of Moray and Aberdeen, the earls of Argyll, Morton, Glencairn, Marshall, and the lords Ruthven, Hay, Glamis and Grey. She then went to Edinburgh Castle to meet her son the King, who had recently returned there from Dalkeith. [28]

Events in Scotland became more confusing and dangerous when the French ambassador Lafiot and a clerk Cordell arrived in Edinburgh during December, along with the Clarencieux herald, to invite Scotland once more to comprehend into a French-English treaty. They would also witness the complicated relationships within Scotland. Whilst Angus held Edinburgh town and made the visitors welcome, the young King James, with Lord Ruthven as governor, occupied Edinburgh Castle. The envoys also sought to address parliament. At their insistence invitations were sent out to Arran and the Archbishop of Glasgow to come to Edinburgh. They declined this and an offer to meet in Linlithgow. The French envoys suggested Stirling, but this was not accepted by Angus and his following.

Nevertheless, the French were not impressed by Angus' efforts to negotiate the terms of the treaty and decided to attend a Council meeting at Stirling for December 15th and fronted by the Archbishop of Glasgow and Arran. Lafiot and Cordell informed the Scots that if they did not enter into the treaty then the King of France would find it difficult to intervene on Scotland's behalf in the event of a Scottish war with England. The Lords of Council also wrote to Angus and the bishops of Dunkeld and Aberdeen, but their council refused to accept the letters and decreed that they would not attend the parliament at Stirling. The Council at Stirling decided on December 18th 1519 to accept the terms of the treaty, and a truce with England was proclaimed, to last until St Andrews Day 1520. This was an insult to Angus, and when the French envoys were returning home by way of England he gathered sufficient forces and stopped them at Caerlaverock in the south west. He upbraided them for taking the part of his enemies so such an extent that they were concerned for their safety. Angus allowed them to cross the border, his rough methods no doubt gifting them once more with a picture of the poisonous divisions within Scotland. [29]

Further dissention involving the Douglases would occur during January 1520 when Andrew Kerr of Ferniehurst entered into a dispute about jurisdiction over Jedworth Forest, which the Earl of Angus held in regality but where Kerr claimed he had authority to administer justice, as he was Baillie. Sir James Hamilton of Finnart, illegitimate son of the Earl of Arran, sided with the Kerrs of Ferniehurst, whilst Kerr of Cessford sided with Angus. At Kelso Hamilton arrived with 400 men from the Merse, but on the advance of Cessford, joined by John Somerville from Carnwath, they fled. Hamilton was chased to Castle Hume, with several casualties. Despite this skirmish, known as the 'Raid of Jedworth Forest', Kerr of Ferniehurst continued to act as Baillie of Jedworth Forest whilst Angus held a rival court several miles distant. [30]

With the capital Edinburgh being a divided city, fought over by the factions of Arran and Angus, Albany sent a command from France that none of the family of Hamilton or Douglas were to be provost of Edinburgh. At this Archibald Douglas, of Kilspindie, resigned the position to one Robert Logan. This weakened the power of the Douglases within Edinburgh. Arran entered Edinburgh in strength and a convention was called for April 29th 1520 to address the divisions with Scotland. A plan appears to have been conceived by Arran and Beaton at the latter's Edinburgh home on Blackfriars Wynd to capture Angus, as it was considered 'that his surpassing power' would disrupt the planned convention. The Earl of Angus, learning of this meeting, sent his uncle, Gavin Douglas, Bishop of Dunkeld, to intermediate. Angus offered to lead all his followers out of Edinburgh if they were not harmed or attacked. Upon meeting with the Bishop of Dunkeld, Beaton appeared to concede that he could do nothing to stop any forthcoming battle, saying 'there is no remedy, upon my conscience I cannot help what is going to happen'. Under his tunic there was armour which made a metallic sound when Beaton dramatically beat his chest. Dunkeld replied, 'How now, my Lord, methinks your conscience clatters'. [31]

Dunkeld returned to his nephew and warned him that violence was imminent. Angus also learned that the gates and passages that could offer escape were blocked, so he steeled his men to prepare to fight. According to Calderwood they formed a body of 80 to 100 and made their way to Blackfriars Wynd. As Angus was popular within Edinburgh, his men were allowed to take pikes and spears from stores which made and sold these weapons, and citizens handed out spears and weapons out of windows and doorways as Angus' men passed by. This gave the outnumbered Angus faction something of an advantage as their enemies had few spears or lances, and were armed with mostly swords, daggers and axes.

Sir Patrick Hamilton, the half-brother of the Earl of Arran, perceiving that the Angus faction were strongly arrayed, suggested that a peaceful solution should be sought. But Sir James Hamilton of Finnart accused his uncle of cowardice, and in answer Patrick and a few of his followers rushed at Angus and were slain. John Montgomery, the Master of Eglinton also lost his life.

The Hamiltons joined the street fight but the Angus faction were better organised, managing to defend against and drive back enemy bands arriving out of the narrow closes to attack them. Angus' brother William, the priory of Coldingham, and Hume of Wedderburn forced the gates of the city and joined with several hundred borderers. Eight hundred horsemen belonging to the Arran faction were given permission by Angus to exit Edinburgh with some disgrace. Beaton himself had entered the fray but when the fight was lost he fled into Blackfriars church, and was saved from being slain by the intervention of Gavin Douglas, Bishop of Dunkeld. Arran and his son James escaped by a ford, passing by the North Loch. Others sought refuge in the Dominican Church. The skirmish would become known as 'Clean the causeway'. The following day the Humes and John Somerville would array at the Boroughmuir with a 'multitude of thieves and evil-doers' in sight of King James who may have witnessed these provocative demonstrations from within Edinburgh Castle. Although no fight ensued, the Humes would then use the advantage gained to regain the strongholds of Hume and Wedderburn. [32]

Arran would try to strike back by attacking Angus' adherents, such as Robert Boyd, who unsuccessfully laid siege to his castle of Kilmarnock. Angus however was not at that time confident enough to continue to hold Edinburgh and would be forced to leave. By August 1520 the civic authorities, weary of the strife, would enter into a bond of maintenance with Arran, where both agree to support the other as long as Arran holds power in Edinburgh. [33]

Like the people of Edinburgh many of the lords and prelates were yearning for some law and order and supported the return of Albany. The main stumbling obstacles were the English propaganda campaign in which they envisioned an Albany who would persecute the Queen, and harm the young King. On the first point there was a counter-belief from the French court that Queen Margaret was supportive of Albany's return. In respect to any threat to James, the French would propose in a forthcoming meeting with the English allowing ambassadors from the English, Danes, French and Vatican to live in the vicinity of the King, to have free access, and ensure the safeguarding of treaties and co-operation between all players. The French were offering terms to Henry VIII, in that his sister Margaret should get all her dowry and property restored to her, that she should continue to visit her son when she pleased, and that she would be consulted on any matter regarding the safety or wellbeing of the King.

Whilst Margaret was custodian of Stirling Castle, if she handed the keys to Albany then her son could be removed from Edinburgh Castle and placed in Stirling. The French, whilst forwarding these ideas, were also well aware that the English did not want Albany's return, as they sought to formant feud and dissention and keep Scotland divided. The murder of de la Baste, the abduction of Poillot the ambassador, the killing of the Abbot of Coldingham and other incidents were done with English support and in some cases with English manpower. Around 50-60 Englishmen were said to have been involved in the recent skirmishes between rival Scottish parties. [34]

English spies and intelligence networks across the continent thrived on news of Albany. In Rome he is reported to have given homage to the Pope in the name of Scotland on June 18th. Possibly as a response to this new development, representatives of the Archbishops of Glasgow and St Andrews were reported to have travelled to France in the summer to petition Francis to allow the Governor to cross the waters to Scotland.

It is significant that Andrew Forman, Archbishop of St Andrews, was now siding with James Beaton, the Archbishop of Glasgow, to request the return of Albany, the former still associated with the party of Angus. Forman obviously wanted an end to the civil strife tearing Scotland apart. It would also be his responsibility as papal legate to support Albany, as the pope had recognised him as Scotland's Governor and the King's tutor. A Bull was also issued on June 19th in which Pope Leo X opposed any attempts by other parties to claim Albany's legal post of Governor of Scotland, and he also announced that he would take King James and the kingdom of Scotland into his protection. Anyone disrupting Albany's right to govern would suffer excommunication. Forman would have no choice but to support Albany. [35]

It appears that Francis, fearful of provoking the English, decided against sending Albany to Scotland and would instead authorise Robert Stewart, Lord of Aubigny, to travel as his ambassador. Robert was the son of John Stewart, 1st Earl of Lennox, born in 1470. He travelled to France and joined the army around 1495 soon after his father's death. He served with a cousin, the famous Berault Stewart, and married Berault's daughter Anne. He also served with his brother William's regiment. He fought with Louis XII in the Italian wars and was involved in the capture of the Duke of Milan in 1500. After Berault Stewart's death he inherited the Lordship of Aubigny. He was appointed Captain of the King's Scots Guards in 1512, and whilst he earned a reputation for military courage and skill Francis sought to use Aubigny's diplomatic skills, by sending him to Scotland to explain French policy. Francis' aim was for the Scots to settle their differences and to keep the peace with England. He was accompanied by John Planis, a doctor of law, and a previous diplomatic visitor to Scotland. [36]

There were efforts to break the peace between England and France. Charles V shocked Europe when he suddenly arrived at Sandwich in May 1520 to meet with Henry VIII to lobby for military support in a future war. King Francis countered by agreeing to meet Henry on the border between Calais and France in June 1520. This was known as the 'Field of the Cloth of Gold' in reference to the elaborate and expensive clothing worn that day by both parties. Having gained the restoration of Tournay through diplomacy with Wolsey in 1518, Francis was now hoping for France to regain Calais. The Lord of Aubigny was also present at this occasion and would have met Henry and Wolsey. Here he would gain an insight into the objectives of the English in respect to Queen Margaret, the Scots lords and the Duke of Albany.

Charles V would meet Henry soon after this at Gravelines on July 10th, and although details are unknown it is likely that no agreement was made. Nevertheless Francis would be well aware of the danger of England joining the Empire to attack France, and in order not to antagonise Henry VIII Francis had the Duke of Albany briefly detained, as he was suspected of planning to travel to Scotland without royal permission. Later the Pope would call him to Rome to spend winter there. As noted earlier Lorenzo di Medici, Duke of Urbino and nephew of Pope Leo X, had married Albany's sister-in-law, Madeleine de La Tour d'Auvergne. The Duke and Duchess had a daughter, Catherine, born at Urbino on 19 April 1519, but both her parents would die within a month and she was warded with her great-uncle, Leo X. Not only would Albany develop a working relationship with the Pope he would get to know his niece Catherine de Medici, who would in the future marry Henry II and become Queen of France. [37]

Whilst English spies observed the Scots representatives of the Archbishops of Glasgow and St Andrews returning to Scotland after meeting Francis, they would also learn that whilst Albany was not returning to Scotland in the foreseeable future he had outfitted four galleons at Honfleur for Aubigny to use. [38]

Besides seeking peace in Scotland, Aubigny was also tasked to settle the grievances of Queen Margaret regarding her dowry, a cause which Henry was using as an excuse for hostility against the Scots. Queen Margaret herself would report widely of the dire straits she now was in. Whilst able to claim the revenues of Stirling and Linlithgow, she could get no access to rents or revenues from the Forest of Ettrick, or within the Earldom of March and other places. She had limited access to her son, and whilst he was closely guarded she feared that in order to acquire power certain nobles would conspire to capture him. Possibly she meant her husband. [39]

Aubigny and John Planis arrived at Dunbar on November 27th after a stormy obstructive journey. They were at Edinburgh in the beginning of December and were met by the nobles representing the Angus faction. They were allowed to meet the King, although it was a sign of the fears and suspicions of the times that the lords were only allowed to enter the castle with one servant each. The Earl of Arran and his faction were reluctant to join with that of Angus, however the Lord Treasurer Campbell managed to get Archbishop Beaton to agree to a continuance of the truce to last until Christmas, and the former wrote to Lord Dacre to confirm this intention. A parliament was arranged in mid-December between the rival factions, although it is not recorded where it was held or who attended. James Beaton, the Chancellor and Archbishop of Glasgow, suggested that ambassadors should be sent to England to negotiate terms for a longer-term truce. Francis also sent a letter to be read out in the Scottish parliament in which he asked the Scots 'to compose their quarrels' which had left Scotland 'lacerated with civil wars'. Whilst Francis expected the two ambassadors to contribute towards peace, he suggested that Albany's presence in Scotland would be counter-productive - 'things being as they are, he had better remain in France'. Queen Margaret reported that these sentiments against Albany were resented by some of the Lords of Council as they directly challenged their constitutional right to choose their governor. (40)

The Lord Aubigny met Andrew Forman, the Archbishop of St Andrews, on January 8th 1521. He explained to Forman how King Francis believed that for the sake of peace Albany should stay in France. Although Forman was still associated at that time with the Angus faction, possibly acting in a role to moderate the violence between the rivals, as already noted he was also supportive of recalling Albany to Scotland. Aubigny would have been attempting to keep Forman to the French agenda, although he would be up against the papal bull which arrived in Scotland and granted papal authority to the governorship of Albany. The Archbishops of Glasgow and St Andrews and the Bishop of Aberdeen were ordered to publish the Bull and support it.

The papal bull would suddenly change the national policies of the Scots and whilst mindful of the importance of the alliance with France they were not going to allow themselves to be dictated to by the French King. Forcefully taking the initiative, the Scots called a parliament for January 21st 1521, demanding the recall of Albany by August 3rd or he would be deprived of the Governorship. Albany, the French national, loyal to his King, was now being sent conditions from the Scots to serve them. As a further challenge

Beaton and the Arran faction decided not to send the promised ambassadors to England. [41]

Localised truces however were negotiated on the borders between Thomas, the priory of Kelso, Andrew Kerr of Cessford and Adam Otterburn on the Scottish side, and Lord Dacre for the English. The truce was to last from January 30th 1521 to June 30th 1521. Whilst Cessford was commissioned by King and council to act as Warden, he would admit to Dacre at a later date that he could not command full obedience, and many borderers were committing raids without fear of redress. It seems clear that the Scots were not looking for anything other than temporary truces, whilst rejecting or postponing any embassies being sent to England to finalise a more concrete treaty. One excuse for delay was the sudden death of Andrew Forman, Archbishop of St Andrews, in March, which caused some upheavals with the Earls of Arran and Lennox disputing over the Abbey of Dunfermline and John Hepburn having re-entered St Andrews. [42]

Henry VIII complained of the reluctance of the Scots to send ambassadors, whilst Francis I in conversation with the English ambassador Fitzwilliam agreed, and insisted that he had asked the Scots to send embassies to England. He claimed that he had even threatened Albany with losing land and influence if he went to Scotland. There is an impression that Albany wanted to return and Francis was doing all he could to keep him in France. It is possible that this was a stratagem to practise with Henry. Francis was concerned that war could break out between France and the Empire and he wanted England to stay out of it. However if England went to war with France alongside the Habsburg Empire, then Albany could provide distractions in Scotland. So whilst Francis wanted peace, he also needed more aggressive options if it failed. [43]

The King of England would also learn during March that his sister, the Queen of Scotland, had once more left the side of Angus and had been spirited away from Edinburgh to Linlithgow by Sir James Hamilton, described as Angus' 'deadly enemy'. It seems likely this was the twenty-six-year-old Sir James Hamilton of Finnart, the illegitimate son of the Earl of Arran. According to reports, Albany had persuaded her on this course by 'fair words' in a letter to her. Besides having a reputation as a ferocious and bloodthirsty individual, Hamilton of Finnart was an ally of Albany, having travelled to France firstly as a hostage and later as a diplomat. He also showed an interest in continental architecture, and possibly met Leonardo da Vinci whilst accompanying Albany to Amboise. He would later be responsible for introducing innovative continental designs to the construction of castles, palaces and even prisons. As Margaret herself would show an interest in building designs, these interests may have helped her bond with the dangerous Finnart, added to the fact that he was an enemy of her husband, which antagonised Angus more. She would also be aware that Albany intended to return to Scotland, which would lead to Angus being expelled. She hoped for a more favourable outcome, where she gained access not only to James but also to her daughter Margaret, who was still under the care of Angus. We know little if nothing about the relationship between Queen Margaret and her daughter up to that time. It is likely, as the five-year-old Lady Margaret is not mentioned in the official records, that she continued to be housed in Tantallon under the care of the ladies of the Douglas faction. It is possibly that Queen Margaret could have been allowed some access, but under conditions set by Angus. [44]

During the disputes between Arran and Angus, Queen Margaret had been a virtual spectator, although she would waver between both sides, which were too equally matched for one to win outright. She would complain to the English about her poverty and her treatment, whilst seeking some opportunity for herself. The most promising alliance offered was that from the Duke of Albany; he had the money and will to regain power in Scotland if he returned and he had widespread contacts on the Continent, and most importantly with the papacy, which would offer the prospect of divorce from Angus. Her reported dalliance with Sir

James Hamilton of Finnart infuriated her husband and her brother, yet it sent a message to Albany that she was now prepared to support him.

In May 1521 the French invaded the contested kingdom of Spanish Navarre in May 1521. This aggression was an excuse for Charles V to persuade Henry VIII and Pope Leo to join him in an alliance against France. Whilst Cardinal Wolsey would seek to mediate some type of diplomatic solution that would benefit England, there was an effort, as European war was looming, for the truces between Scotland and England to continue. There were also troubling reports of the Earl of Argyll supplying Scots to Ireland to cause mischief there and support Irish lords. Henry sought to get a meaningful treaty with the Scots, knowing full well he could not fight on three fronts - Ireland, Scotland and the continent. He wrote to the Lords of Council requesting a continuance of the truce and for an embassy to be sent to England. James, having been persuaded through French envoys, replied to Henry's letter, agreeing to a truce to extend the 'Purification' but also requesting that in the event of a truce Albany would be comprehended into it. [45]

The English however did not let the pretence of seeking a truce to stop them interfering in Scotland. Earlier in March Dacre had written to Wolsey regarding the 'great service' that Angus and the Humes could provide against the Scottish government. Dacre was providing support to the Scottish rebels whilst providing 300 borrowed troops from Berwick to lie in the marches, paid 6d per day. When Angus and David Hume of Wedderburn brought a considerable force into Edinburgh on July 2nd, 1521, they would have had English auxiliaries paid by Dacre in their force. The Humes took down the heads of the executed Alexander and William Hume from the Tollcross. The following day a large war band made for Linlithgow, then passed to Stirling before returning to Edinburgh on July 25th. The purpose of this round trip was to capture Beaton. They also were arrayed to intimidate and provoke the Earl of Arran into battle, but the latter sensibly avoided this.

In Edinburgh funerals were held for Alexander and William Hume, and prayers were said for their souls. [46]

Angus was once more the dominant power in Edinburgh, and he became more overbearing and imperial in his attitude. His uncle, Archibald 'Greysteel' Douglas of Kilspindie, would retain the office of provost. By savage means his brother William would continue to retain the Abbey of Coldingham, although there was a continued dispute with his nearest rival Patrick Blacadder, who wisely kept a safe distance from the Douglases. Through the mediation of common friends Angus offered to make reparations towards Patrick Blacadder for his loss of rights to the Abbey of Coldingham. He invited Blacadder to Edinburgh to discuss the dispute and the invitation was accepted.

As he approached the city with six attendants they were intercepted by the Humes, and all were slain. News of the murders compelled a party of men to gather and give chase, but upon seeing Sir George Douglas in the company of the Humes, they decided to withdraw. [47]

Whilst Henry VIII saw Angus as important to his designs on Scotland, his sister Margaret continued to look towards France, as her hatred of Angus compelled her to side with her husband's enemies. She would write letters to Albany asking him to return and govern Scotland. It was also said that Albany was making use of an agent in Rome to arrange a divorce between Queen Margaret and Angus, an act that would have huge implications for the ambitions of the Douglas faction. Wolsey also believed reports that Albany's wife was suffering from a fatal illness, and in the event of her death Albany had secretly agreed to marry Margaret, if Rome granted her a divorce from Angus. Such a plan would damage Henry's ambitions towards Scotland, and it would no doubt cause him grave humiliation that his sister would marry a dangerous enemy. [48]

On October 10th 1521, James Beaton, chancellor of Scotland and Archbishop of Glasgow, was by papal decree translated Archbishop of St Andrews and Abbot of Dunfermline. The

Archbishopric of Glasgow would be nominated to Gavin Dunbar, the King's tutor and nephew of his namesake Gavin, Bishop of Aberdeen. Whilst Albany would recognise him as such in 1523, it would be not until July 8th 1524 that he would provided in this position by the pope. Beaton seems to have been supported in his appointment by Wolsey himself, who authorised his clerk in Rome to act on Beaton's behalf. It appears that in order to win Wolsey's support in Rome, Beaton had over the past few months been, according to Wolsey, a promoter of peace between Scotland and England. Like Beaton, Wolsey appeared to be playing a duplicitous game, as the English, whilst outwardly supporting peace, were also secretly supporting the less than peaceful Douglas faction. The Abbey of Coldingham was long thought to be under the ecclesial authority of the Archbishop of St Andrews. Wolsey's clerk in Rome conceded that this matter was concluded in favour of the 'opposite party', not by papal decree but through bloody murders committed by William Douglas and his Hume allies. [49]

In November 1521 England entered into a league with the Emperor and Pope Leo, and promised to supply troops. However Henry VIII did not send over an army, and the papal and imperial forces would not need them as they defeated the French in Italy and recovered Milan, Parma and Piacenza before the end of the year [50]

Chapter Four: References

(1) (ALCPA, May 25th, 1517, xxx, f.11, pp. 93-94. ALHTS, pp. xlviii-xlix. Fraser, pp. 186-188. Holinshed, pp. 488-489. Lesley, pp. 109-111. LP, Magnus to Wolsey, June 16th, 1517. ODNB, vol.24, pp. 823-826, ODNB, vol.24, pp. 823-826. ODNB, vol.52, pp. 684-685. RPS, May, 1517.Thomson, vol.2,pp. 549-550). (2) (ALCPA, May 25th, 1517, xxx, f.11, pp. 93-94. ALHTS, pp. xlviii-xlix. CSPS, vol.1, Queen Margaret to Henry VIII, Aug 7th, 1517. Fraser, pp. 186-188. Lesley, pp. 109-111. LP, Magnus to Wolsey, June 16th, 1517. RPS, May, 1517. Strickland, vol.1, pp. 136-138. Thomson, vol.2,pp. 548-549). (3) (LP, Dacre to Wolsey, June, 1517. LP, Dacre's correspondence, June 24th. LP, Dacre to the Lord Chancellor, July 6th, 1517). (4) (ODNB, vol.52, pp. 709-715.

Thomson, vol.2,pp. 549-550). (5) (ALCPA, p.149. Calderwood, vol.1, pp. 60-61. Holinshed, pp. 489-491. Thomson, vol.2, pp. 550-551). (6) (ALCPA, September 24th, 1517, xxx, f.166, pp. 102-104. Holinshed, 489-491. Hume, vol.1, pp. 70-71). (7) (ALCPA, November 21st, 1518, xxx, f.180, pp. 108-109. ALHTS, pp. 152-153. Holinshed, pp. 490-492). (8) (Lesley, pp. 111-113. SHD, Treaty of Rouen). (9) (LP, The General League, 1518. ODNB, vol.52, pp. 709-715. Pitscottie, pp. 302-304). (10) (ALHTS, vol.5, p.154, p.159. Pitscottie, pp. 302-304). (11) (ALCPA, February 22nd, 1518, xxx, f.188, pp. 110-111. ALCPA, February 27th, 1518, xxx, f.208, pp. 115-116. Buchanan, pp. 277-279. Leslie, pp. 110-112. LP, The Estates of Scotland to Francis I, March 29th, 1518. LP, James Abp. of Glasgow to Francis I, March 29th, 1518). (12) (ALHTS, pp. li-liii, pp. 152-159. Buchanan, pp. 277-279. Leslie, pp. 110-112. LP, The Estates of Scotland to Francis I, March 29th, 1518. LP, James Abp. of Glasgow to Francis I, March 29th, 1518. rgss, vol.1, 2970). (13) (Gordon, vol.3, pp. 393-395. Holinshed, pp. 491-493. Lesley, pp. 111-113. Pitscottie, pp. 303-305. SP. vol.2, pp. 153-154). (14) (Lesley, pp. 111-113. LP, Dacre to Wolsey, June 8th,1518. LP, David Hume of Wedderburn to Wolsey, July 25th, 1518. LP, France and Scotland, June 22nd, 1520. Pitscottie, pp. 303-305). (15) (Johnson, pp. 83-84. LP, The General League, 1518. LP, Wolsey to Dacre, 1518. LP, The Estates of Scotland to Leo X, January 4th 1519. LP, Dacre to Wosley, March 5th, 1519). (16) (Strickland, vol.1, pp. 137-139). (17) (Fraser, pp. 187-189. Lesley, pp. 112-113. ODNB, vol.36, pp. 648-652. Strickland, vol.1, pp. 138-141. Strickland, vol.2, pp. 250-254. Thomson, vol.2, pp. 554-555). (19) (ALCPA, December 13th, 1518, xxxii, f.60, pp. 133-134. ODNB, vol.16, pp620-621). (20) (Buchanan, pp. 290-291. Gordon, vol.2, p.395. LP, The General League, 1518. LP, Wolsey to Dacre, 1518. LP, The Estates of Scotland to Leo X, January 4th 1519. LP, Dacre to Wosley, March 5th, 1519). (21) (Johnson, pp. 129-135). (22) (Buchanan, pp. 290-291. Gordon, vol.2, p.395. Lesley, pp. 112-113. ODNB, vol.20, pp. 369-370). (23) (Lesley, pp. 113. LP, Queen Margaret to Henry VIII, May, 1519. LP, Dacre to Queen Margaret, July 10th, 1519. LP, Queen Margaret to Dacre, July 14th 1519. ODNB, vol.36, pp. 649-650. Strickland, vol.1, pp. 141-143). (24) (ALCPA, October 27th, 1519, xxxii, f.185, pp. 146-148. LP, Dacre to Wolsey, October 22nd, 1519). (25) (ALCPA, November 26th, 1519, xxxii, f.189, pp. 149-150. Calderwood, vol.1, pp. 60-61. Holinshed, pp. 491-492. Lesley, pp. 114-116. LP, Queen Margaret to Dacre, October 13th, 1519. Tytler, pp. 162-164. LP, Dacre to Wolsey, October 22nd, 1519. Thomson, vol.2, pp. 552-553). (26) (Calderwood, vol.1, pp. 60-61. Herkless & Hannay, vol.2, pp. 187-191. Herkless & Hannay, vol.3, pp. 65-68. LP, Queen Margaret to Dacre, October 13th, 1519. LP, Dacre to Wolsey, October 22nd, 1519. ODNB, vol.36, pp. 650-651. Strickland, vol.1, pp. 139-141. Thomson, vol.2, pp. 551-552. Tytler, pp. 162-164). (27) (Calderwood, vol.1, pp. 60-61. Herkless & Hannay, vol.2, pp. 187-191. Herkless & Hannay, vol.3, pp. 65-68. LP, Queen Margaret to Dacre, October 13th, 1519. LP, Dacre to Wolsey, October 22nd, 1519. ODNB, vol.36, pp. 650-651. Strickland, vol.1, pp. 139-141. Thomson, vol.2, pp. 551-552. Tytler, pp. 162-164). (28) (Herkless & Hannay, vol.2, pp. 188-189. LP, Dacre to Wolsey, October 22nd, 1519). (29) (ALCPA, December 16th, 1519, xxxii, f.190, pp. 150-151. Herkless & Hannay, vol.3, pp. 68-69. Lesley, pp. 114-116. Tytler, pp. 164-166). (30) (Buchanan, pp. 277-279. Calderwood, pp. 60-62. Fraser, pp. 190-192. Hume, vol.1, pp. 70-72. Leslie, pp. 110-112. Leslie, pp. 115-117). (31) (ODNB, vol.16, pp. 620-621. Small, pp. lxxxv-lxxxviii). (32) (Buchanan, pp. 279-281. Calderwood, pp. 61-63. Herkless & Hannay, pp. 69-73. Lesley, pp. 115-116. ODNB, vol.38, pp. 848-849. RPS, Judicial proceeding: reduction of forfeiture, July, 1525. Small, pp. lixivia-lixivia). (33) (Buchanan, pp. 279-281. Fraser, pp. 193-195). (34) (Herkless & Hannay, vol.2, pp. 190-192. Herkless & Hannay, vol.3, pp. 72-74. LP, France and Scotland, June 22nd, 1520. LP, Spinelly to Wolsey, August 29th, 1520). (35) (Herkless & Hannay, vol.2, pp. 190-192. Herkless & Hannay, vol.3, pp. 72-74. LP, Sil. Bp. of Worcester to Wolsey, June 22nd, 1520. LP, Hector de Vicquemare, August 20th 1520. LP, Spinelly to Wolsey, August 29th, 1520. ODNB, vol.52, pp. 709-710). (36) (Herkless & Hannay, pp. 73-74. ODNC, vol.52, p.743). (37) (Herkless & Hannay, vol.2, pp. 190-192. Herkless & Hannay, vol.3, pp. 72-74. Johnson, pp. 135-137. LP, Sil. Bp. of Worcester to Wolsey, June 22nd, 1520. LP, Hector de Vicquemare, August 20th 1520. LP, Spinelly to Wolsey, August 29th, 1520. ODNB, vol.52, pp. 709-715). (38) (Herkless & Hannay, vol.2, pp. 190-192. Herkless & Hannay, vol.3, pp. 72-74. LP, Sil. Bp. of Worcester to Wolsey, June 22nd, 1520. LP, Hector de Vicquemare, August 20th 1520. LP, Spinelly to Wolsey, August 29th, 1520). (39) (Herkless & Hannay, pp. 73-74. LP, Queen Margaret to Dacre, Oct 17th, 1520. ODNC, vol.52, p.743). (40) (LP, Francis I to the Three Estates, 1520. LP, The same to the same. 1520. LP, Queen Margaret to Dacre, [1061] 1520. LP, John de Planis to Dacre, November 27th, 1520. James Chancellor of Scotland to Dacre. LP, LP, Dacre to Wolsey, December 10th, 1520. Tytler, pp. 164-166). (41) (Herkless & Hannay, vol.2, pp. 191-192 .Herkless & Hannay, vol.3, pp. 72-76). (42) (LP, Scotland, January 30th, 152. LP, Scotland, February 27th, 1521. LP, Dacre to Wolsey, March 17th. LP, Scotland, April 18th, 1521). (43) (LP, Fitzwilliam to Wolsey, March 29th, 1521. LP, Henry VIII to Sir William Fitzwilliam, April 18th, 1521). (44) (LP, Dacre to the Queen of Scotland, March 6th, 1521. ODNB, vol. 24, pp. 826-825. ODNB, vol.36, pp. 651-652. Strickland, vol.2, pp. 250-252). (45) (Johnson, pp. 160-161.LP, Instructions for Sir John Petchie, May 1521. LP, Henry VIII to the Scotch, May 1521. LP, James

V, May 21ˢᵗ, 1521). (46) (Buchanan, pp,280-281.Lesley, pp. 116-117. RPS, Judicial proceeding: reduction of forfeiture, July, 1525. Tytler, pp. 164-167). (47) (Buchanan, pp. 290-291. Herkless & Hannay, pp. 76-77. LP, Clerk to Wolsey, October 10ᵗʰ, 1521. Thomson, vol.3, pp. 552-553. Tytler, pp. 165-167). (48) (Herkless & Hannay, pp. 76-77. LP, Clerk to Wolsey, October 10ᵗʰ, 1521. Thomson, vol.3, pp. 552-553. Tytler, pp. 165-167). (49) (Dowden, pp. 40-41, pp. 343-345. Lesley, pp. 118-120. LP, Clerk to Wolsey, October, 1521). (50) (Johnson, pp. 160-161).

Chapter Five

OF SPRITES AND FEARFUL
SIGHTS, 1521-1523

Word was passed around Scotland that Albany was about to return, and this coincided with an increase of Scottish raids into Northumberland, with villages being burned and prisoners taken. Wolsey would order Dacre to make use of Angus and the Humes, and also provided 500 to 1,000 marks to cause mischief within Scotland. Albany arrived in Scotland on November 19th 1521, landing on the Gareloch in Lennox. He was backed by strong companies of French soldiery, arms, ammunition and money. He met with Queen Margaret at Stirling, and there was reported affection between the two which would feed hostile rumours, many given artistic licence by Lord Dacre, who claimed that the affection they expressed for each other spread from the daytime into the night. Queen Margaret was accused of being 'inclined to the pleasure of the duke in all manner of things'.

Albany would meet with Gavin Dunbar, the new Archbishop of Glasgow, and many other lords and prelates who through the Frenchmen saw the beginnings of the end of chaotic government. Albany and Queen Margaret spent a few nights at Linlithgow, and then on November 23rd they led an army towards Edinburgh. Angus and his people fled towards the borders, where he sent his uncle Gavin Douglas, Bishop of Dunkeld to plead for help and assistance from Cardinal Wolsey in London. Angus would claim that Albany sought to gain possession of James in order to cause his death and take over for himself the crown of Scotland.

Queen Margaret and Albany entered Edinburgh together, and in a ceremonial ritual to display Albany's regal power he gave Margaret the keys of the castle, which housed King James, and symbolically she handed them back to Albany, appointing him tutor to her son. The obvious growing friendship between Albany and Queen Margaret was a grave and humiliating insult for Angus, and a threat to Henry VIII who now had French power once more north of the border. Albany however wrote to King Henry and his Queen Katherine of Aragon, and to Cardinal Wolsey, insisting that he had arrived in Scotland to preserve peace, and to do service to King James and Queen Margaret. [1]

The Earl of Angus, Lord George Hume, John Somerville and other allies reached the Kirk of Steyle and vowed not to make peace with the Duke of Albany without taking the advice of Henry VIII. They also asked that in the event of peace between Scotland and England their security should be considered. Angus in his bitterness repeated dark accusations against Albany and Queen Margaret. He claimed that they were now lovers, and that Albany was a threat to the wellbeing of the King. They ask that Henry should use whatever influence was available to insist that none of the Duke's appointments should be allowed within 30 miles of the royal person, alluding once more to dangerous intent towards the King. [2]

Lord Dacre elaborated colourfully on the allegations of Angus, claiming that he had received collaborative reports that Queen

Margaret had offered him Ettrick Forest in return for a divorce. Dacre accused Albany of corruption through his kinship with the Pope, having taken authority to bestow vacant benefices on those whose support he sought, including sons of nobles, even those that were not of the church. Lord Fleming's son was granted the rich abbey of Holyrood in this way. Albany is also said to have sold benefices for personal profit, by which it was claimed he had amassed a fortune of 40,000 Scots merks.

The most damning charge was that Albany sought to usurp the throne of Scotland by killing James. Dacre did not reveal the sources of his information, apart from Angus, yet this black propaganda was aimed at testing the temper of Henry. He suggested that Henry should support raids and incursions across the border which would serve to undermine confidence in the governor at less cost than financing an army. [3]

Gavin Douglas, the Bishop of Dunkeld, also fled to England, and would be granted by Henry VIII a residence at the Savoy. Whilst in London Dunkeld would compose a memorial for Henry VIII in which he outlined all of Albany's crimes, his garrisoning of French troops in Scottish castles, the selling off of crown land, the selling of three Scottish ships to the French navy for half their worth, the trading of benefices and the theft of movable royal possessions, including silver jugs, tapestries and robes. He repeated the rumours that whilst in Rome Albany had attempted to procure the divorce of Queen Margaret and Angus so that he could marry her. These claims were written down by Henry in a letter to the Three Estates of Scotland dated January 14th, 1522, which also accused Albany of intending to claim the kingdom of Scotland for himself, saying the young King's James' life was in danger from Albany's ambition. Henry threatened war if Albany was not expelled.

The Scots replied to these accusations, dismissing them as smears and 'false reports' instigated by Dunkeld. They reminded him that Albany had been chosen by the Three Estates and was no usurper. They questioned Henry's reasons for insisting that the

King of France should keep Albany from travelling to Scotland by reporting that James 'is to be destroyed' and Queen Margaret through divorce would be condemned 'to the point of perdition'. The estates reminded Henry that he had been encouraging his wardens on the borders to support Scotland's 'traitors, rebels and broken men' by challenging the authority of King James and his regents. They also stated that Albany arrived in Scotland to heal the divisions after Flodden, in which he had proved successful when he was present in Scotland, and if Henry VIII further threatened the independence or sovereignty of Scotland then they would 'take God to our good quarrel in defence'. [4]

Albany would purge the Douglases and their supporters from the positions of provost and other official posts in Edinburgh. Tantallon, Angus' powerful castle on the North Berwick coast, was soon taken by Albany in the company of the earls of Huntley, Argyll, Arran, Lennox and others. At the advice of the Lords of Council a parliament was called for January 26th 1522, and proclamations made at the Market Cross in Edinburgh, where the Earl of Angus, William Douglas, Abbot of Coldingham, David Hume, Laird of Wedderburn, William Cockburn, John Somerville of Cambusnethan and other followers and adherents, were summoned to parliament to face charges of committing treason against the King's regents. On February 21st at Edinburgh James V proclaimed that Gavin Douglas through residing in England and entering into meetings and correspondence with Henry VIII and his counsellors was guilty of High Treason and was deprived of the bishopric of Dunkeld and other possessions. [5]

As compensation for the rumours spread by Gavin Douglas that Margaret was the mistress of Albany, she received the profits and revenue of Dunkeld. When Henry wrote to his sister accusing her of infidelity she responded with an angry letter, scolding him for his 'sharp and unkind' words. She insisted that Albany had shown her 'good bearing' whist Gavin Douglas, who she had formerly helped become Bishop of Dunkeld, now made 'false and evil' reports. She also admitted that whilst she had sought 'remedy'

for her 'quarrel and defence' through friendship with Albany, this
course of action had been forced on her by lack of support from
Henry. Guardians had been appointed to oversee James' wellbeing
and Margaret had been allowed to reside in Edinburgh castle with
her son. [6]

The Earl of Angus, fearing the possibility of forfeiture, asked
permission to meet with his wife, which Albany allowed, along with
a safe conduct. He asked Queen Margaret to plead that he and his
brother instead of forfeiture should be allowed to exile themselves.
In an extraordinary show of clemency Queen Margaret pleaded
mercy for her warmongering and treacherous husband, and Albany
agreed to it, also a remarkable judgement considering his previous
judicial slaughter of the two Hume brothers. Albany later attested
that he showed mercy out of respect for Queen Margaret. He
allowed Angus and his brother Sir George to leave for exile in
France. Queen Margaret's leniency might have been down to
ensuring that the earldom of Angus stayed intact and was not
forfeited and cut up. Margaret's daughter Lady Margaret Douglas
would be heiress in the event of Angus' death.

Angus and George appear to have been transported on one of
two of Albany's ships which sailed from Leith on March 11th 1522,
in the company of their brother William and an embassy
comprising Lord Fleming and Thomas Hay, the King's secretary.
According to Pitscottie, whilst Albany had agreed to Angus exiling
himself, he claims that before arriving at Calais he and his brother
had been made prisoners. However if this is true they were not
imprisoned for long and were free to travel anywhere in France,
even to the court of Francis, where Angus was mistaken by an
English spy for an ambassador. He was ordered to stay within the
borders of France.

In writing to Wolsey Gavin Douglas would call his nephew the
'unworthy Earl of Angus', no doubt due to the deal he made with
Queen Margaret and Albany. Gavin Douglas would continue to
reside in London, keeping company of the likes of the Italian
historian Polydore Vergil and the scholar John Mair. He still

intended to promote his right to the Archbishopric of St Andrews. Before September 1522 when his will was produced, he would die of the plague. [7]

Due to lack of information it is difficult to determine what happened to the Queen's six-year-old daughter, Lady Margaret, as there is no account of her amongst the household of Queen Margaret or elsewhere, even England. In late 1524 Queen Margaret would write a letter condemning the Earl of Angus for not allowing access to her daughter. 'In especial, these three years bypast, not having consideration for our person, which was over piteous and great marvel to report ; and after, would not suffer our own daughter to remain with us for our comfort, who would not have been disherest [disinherited] had she been with us'. It is possibly that the Lady Margaret continued to be under the care of the ladies of the Douglas, although we do not know where they resided. There is also a belief that Angus may have sent for his daughter to come to France, as when older she is said to have had a good understanding of the French language. [8]

Whilst Albany had won the contest against the Douglases and the Three Estates were making a strong verbal defence of his governorship to Henry VIII, there was still some reluctance within the Scottish nobility to give full-hearted military support for France against England. Albany wrote to Francis asking for more arms, money and men as he was certain that the Scots sought a peace treaty with England, and they were 'weary of fighting for others'. They sought a commitment from the French King by the next parliamentary session on May 12th, for an account of what he was prepared to supply to Scotland, otherwise if there was no offer or an unsatisfactory one, Albany might be compelled to leave the country and return to France. [9]

Matters on the continent would determine the political swings in Scotland. Pope Leo X had died in December 1st 1521, and the wardship of Catherine de Medici would ultimately pass to Albany as he was the nearest male relative. Obviously he could not exercise that responsibility, but as Catherine had extensive French possessions he appointed his wife to administer them. The new pope Hadrian VI, elected on January 9th 1522, did not join the Holy League and fell out with Francis I. He was more concerned with creating a Christian coalition to challenge the Turkish Sultan, a project that neither superpower was interested in. The French, whilst regaining some influence in Italy, saw a reversal at the Battle of Bicocca on April 27th 1522, when they lost towns and strongholds and were driven out of Genoa and Milan. Elated by these imperial victories, the Emperor Charles V came to England in June 1522, and signed the Treaty of Windsor, whereby Henry agreed to declare war on France. Henry would send part of his army across the channel to France, whilst taking harsh unjust measures against Scots and French living in England, stealing their properties and goods and banishing them. The exiled Scots were forced to march to Scotland with white crosses marked on their shirts.

Francis wrote to the King of Denmark that since Henry VIII was now waging war against France and Scotland, he intended to attack the English at Calais and would send arms, ordinance, money and men to Scotland. War was approaching, yet the Scots were hesitant about waging war on France's behalf remembering the lesson of Flodden that the Scots could be discarded by French kings depending on the ebb and flow of European politics. The Scots would fulfill their commitments to France but on their own terms. The Bishop of Carlisle did not believe there was any wide support in Scotland for war amongst the common people. If an army were to be raised, or a war fought, the strategic aims would be defensive. Albany would however attempt to raise an army in June but heavy rain soaked the ground to such an extent that it was too difficult to transport the artillery. [10]

Henry continued to demand that the Three Estates expel Albany from Scotland, and to show his intent the northern levies were raised and were led by the Earl of Shrewsbury in July. Part of the town of Kelso and the surrounding area was attacked and put to the flames. The Scots from the Merse and Teviotdale responded and beat back the invaders over the border, inflicting heavy losses and capturing many prisoners. Albany called a parliament on July 19th for the purpose of declaring war against England and raising an army. King James, now eleven years of age, was escorted to Stirling Castle under the protection of Lord Erskine, the governor of the castle. [11]

In August the English were expecting an invasion, and the Earl of Shrewsbury was made Lieutenant-General. Fresh garrisons were placed in the strongholds on the border. All the great lords of the north, including the Earl of Northumberland, were placed in his council, and he was commissioned to raise manpower, supplies and money in Yorkshire and within the bishopric of Durham. He would have authority to send out proclamations to the Scots, and advertise the reasons why the English army would be advancing to the border. [12]

The English invaded Picardy, and blockaded the French ports. Francis called on the envoy François Charron to visit Scotland and inform Albany and the Three Estates that there would be difficulty in fulfilling the terms of the Treaty of Rouen due to the English naval blockade. Having to garrison and victual troops in Italy, Picardy and Guienne, as well as recruiting in Normandy, Bretagne, Provence, and Languedoc, meant that the amount of aid available to the Scots would be small. Nevertheless, despite this lack of aid Albany decided to support the French King with a diversion in northern England. [13]

Aware that a Scots invasion was now a strong possibility, Dacre entered into a correspondence with Queen Margaret where he sought a peace conference. Possibly suspecting some delaying tactic, Margaret sought clarification on whether Dacre had the authority to treat for peace, whilst she knew that Shrewsbury did have this authority. Dacre however claimed he did not have official authority, yet sought to work towards a dialogue to prevent 'invasions on both sides'. He offered to delay Shrewsbury's army if Margaret would make efforts to do the same with Albany's army. It has been claimed by some historians that the correspondence that Margaret opened with Dacre was close to treason, in that she was revealing details of Albany's plan. This opinion appears wrong as it was later claimed that Albany had raised the army at 'the earnest solicitation of the Queen, for the defence of the kingdom and revenge of its cruel invasion'. Any correspondence was done with apparent knowledge of Albany, who was privy to copies of much of the correspondence. The purpose of the muster was to discourage the invasion of Shrewsbury and to pressure the English to enter into meaningful peace talks. Margaret used the threat of invasion to convince her brother that peace was better than war, and her letters were a method of opening up such channels of discussion. [14]

An army assembled at Roslin on September 2nd, including a great artillery train. It was estimated by Dacre that it had 80,000 troops, which was unlikely. It was also said to have 45 pieces of brass ordinance and 1,000 harquebusiers, although this also seems an over-inflated count. There were reports that a form of light artillery was introduced to Scottish warfare with hag buts placed upon trestles. The army was well supplied with food and beer so that there was little need to feed off the countryside.

Knowing the bitterness caused by Flodden with a Scots army fighting for French interests, Albany ensured that the reason given for mustering was to counter the threat posed by Shrewsbury. The army was then ordered to travel towards the borders, with severe punishment threatened for any who disobeyed. The van was commanded by Arran and advanced past Hume Castle, apparently threatening Wark, which was deserted by its captain. This seems to have been part of a feint in order to deceive not just the border captains, such as Dacre, who rode towards Berwick, but also Shrewsbury, who was at York with the bulk of his army.

The Scots then moved to the western marches, reaching the Dumfries area around September 7th. They were now in a position to threaten Carlisle. Shrewsbury sent 20,000 men to Dacre. Because of lack of funds he himself could not proceed, and he claimed he would have problems transporting the artillery and cannon across Stainesmoor to Carlisle. [15]

When the army approached Solway on the borders, Alexander Gordon, 3rd Earl of Huntley, halted his adherents three miles from the border. The Governor, aware of the dissention and uncertainty in the muster, called a Council meeting within his tent. Under questioning by the Earl of Arran, he revealed the true purpose of this invasion, to use all means to attack England and divert forces away from France. Huntley argued that this purpose had been met, as English forces were now marching towards the borders to meet the Scots. Others put forward the point that the advance to the border was defensive in that it was a show of force against any further English incursions by Shrewsbury, and that if the Scots crossed the border this could be viewed as an unjustified invasion. One speaker made an argument based on reason and logic, that Scotland did not have the resources to fight pitched battles with England. He gave the example of how James IV brought prosperity and peace to Scotland, yet threw it all away at Flodden. Scotland had struggled with itself since that battle. He also reminded the Scots that their present King was in a minority and it was the duty of all to protect him, and not to risk all in an invasion of England. Whilst the Scots might win one battle against the English, the old enemy had the wealth and manpower to raise more armies. Winning one battle might bring glory, but it would also weaken the army with casualties.

Albany responded by saying that Scotland had the right to invade England by fire and sword in respect to recent incursions. He even went so far as to say that invading and conquering England would be a just cause, since both Scots and English seemed incapable of sharing the Island without fighting. Despite these points made, with no apparent English army preparing to cross the border into Scotland, and the nobles declined towards invasion, Albany decided to see if he could at least score a diplomatic victory of some nature. According to Lesley, Margaret sent word to Albany at his camp asking him to open discussions with Dacre. Buchanan added that Albany sent a secret message via a merchant to Lord Dacre inviting him to a conference with the

Scots. Dacre accepted and sent a herald to Albany for the purpose of obtaining a safe conduct. Dacre was looking for a truce, knowing that Henry VIII and Cardinal Wolsey were reluctant to fight Scotland whilst fully engaged with France. Carlisle's defences were said not to be strong enough, and there was uncertainty about the number of men Dacre and Shrewsbury could muster, especially at that time of year. In exchange for hostages, Dacre was granted a safe conduct for himself and around 100 men to visit Albany's camp. Dacre claimed that he gave the Scottish nobles 'sharp words' for their invasion. [16]

An indenture for a month-long abstinence of war was agreed between Albany and Dacre at Solane Chapel on September 11th. Dacre agreed to cease all English invasions into Scotland and allow safe conducts for ambassadors to travel to England and negotiate a peace treaty. Albany insisted that France should be allowed to comprehend into it. It was an ambitious initiative and Dacre in principle agreed to it. Albany disbanded the army and returned home. Shrewsbury's army also disbanded. [17]

Wolsey would later gloat that it was a missed opportunity for the Scots as Carlisle and Cumberland could not have resisted such an invasion, if Dacre's unlikely account of a Scots army of 80,000 is to be believed. Dacre was trying to play up the numbers of the invading army so as to boost his achievement in having apparently outplayed Albany and compelled the Scots to disband. Buchanan would repeat rumours that Albany had accepted a bribe from Dacre to agree to peace. He would also claim that these rumours were spread by those Scots who wanted to blacken the Governor's name and blame him for not crossing the border. Lesley also mentioned a bribe and stated that the men of Carlisle 'promised to him [Albany] a great sum' not to besiege or attack the city. What seems clear is that the Scots army had crossed the border and was within five miles of Carlisle before agreement was made. [18]

Whilst the result of these military manoeuvres could be considered a stalemate, Queen Margaret had through her efforts, by interceding with both Albany and Dacre, contributed to stopping the planned invasions by both armies. Cardinal Wolsey, in a letter to Albany, gave Queen Margaret the credit for procuring the truce, which he would also state was 'displeasant' to Henry, who wanted to try 'his righteous quarrel with the aid of God, by force of Battle'. Henry VIII would give a contradictory message through the Clarencieux Herald in November which praised Queen Margaret 'for the labour she has taken in the peace'.

Although she supported the initial mustering of the army she understood that to negotiate peace terms with her brother, it was best to do so from a position of strength and determination. Whilst she would be accused of interceding on behalf of England, this can be countered through correspondence she sent to her brother Henry VIII calling on France to be comprehended into any peace between Scotland and England, and speaking favourably on behalf of Albany.

In context her situation was difficult, with her brother recognising her rule of Scotland yet at the same time supporting enemies of the Scottish government whilst sanctioning brutal raids across the border. Queen Margaret was also acknowledged by French envoys to be taking a leading role in peace negotiations, to prolong the truces and comprehend the French as allies. Three ambassadors would be granted safe conducts and passed to England during October, but negotiations were difficult as the King refused to allow the comprehension of the French into any treaty, and forwarded other unfavourable conditions that the ambassadors considered 'contrary to honour and the commonwealth of the kingdom of Scotland.' Henry, whilst roaring against the Scots, and threatening more war against his sister and nephew with the logic that he did so to protect them, would never don armour himself and take to the borders. Always he sought to work through proxies, never risking his own limbs.

Albany left leave Scotland on October 25th to seek conference with Francis with the possibility of returning with more arms, money and manpower. He appointed the Archbishop of Glasgow, Huntley, Argyll, Arran and a French commander, Gonzales, as joint regents until his return. Gilbert Kennedy, Earl of Cassillis, would be a companion to James, and was paid £120 for staying close to the young King. [19]

Whilst he was warmly received by the King once arriving in France, Albany had learned that the Scots would not fully commit themselves to war against the English unless the French matched such commitment with sufficient arms, men and money. Albany asked Francis II for 5,000 horsemen and 10,000 German mercenaries to take to Scotland, and was confident that with this commitment the King of England would be toppled. Francis however was not convinced by what Holinshed termed a 'vain brag', and reiterated that he needed as many men and resources as possible to counter the Imperial and English forces on the continent. He did promise to give whatever help he could. [20]

The peace negotiations would continue in Stirling during November and December when Henry sent Clarencieux Herald. A truce was agreed to last until the end of February, and was accepted by Arran and the Lords of Council. There were also discussions during this meeting regarding a marriage between James and Princess Mary, daughter of Henry. A sixteen-year truce was proposed and the possible return of Berwick into Scottish hands. As the negotiations had been made at Stirling, where Queen Margaret had been residing with her son, she would have been supportive of a meaningful treaty being agreed between Scotland and England. The prospect of a marriage treaty would open the possibility of one of her linage becoming King of England in the event of Henry dying without male heirs. The Scots expressed an interest in these possibilities, although in the end nothing would come of them. Albany, living in Auvergne, was aggrieved at the three-month truce agreed as it did not comprehend France, and was done without his approval. He wrote complaining to Wolsey about these negotiations without his sanction. [21]

During the autumn Queen Margaret contracted smallpox, and it became more severe during the winter while she was residing in Stirling with her son. She reported that the disease was so prevalent that she had difficulty moving her hands or sitting up, or talking. Because of this incapacity Margaret could barely write during those winter months. She would recover in the New Year, but the bout of smallpox would reportedly scar her physically. Later portraits in middle age display a sterner countenance than her earlier colourful and brighter depictions, and Strickland suggested that this was a result of the rigours of the disease. It is more likely that the intense intrigues and stress of war would have laid a severe psychological impact on her personality. However, as history would show, she did not become a weaker person and would continue to throw herself as fully as she could into the politics of the period. [22]

The Earl of Northumberland was appointed Warden of the three marches, replacing Shrewsbury, and he would be able to testify to the falseness of the truce as he would have to contend with regular raids and incursions into Northern England. Unable to stop the flow, he was discharged of his duties and Thomas Howard, Earl of Surrey, and second son of the victor of Flodden, was appointed Lieutenant-General and Lord Admiral on February 26th 1523. With the end of the truce by the end of February, English raids would recommence. The Earl of Surrey would make plans to raise an invasion force of 10,000. The town of Annan was burned by Dacre in April. A small fleet made raids along the North Berwickshire coastline, with a failed attempt to burn Tantallon and a fight at Kirkholm. From May these raids would intensify, although lack of supplies and lack of fodder made it difficult for the raids to last longer than a night. The lack of forage in Northumberland was a serious problem, and this was partly a result of Scots conducting retaliatory raids, although the musters would not be as large as that commanded by the English.

Surrey led 2,000 men to Cessford Castle and bombarded it with artillery, a vain endeavour as the walls of the castle were thick enough to withstand the impact of the cannonballs. Surrey sent out forces to storm the castle with scaling ladders and covering fire from archers and firearms, but was met with a vigorous defence, resulting in casualties. The conflict ended when Kerr of Cessford, the March warden and owner of the castle, who was near the conflict, decided to surrender it under condition that men and baggage were allowed free passage. Surrey accepted, although in his estimation this was a mistake as he did not believe the castle could have been taken by force. His men cast the castle down.

A raid into the Merse and Teviotdale in June was met with hard resistance and losses, although Dacre would claim a large number of villages put to the flames and towers cast down. Dacre also led a large foray to Kelso. The town was burned and the gatehouse demolished. The priory lodgings were burned and cast down, as well as the church and dormitory. Albany, when he received reports, claimed that actions such as plundering Kelso were sacrilegious and devoid of mercy, as age or sex was no barrier to the slaughter. [23]

The Scots begin to prepare for another invasion, believing the raids and destruction into the Merse were a prelude to this. The Lords of Council ordered the wardens and border lords to exploit their spies and informers amongst the English to gauge as much information as possible about future plans. A system of scouts and combustible bales upon mountains was put in place to give warning across the country in event of serious invasions. The sheriffdoms and towns were ordered to organise effective defences and to be ready at short notice after a proclamation to march to muster points in Edinburgh or elsewhere south of the Forth. A rotation system of lords and companies was stationed on the border, each to serve for a certain amount of time until another lord and company took over. [24]

The raids, though terrible to the inhabitants along the border, had no real impact on the political situation in Edinburgh except that the Scots could exaggerate the threat to their French allies. On hearing of these incursions, Francis promised the Scots the return of Albany and fresh aid. Five hundred French infantry had already passed to Leith, and 1,000 crowns were paid to each regent, and reportedly the Queen. The Scots also threatened to open peace negotiations, and a message from a French envoy to Francis outlined the possibility of the Scots entering into talks with England, and the need for a stronger French presence to counter English influence and promises. Francis set out to offer the Scots assistance greater than that agreed in the Treaty of Rouen. [25]

Overall there were 800 Frenchmen in Scotland commanded by Gonzales, who is one of the regents of Scotland. The bulk of the French forces had retired to Dunbar, and Dacre considered it one of the strongest fortresses in Scotland, with a bulwark recently added to it and strongly defended with ordinance. There was also the advantage that it could be supplied from the sea. Dacre added in correspondence to Wolsey, who had suggested an invasion of Scotland, that he did not think it would succeed and despite reports to the contrary the Scots were not as disunited as appeared. Dacre suggested that the strategy of wasting the borders was the best policy as a large number of strongholds had been cast down and communities and villages wasted. He believed a few more large raids would 'entirely destroy the Borders'. His reporting though was selective, and would fail to mention the 'incessant plundering incursions' that the Scots borderers were continuing to make into northern England. [26]

Dacre failed to explain how this economic warfare could damage the Scots whilst not damaging the economies of Northern England, which would have to provide victuals as well as being vulnerable to Scottish retaliations. Such wasting would have a negligible effect on the economies of cities like Glasgow, Edinburgh, Perth, Dundee and Aberdeen, which with access to the sea could export from abroad, despite the English embargo. With the mercantile deal that Albany had done in 1517, the Scots were interconnected with European economies and commerce. It was the people who suffered, forced to endure the wasting of their lands, homes and properties. Dacre suggested an invasion after Michaelmas, which during that season would make it difficult for the Scots, even with Albany's presence, to conduct a counter-invasion. [27]

For the Scots there were several false alarms throughout the spring and summer. Invasion had been expected in June, and word was sent to the regions north of the Forth to march south. On June 19th a muster was to be called for June 23rd at Deridounlaws, although there is no record of whether it occurred. (28)

Queen Margaret would enter into correspondence with Surrey during the summer. She complained about the hurt the raids were making on her subjects, whilst explaining that the best way to win friendship with the Scots was by winning over those most likely to oppose Albany, and to do so with a reasonable policy. There is a strong implication that her prior amicable relationship with Albany had broken down, and she was no longer fully trusted by Albany's supporters. She would complain that Albany had turned against her because she had acted against him, and he had apparently stopped her pension, worth 150l Scots. It was possible that the peace negotiations during November and December 1522 at her castle of Stirling angered Albany, in that they had been conducted without his authority. It had also shown that she was willing, if the opportunity offered itself, to follow actions contrary to the authority of the governorship. This growing distrust may have been the reason the King was kept under close surveillance by Albany's people in Stirling, a situation that she complained of. She herself used Edinburgh Castle as her base.

Margaret suggested that if Henry wrote to the Lords before a forthcoming parliament in Edinburgh with an offer of support, they might be moved to 'liberate the King', otherwise they would hold him 'for the Governor's pleasure'. Henry apparently wanted Margaret to escape to England, although she preferred that her brother should offer a truce with Scotland and allow her to take credit for it. Unfortunately for Margaret, Henry was suspicious of her correspondence and believed she was working with the French to gauge the conditions for peace he might consider.

Surrey responded to Queen Margaret's pleas and offered a plan by which, if she could somehow get King James free from Stirling, Surrey, if able, would ensure her and her sons' safety if they could make their way to the borders. He suggested that she should travel to Bonkle under the cynical pretence of consoling the borderers who were suffering through the raids. She was to bring plate, jewels and other goods to sustain her, and would depend on being able to pass through lands administered by Lord Maxwell. Her safe passage would also depend on being able to avoid the warfare, and throughout August and September the Scots would send out warnings and mobilisations in response to the incessant raids and incursions.

The plan was unfeasible. It relied first on the King escaping from his guardians, and then on his passing through to a war-torn border. Surrey was probably trying to humour Margaret. Nevertheless her diplomatic efforts did result in Henry instructing Surrey to cease the raids for a while in the hope that the Scots would see the benefits of peace and throw off the French partnership. [29]

Margaret's motives were the safety of her son and his destiny as King of Scotland. She first allied with Angus to ensure he was protected and to ensure her own rights. Then, when this failed and Henry's support was meagre, she allied with Albany for the same reasons. Now she claimed she was in financial difficulties, having had to pawn or sell off her personal belongings. She complained that she could only claim 1,000 libres per year, whilst receiving nothing from the Ettrick Forrest or the Earldom or March. Now with Albany gone she sought to influence the political situation. She began to form around her a body of nobles who were supportive of James, taking the full power of a king. They needed to agree that whilst James was not legally aged by Scottish laws and custom to take government, he should be appointed King anyway, with full regal powers so as to make him independent of regents and foreign interference. [30]

Dacre and Surrey offered to support her son as King of Scotland, and would support Margaret as head of the council governing his affairs if she could form a party strong enough to challenge Albany. This party should bring James from Stirling, armed with a mandate to open negotiations with England. [31]

As suggested by Margaret, Henry also wrote to the Scottish nobles asking that they support James in assuming full regal power. For the sake of peace Henry would promote a marriage between his daughter Mary and James. By throwing off alliance with France and opening up to friendship with England, Scotland would benefit from trade and prosperity. Many of the Scottish nobles were being won over by this argument, remembering that the death of James IV had brought blood and toil to Scotland, and constant war had brought no benefits. They would need a strong commitment of support from Henry, strong enough to counter the French influence. [32]

The possibility of Albany failing to appear at his appointed time on September 1st compelled a council meeting in St Giles, Edinburgh, when the French contingent under Gonzales warned that they intended to appoint four new regents and enter into peace negotiations with England. Queen Margaret wanted this and had successfully brought together a strong party of allies. The regents proposed were the Earls of Argyll, Arran, Huntley and Lennox. The French, supported by Beaton, the Chancellor and the Archbishop of St Andrews, asked for 40 more days, but the Lords refused.

After a few days a herald from France and Master Gaultier, Albany's secretary, arrived with letters from Francis and Albany asking the Scots to wait longer as weather conditions had made it difficult to travel. The lords sent four envoys to Stirling to meet with King James and gain his decision on whether to wait for Albany. He replied that he himself was prepared despite his young age to govern Scotland, and that Albany had not fulfilled his obligation to defend the nation as governor. James however decided to give Albany until the end of September to return to Scotland.

The Abbot of Kelso, writing to Dacre, suggested that the Lords who supported this new motion to give Albany more time were possibly 'seduced by French gold'. Queen Margaret was reported by Surrey's contacts in Scotland to have changed her mind over the plan to escape to England and had also received some cash bribes from Gaultier. [33]

The Lords of Council suggest four lords should be appointed guardians of the King: his half-brother James Stewart, the Earl of Moray, the Earl of Cassilis, the Bishop of Galloway and the Abbot of Cambuskynnell. The King was to remain in Stirling and only allowed to travel to the park and back for hawking and hunting and such. The Queen and her supporters wanted the King brought to Edinburgh and put under the guardianship of the Bishop of Aberdeen, the Abbot of Holyroodhouse, the Lord Erskine and Lord Borthwick. The appointments were discussed and the lords made a compromise with the Queen and appointed Lord Erskine, the Abbot of Cambusskynnell, the Earl of Cassilis and Lord Fleming. [34]

Despite Surrey's reports that Queen Margaret had received French money, she came up with another plan to get the King out of Stirling and bring him to Edinburgh to address the Lord's Council. The plan was for Queen Margaret to form a strong party around King James which would appeal to his uncle, King Henry, to hold back Surrey from invasion. Thereby if hostilities ceased the young King would successfully impose his authority and challenge the faction of Albany. However it is believed that Margaret was losing support amongst the lords and prelates and more of them were gravitating back towards the French. With this development she wrote to Surrey asking him to draw close to Edinburgh so as to intimidate the pro-French faction, and also to meet with the pro-English faction. Surrey wrote to Margaret that he would attempt a march to Edinburgh if assured of support from her supporters; however this was not a genuine offer as he informed Wolsey that he could not invade so deep into Scotland as he did not have enough carriages or victuals to make the journey.

A consultation with Dacre outlined the dangers, with the Scots having the option of hindering an invading army or effecting a counter-invasion into England. Surrey offered an opinion that Margaret was asking him to come to Edinburgh so that she could find means to escape. He would later offer a different opinion: that the plan to bring King James to Edinburgh was not genuine and was a stratagem used by the Lords Council with the compliance of Queen Margaret to gain time to prepare for the English invasion. Surrey was generous in stating that the Lords Council 'deceive the Queen', however there is no way of truly knowing if this was a stratagem or a genuine attempt by Queen Margaret to free her son. [35]

To give Queen Margaret the benefit of the doubt, the attempt to set up an alternative government around her son appears genuine, but it was reliant on support from her brother. Her letters to Surrey were her attempts to buy time, gather more support amongst the Scots and gain the government through her son. She was up against the financial power of the French, who were able to offer expensive gifts and bribes, and also to contend with the eminent arrival of Albany with an army. Her invitation to Surrey to march to Edinburgh was meant to act as a diversion, allowing her the opportunity have her son take power, and then order the Lords to accept his authority. King James would then request that Surrey stop the warfare, an action that would score a huge propaganda coup for the young King and Queen Margaret. The Abbot of Kelso wrote to Lord Dacre that the common people of Edinburgh, weary of the war, also wanted the King freed and in his opinion were 'beseeching God for sudden vengeance on Albany', this being a public perception that the French were the main obstacles to peace. [36]

Reports of events on the continent were also used as propaganda, to soften up the Scots with the possibility that France was about to be conquered by several aggressive powers, the Duke of Bourbon having defected from allegiance to France and now being paid by the Emperor, while Henry VIII was preparing to launch 28,000 men against King Francis. The Emperor was invading Guienne and Languedoc, and England had entered into alliance with Burgundy. The Scots were faced with the possibility of fighting England whilst losing the support of her oldest ally. Yet Albany was still determined to sail to Scotland and threaten England. [37]

Any success for Margaret's cause would have been reliant on Surrey marching north before Albany arrived in Scotland, and entering into peace talks with the Lords' Council. In return Surrey was given by Henry 'full authority to treat, and assist them with men and money', against those French stationed at Dunbar and elsewhere. He was also hopeful of support from Sir George Douglas and from Lord Hume, which if genuine would give him local support in a march up the eastern and middle marches. Surrey however was not intending to march so far north, for reasons already given to Wolsey; he instead contended himself with incursions along the borders, actions which would serve no political value. [38]

Surrey managed to raise 10,000 men and advanced towards Jedburgh. The Scots, under Andrew 'Dandy' Kerr, of Ferniehurst, raised 1,500 men and occupied the six towers of Jedburgh and the fortified abbey. The English invaders and Scottish defenders indulged in savage street fighting. The town was put to the flames and the town dwellings practically erased, although Surrey would write to Henry that the outnumbered Scots were 'the boldest men and the hottest' during this campaign. Lord Dacre led an attack on Ferniehurst Castle, and as the English tried to draw close to the castle with artillery, they were met by Scots darting out of the woods and engaging in hand-to-hand combat. Fresh English forces managed to decide the matter; Dandy Kerr was captured and the castle taken. The fighting did not finish then. As darkness fell 1,500 English put up a makeshift camp, and during a night attack around 800 horses were lost through an unexplainable mass panic. Many of the mounts were mistaken for Scots on horseback and assailed by volleys of arrows. Others galloped towards the flames of Jedburgh and were captured by Scots women glad of these unexpected prizes during a night of violence and mayhem. Surrey would sarcastically quote the words of Lord Dacre, who claimed that the Scots had allied themselves with the devil, and that 'sprites and fearful sights beset' the camp in 'six distinct inbreaks amongst the tents'. [39]

Prior to the above engagements Albany was preparing to return to Scotland. The French King could only spare a limited amount of money due to the war with the Emperor and Henry VIII, but the support he did grant was significant. During the spring and summer, 87 small ships were outfitted with arms and men in different ports across France and Brittany, which deceived the English since their ships were blockading the French ports, and their spies were searching for heavy concentrations of shipping. The armed force made ready was 4,000 foot, 1,000 harquebusiers, 500 men-at-arms, 600 horsemen and a range of artillery; large and small cannon, double cannons and ordinance set on wheeled carriages. Albany was also planning for 3,000 experienced Swiss infantry and the arrival of Richard de la Pole, a pretender to the throne of England through linage with a sister of Edward IV. When the English admiral by August 13th could find no evidence that any large number of French ships was preparing to go to Scotland, he disbanded his fleet. Albany, not able to assemble his full force, quickly organised 50 ships with 3,000 foot. He sailed from Brest in Bretagne west towards Ireland and through the Irish Sea to Kirkcudbright, arriving there on September 21st, before sailing on to the Isle of Arran on September 24th. [(40)]

Albany's stores of arms and ammunition were sent up the Clyde to Glasgow and from there he presented his army and called the lords to meet him. He then marched to Edinburgh. Once in the capital and joined by the lords and a growing number of Scots, Albany praised those Scots that continued the fight against England and stayed loyal to the league with France. He called on all Scots to unite and revenge themselves against the incursions committed almost daily on the borders. He used money to buy over those Scots who were undecided or reluctant to invade, and even tried to sway Queen Margaret with personal charm and French coin, although she stayed in Edinburgh, where she felt safer. She possibly feared that if she travelled to Stirling she would be kept against her will. Queen Margaret informed Surrey that if she or her son were not assisted by her brother, then she would have no choice but to ally herself with Albany, and said the French King had offered her a pension of 6,000 which she claimed to have refused. [41]

Surrey wrote to Wolsey that Queen Margaret was better in Scotland than England. She would be more useful to English interests and less an expense, as the cost of living was higher south of the border. Margaret would write to Dacre and Surrey concerned about the potential threat to her son with the coming of the French, and even a gift of 12 Scottish archers from the French King to James was perceived as dangerous. Soldiers funded by a foreign King would now have access to her son. With Albany her relationship was now barely warm. The Prioress of Coldstream, a resolute double agent who plied information to both sides to save her nunnery from raids, would report that Albany 'was evil-disposed' towards Queen Margaret and despite a few short meetings they kept their distance from each other. Albany would, according to Margaret, compel her to write to Surrey regarding peace negotiations, and she 'dares not refuse to write'. Margaret's fear of the French however does not stop her reportedly 'singing and dancing' for a marathon nine hours at a party with the foreign visitors. [42]

Having failed to gain the release of her son and helped him to claim power and kingship, Queen Margaret was now once more under the sway of the Duke of Albany. It was claimed that she composed letters dictated by him. She would write that the Governor sought peace between Scotland and England, and also wanted France to be comprehended into this peace. Surrey would write to Margaret claiming that Albany's actions were determined by news from France, where the French army was under pressure from the Emperor and the King of England, who were also joined by the Duke of Bourbon. Albany wanted to cause a diversion. It appears that Queen Margaret had been bought over by the French, and the fact that she was informing the English on information about the numbers of troops and armaments was not treachery on behalf of England as suggested by Strickland, but was in line with

French strategy to lure as many English troops as possible to the borders.

Surrey wrote to the Chancellor of Scotland and the Earls of Huntley, Argyll, Arran and Lennox stating that he was authorised to treat for peace with the Scots, but he had no authority to deal with Albany, or comprehend France into a truce or treaty. In other words he sought to divide the Scots from the French by offering peace to the former but not the latter. Dacre also believed that the letters of peace by Queen Margaret had been dictated by Albany as part of a ruse to buy some time as he learned that troops were mobilising at Moffat to await Albany's main army, and that half of his artillery pieces and cannon had been brought to Edinburgh. On October 20th the army mustered at Boroughmuir, to march southwards on October 22nd. [43]

There was reluctance from some Scots to actually invade England, and they repeated rumours that Surrey had been ordered by Henry to fight a defensive war. Wolsey advised the commander to avoid direct combat and wait out the Scottish effort whilst the worsening weather caused supplies to become scarcer, and the common soldiers served out their compulsory period of service, which he thought was 20 days, although it was actually 30.

Discontent became more evident as the army slogged south through roads made difficult by the approaching cold winter weather. The burgesses complained about the transports and wagons they had been ordered to supply, as well as food and drink, whilst the Earl of Argyll at Glasgow absented himself from the march as he waited for Highlanders and Isleman to arrive. The Earl of Huntley blamed illness for his non-attendance. News on the continent may have caused much of this reluctance, as a massive army was said to be marching towards Paris, and if Scotland's only ally were destroyed then Scotland would be alone and vulnerable against a powerful neighbour supported by the Empire. Albany on the other hand wanted this Scottish army to invade England and force the English to consider diverting forces from the continent to Scotland, through either defeating an

English army or capturing strongholds. [44]

At Melrose, where a bridge was thrown across the river, companies of Scots refused to cross. In the van were the Earls of Arran, Argyll and Lennox, the Earl Marshall, the Lords Maxwell, Lisle and Ruthven and the Kerrs and other borderers. David Hume, the Laird of Wedderburn, had been invited to defect from the English and join the Scots. The army stayed at Melrose for a few days. Albany, in an attempt to encourage the reluctant, decided to lead the vanguard across, but the bulk of the army refused to follow; perhaps they thought that being so near the field of Flodden was a bad omen. Nevertheless, with the French and those Scots available, Albany travelled to Coldstream. Horsemen crossed the Tweed and blocked the passages around Wark Castle and wasted the surrounding areas. Albany left a proportion of his forces on the Scottish side of the Tweed with artillery and cannon aimed at Wark, then 2,000 of his French crossed with boats to lay siege to the castle, which was defended by Sir William Lyle and well supplied with men and victuals. [45]

The Earl of Surrey's army, stationed at Alnwick, was said to number 40-50,000, although this appears unlikely. Surrey himself was stationed at the Holy Isle. Dorset was sent to bolster the forces at Berwick, which were said to be 6,000. Surrey's forces probably outnumbered those of Albany, who had lost the bulk of the Scottish army through a reluctance to invade.

Albany sent a herald to Surrey inviting him to come to Wark and do battle. Surrey replied that he had no commission to invade Scotland and only to defend, despite Albany having clearly invaded England. He invited Albany to come to Alnwick. To further provoke Surrey, companies of Scots lead by the Laird of Wedderburn crossed the Tweed, burned towns and communities and dismantled peels. Surrey kept his army intact. On November 2nd Albany then sent his French forward to storm the outer walls of Wark, which was taken, but the English within the inner walls set fire to the barns and booths which stored the straw and farm produce. The smoke was heavy enough to cause the French to withdraw.

Artillery from the Scottish side of the Tweed began to batter breaches in the inner walls. The French once more assaulted the castle and were met with a fierce defence as from the towers and walls every available missile, from bullets, arrows and rocks to boiling liquid, was thrown on the attackers.

By nightfall the French withdrew, determined to start up again the following day. However it was winter time, and throughout the night and early morning of November 3rd a great storm came with torrential rain which threatened to flood the Tweed and cut off the besiegers from the army on the other side. They quickly ended the siege and re-crossed the river. Three hundred dead, mostly French, were said to have been left at the siege, although George Buchanan, a participant and witness to the campaign, wrote that Albany had lost 'a few men', and this would be later corroborated by Surrey, who also added that 160 were injured. Lesley said that the defenders had lost a large number during the artillery bombardment, which damaged much of the castle structure.

Upon hearing of the assault on Wark, Surrey was duty bound to confront Albany, as he had invaded England. Surrey left the Holy Isle and met his army once it reached Barmoc Woods several miles from Wark. [46]

Albany was not confident that the nobles within his army could be relied upon to confront the English, and those he could rely on, his French troops and assorted Scots, were not enough in number. Lesley also claims that Surrey had sent 'secret messages' to the Queen, who was near the army, asking her to intercede and persuade Albany to disband his army. Queen Margaret would intervene to halt the hostilities and published a public letter calling for peace and dated November 10th. In it she declared her credentials to speak, being Queen of Scotland and sister of the King of England, which put her in a unique position to mediate. She would write that 'considering the great trouble that is like to be, and hath been, betwixt the two realms, and being so tender on both the sides, methink the reason there should none be so well heard as I.'

Whilst as Governor Albany had no obligation to obey Queen Margaret's command, he would nevertheless disembark his army the following day, November 11th. He withdrew to the monastery of Eccles six miles from Wark, and then the next night marched to Lauder. Whilst Surrey would deride Albany for having withdrawn from Wark, he himself was having problems holding his army together as many had used up their own funds. Heavy and freezing snows decided the outcome; Surrey did not cross into Scotland and disbanded his army. (47)

Whilst Surrey would claim that he had done more damage against Scotland than the meagre returns of the Scots in England, the Lords of Council would receive complaints that the Scots army whilst marching south had done damage to 'abbeys, religious places, towns and villages', despite a statute produced on October 12th ordering all soldiers not to harm Scottish property or lands. An inquisition was ordered to examine the claims of compensation that were coming from the districts of 'Teviotdale, Tweedale, Lanark, Lothian, Merse and other places'. War could be an expensive business, not just in the cost of mustering and marching, but possible litigation afterwards.

On November 17th Albany called a parliament in Edinburgh, and came face to face with political opposition to his continued presence in Scotland. He was accused of squandering public funds in a pointless campaign, whilst counter-claims would point to French money paying the wages of the French troops and providing pensions for Scottish nobles. The opposition demanded that the French troops return to France as they were too costly in respect to lodging and daily expenses. The Governor would claim that he had spent 300,000 crowns allocated by the French crown on this campaign, including voyage, supplies, and bribes, and made a demand for recompense by asking to sell off crown lands. This was steadfastly refused as it would further diminish the holdings and revenue of the King. (48)

Albany further alienated Margaret by appointing four new tutors for James; the Earls of Moray and Cassilis, and Lords

Fleming and Borthwick. The Governor was obviously concerned that during September Queen Margaret had been forming a party to challenge the authority of Albany, those being the Earls of Arran, Argyll, Lennox and Huntley. Margaret herself was concerned about the appointment of Lord Fleming, whose sister she claimed was a 'paramour' of Albany. She would also repeat a widespread rumour that Fleming had poisoned his wife and her two sisters, one of whom was James IV's alleged wife Lady Drummond. James was to remain in Stirling, although he would be allowed to reside in Fife or nearby Alloa. Margaret was not allowed to live with her son for more than two or three days, and any time she spent with her son was to be arranged by agreement with the lords.

In correspondence to the Lords of Council and the English powers, Margaret reiterated her fear for her son's safety. She even wrote to the Governor stating that she did not understand why she could not remain with her son, considering she had 'incurred the displeasure of England for Albany's sake'. She pleaded that over the past few years she had suffered disapproval from her brother for apparently favouring Albany and even sending letters to England on his behalf, yet complained of 'evil treatment' by the Scottish government. [49]

Queen Margaret saw two options, one being that if Albany remained in Scotland and her son remained under threat, she should go to England and undermine any moves towards a peace treaty. She would expect her self-imposed exile to pressure Albany and the Lords of Council to change the situation in respect of her son, and it would also pressurise the English as it could possibly lead to full-scale war, one thing they were not wanting despite the threats. Henry VIII rejected this idea as the attempt to escape to England would put Margaret in danger. The Earl of Surrey considered sending 100 marks to keep her quiet. Queen Margaret's other option was for Albany to leave the realm and she should gain the crown authority. The circumstance for his leaving would be a meaningful peace treaty between Scotland and England and his recall to the continent.

With this in mind, Queen Margaret, with Albany's approval, sent her servant John Cantley to England on November 28th with letters lobbying for a period of non-hostility between Scotland and England, and the comprehension of France. Henry VIII declined this offer, believing that a truce would show weakness and bring advantage to Albany, and possibly give an opportunity for the governor to spirit James away to France. Henry repeated his bullish demands that peace would come once the Scots expelled Albany, although his sister believed that this outcome could be achieved through a peace treaty. Henry's policy continued to keep a strain on relations between Scotland and England, and further made it more difficult for Queen Margaret to win over those lords and prelates in the French camp. [50]

Albany and the Lords of Council decide to address Queen Margaret's fears and suspicions regarding the care of her son and other issues. Albany had a private meeting with the Queen and King James at Stirling on December 9th. Unhappily this was not an amicable meeting, as the Queen expressed her displeasure at her treatment by the Governor. The following day she was able to address the Lords Council and accused the guardians assigned by Albany of not fulfilling the terms of their commitment towards her, in that she was not granted free access to her son whenever she felt compelled. The Governor apparently took Margaret's side, explaining that the Lords Council and the guardians had a duty to the Queen, and any infringement of these duties could result in consequences that would be of their own making. Yet despite these words Queen Margaret had heard a sinister report that if she would not be satisfied with the arrangement with the guardians then Albany would abduct King James, and with the armed support of 800 French soldiers take him to the Western Isles. Albany would be in a good position to commit such an act, as he had his ships and equipment in Dumbarton ready to sail away. Surrey would write to Wolsey about a rumour that Albany was intending to return to France with the King. Rumours were part and parcel of political intrigue, yet Queen Margaret would have difficulty ignoring them, in respect to the many political upheavals and tragic events she had already endured.

When Albany visited her and King James on December 11th, he made efforts to convince them both that the appointment of the guardians was for the good. King James expressed his satisfaction with the Governor's explanations. Whether or not he was coached by his mother to hide his real feelings is unknown. Queen Margaret decided at that time not to challenge Albany, and when she later had an audience with the Lords Council she stated, 'if it was for the good of the King her son's person, she would be contented'. After leaving the Council meeting she had instruments drawn up in front of witnesses in which she swore that she agreed to the arrangements due to fears that to do otherwise would bring harm to her son or herself. Such instruments would be kept private until she had the opportunity to use them publicly to revoke the arrangements. [51]

News from France would ease the friction between Albany and the Lords, when it is learned that France has survived the campaigns of the Emperor, Henry, the Duke of Bourbon and their allies. The Imperial troops had crossed the Pyrenees, and the English forces, because of the severe cold, had withdrawn to quarters. However Henry then ordered his troops back to England, and it seems to have been this news that brought calls to renew the alliance with France. The Scots were relieved that France was not destroyed by the multi-national alliance, whilst also concerned that more English troops were returning to England.

The attitude of the Lords of Council towards Albany underwent a rapid change. When he asked the Council for leave to sail to France for five months he was vigorously opposed by Gavin Dunbar, Bishop of Aberdeen. Margaret, often exasperated at these regular changes of political loyalty, would describe the Scots as 'never so fickle lords in the world'. The Bishop of Aberdeen threatened that if Albany went to France without leave he would lose the governorship of Scotland, and be expected to surrender the castles of Dunbar and Dumbarton.

Albany was forced to delay his departure. His reason for wanting to return was apparently that he wished to heal divisions between himself and Francis, as he believed that someone at court had been causing the King to be suspicious of him. The Council appointed Archbishop Beaton's nephew David Beaton, Abbot of Arbroath, to go to France and negotiate a possible marriage between a daughter of Francis and King James. [52]

Chapter Five: References

(1) (CSPS, vol.1, Albany to King Henry, Dec 10th, 1521, p.8. CSPS, vol.1, Duke of Albany to Katherine Queen of England, Dec 10th, 1521, p.9. CSPS, vol.1, Albany to Wolsey, Dec 10th, 1521. LP, Wolsey to Dacre, Dec 3rd, 1521. Small, pp. xc-xcii. Strickland, pp. 144-146. Tytler, pp. 166-168). (2) (Small, pp. xc-xcii. Thomson, vol.2, pp. 554-555. Tytler, pp. 166-168). (3) (Small, pp. xc-xcii. Thomson, vol.2, pp. 554-555. Tytler, pp. 166-168). (4) (RPS, A reply concerning the custody of the kingdom during the minority of the King, February 11th, 1522. Thomson, vol.2, pp. 554-556). (5) (Holinshed, pp. 492-494. Small, pp. ciii-cvi. Small, pp. cxiv-cxvi. Thomson, vol.2, pp. 553-554). (6) (ODNB, vol.36, pp. 648-652. Small, pp. ci-ciii. Strickland, vol.1, pp. 149-151). (7) (Buchanan, pp. 264-281.Fraser, pp. 198-200. Lesley, pp. 97-117. ODNB, vol.16, pp. 697-670. RPS, Judicial proceeding: reduction of forfeiture, July, 1525. Small, pp. ciii-cvi. Thomson, vol.2, pp. 556-557. Tytler, pp. 168-169). (8) (MacGrigor, pp. 24-26. Strickland, vol.2, pp. 251-252). (9) (LP, The Duke of Albany to a Counsellor of France, April, 18th, 1522). (10) (Johnson, pp. 163-165. LP, BP of Carlisle to Wolsey, June 17th 1522. LP, Francis 1st, June 23rd, 1522). (11) (Lesley, pp. 119-121. LP, BP of Carlisle to Wolsey, June 17th 1522. Tytler, pp. 168-170). (12) (LP, The Earl of Shrewsbury, August 13th, 1522.). (13) (LP, Francis I, August 13th, 1522). (14) (LP, Scotland: Margaret to Dacre (I) August 30th, 1522, (IV) September 3rd, 1522. LP, Albany, September 27th, 1522). (15) (LP, Shrewsbury to Henry VIII, September 8th, 1522. LP, Shrewsbury to Wolsey, September 8th, 1522. LP, Dacre to Wolsey, September 12th, 1522. Thomson, vol.2, pp. 556-557). (16) (Buchanan, pp. 280-283. Lesley, pp. 119-122. Holinshed, pp. 493-497. LP, Albany to Dacre, September 10th, 1522. LP, Dacre to Wolsey, September 12th, 1522). (17) (Buchanan, pp. 280-283.

Lesley, pp. 119-122. LP, Indenture made between Dacre and Albany, September 11th, 1522. MacDougall, pp. 124-125. Pitscottie, pp. 303-304. Tytler, pp. 169-170). (18) (Buchanan, pp. 280-283. Lesley, pp. 119-122. LP, Dacre to Wolsey, September 12th, 1522. Wolsey to Henry VIII, September 1522. MacDougall, pp. 124-125. Pitscottie, pp. 303-304. Tytler, pp. 169-170). (19) (Buchanan, pp. 171-172. LP, Scotland: Wolsey to Dacre, December, 1522. LP, Dacre to Wolsey, December 24th 1522. LP, Sir Rob. Wingfield to Wolsey, January 12th 1523. ODNB, vol.31, pp. 241-242. Paterson, pp. 155-156. Tytler, pp. 170-172). (20) (Holinshed, pp. 495-497). (21) (Buchanan, pp. 171-172. LP, Scotland: Wolsey to Dacre, December, 1522. LP, Dacre to Wolsey, December 24th 1522. LP, Sir Rob. Wingfield to Wolsey, January 12th 1523. Paterson, pp. 155-156. Thomson, vol.2, pp. 558-559. Tytler, pp. 170-172). (22) (Strickland, vol.1, pp. 154-157). (23) (CSPS, vol.1, Earl of Surrey to Cardinal Wolsey, March, 1523, p.12. CSPS, vol.1, William Sabin to Surrey, May 21st, 1523, p.12. Fraser, pp. 222-223. Lesley, pp. 123-125. LP, Surrey to Wolsey, April 23rd, 1523. LP, Surrey, May 21st, 1523. LP, Surrey to Henry VIII, May 21st, 1523. LP, Dacre to Surrey, June 12th, 1523. Moffat, pp. 152-153. ODNB, vol.28, pp. 452-455. Thomson, vol.2, pp. 558-559). (24) (ALCPA, May 15th, 1523, xxxiii,f.196, pp. 169-173. Buchanan, pp. 282-283. Holinshed, pp. 496-498). (25) (Buchanan, pp. 282-283. Francis I to the Estates of Scotland, May 30th, 1523. LP, Francis I to M De Langeac. May 30th, 1523. LP, Dacre to Wolsey, June 15th, 1523). (26) (Buchanan, pp. 282-283. LP, Francis I to M De Langeac. May 30th, 1523. LP, Dacre to Wolsey, June 15th, 1523). (27) (LP, Dacre to Wolsey, June 26th, 1523). (28) (ALHTS, pp. lvi-lviii, pp. 213-219). (29) (ALHTS, pp. lvi-lviii, pp. 213-219.Buchanan, 284-287. LP, Queen Margaret to Surrey, August 24th, 1523. LP, Surrey to Queen Margaret (3272), August 26th, 1523. LP, Surrey to Queen Margaret (3273), August 26th, 1523. LP, Surrey to Wolsey, September 4th, 1523. LP, News from Scotland, September 5th, 1523. LP, The Prioress of Coldstream to Sir William Bulmer, Sept 7th, 1523. Strickland, pp. 163-164). (30) (Buchanan, pp. 284-287. LP, News from Scotland, September 5th, 1523. LP, The Prioress of Coldstream to Sir William Bulmer, Sept 7th, 1523. Patterson, pp. 157-158. Tytler 171-173). (31) (Buchanan, pp. 284-287. LP, News from Scotland, September 5th, 1523. LP, The Prioress of Coldstream to Sir William Bulmer, Sept 7th, 1523. Patterson, pp. 157-158. Tytler 171-173). (32) (Buchanan, pp. 284-287. LP, News out of Scotland, September 5th, 1523. LP, Abbot of Kelso to Dacre, September 12th, 1523. LP, Surrey to Wolsey, September 21st, 1523. Patterson, pp. 157-158. Tytler 171-173). (33) (LP, News out of Scotland, September 5th, 1523. LP, The Prioress of Coldstream to Sir John Bulmer, Sept 7th, 1523. LP, Abbot of Kelso to Dacre, September 12th,1523). (34) (LP, News out of Scotland, September 5th, 1523.LP, The

Prioress of Coldstream to Sir John Bulmer, Sept 7th, 1523. LP, Abbot of Kelso to Dacre, September 12th,1523). (35) (Buchanan, pp. 284-285. LP, Surrey to Wolsey, September 14th, 1523. LP, Surrey to Queen Margaret, September 16th, 1523. LP, Surrey to Wolsey, September 21st, 1523. LP, Prioress of Coldstream, September 22nd, 1523. LP, Surrey to Wolsey, September 22nd, 1523). (36) (LP, Surrey to Queen Margaret, September 16th, 1523. LP, Wolsey to Surrey, September 25th, 1523). (37) (LP, Surrey to Queen Margaret, September 16th, 1523. LP, Wolsey to Surrey, September 25th, 1523). (38) (LP, Surrey to Queen Margaret, September 16th, 1523. LP, Surrey to Wolsey, September 17th, 1523). (39) (Buchanan, pp. 283-284. Fraser, pp. 222-224. LP, Surrey to Wolsey, September 25th, 1523. LP, September 27th, 1523. Surrey to Wolsey. Moffat, pp. 152-154. ODNB, vol.28, pp. 452-455. Patterson, pp. 156-158. Strickland, vol.1, pp. 164-166. Tytler, pp. 171-173). (40) (Buchanan, pp. 283-284. Lesley, pp. 123-127. Thomson, vol.2, pp558-559.Tytler, pp. 170-175). (41) (Buchanan, pp. 284-287. Lesley, pp. 123-127. LP, Queen Margaret to Surrey, Sept 26th, 1523. LP, Margaret to Surrey, September 29th, 1523.LP, Queen Margaret to Surrey, September 26th, 1523. LP, Surrey to Wolsey, October 1st, 1523. Thomson, vol.2, pp. 559-560. Tytler, pp. 170-175). (42) (Buchanan, pp. 287-290. Lesley, pp. 123-127. LP, Queen Margaret to Surrey, September 26th, 1523. LP, Margaret to Surrey, September 29th, 1523. LP, Surrey to Wolsey, October 1st, 1523. Tytler, pp. 170-175). (43) (Buchanan, pp. 287-288. LP, Dacre to Surrey, October 19th, 1523. LP, Surrey to Margaret, Oct, 1523. Surrey to the Chancellor of Scotland, Oct, 1523. Strickland, pp. 165-167. Tytler, pp. 170-175). (44) (ALCPA, October 2nd, 1523, xxxiv, f.12, pp. 180-181. Buchanan, pp. 287-290. Lesley, pp. 123-127. LP, Surrey to Margaret, Oct, 1523. LP, Wolsey to Surrey, Oct 1st, 1523. ODNB, vol.28, pp. 452-455. Tytler, pp. 170-175). (45) (Buchanan, pp. 287-290. Lesley, pp. 123-127. LP, Dacre to Surrey, October 31st, 1523. LP, Dacre to Surrey, November 3rd, 1523. LP, Surrey to Henry VIII, November 3rd, 1523. Tytler, pp. 170-175). (46) (Buchanan, pp. 287-290. Holinshed, pp. 497-500. Lesley, pp. 123-127. LP, Wolsey to Surrey, Oct 1st, 1523. Tytler, pp. 170-175). (47) (Buchanan, pp. 287-290. Holinshed, pp. 497-500. Lesley, pp. 123-127. LP, Wolsey to Surrey, Oct 1st, 1523. LP, Surrey to Henry VIII, November 3rd, 1523. ODNB, vol.28, pp. 452-455. Strickland, vol.1, pp. 167-169. Tytler, pp. 170-175). (48) (ALCPA, pp. 185-186, pp. 190-191. LP, Queen Margaret to the Lords of the Council of Scotland, November 26th, 1523. LP, Wolsey to Surrey, November 28th, 1523. LP, Surrey to Wolsey, November 29th, 1523. Thomson, vol.2, pp. 560-561. Tytler, pp. 174-178). (49) (LP, Queen Margaret to Surrey, November 24th, 1523. LP, Queen Margaret to the Lords of the Council of Scotland, November 26th, 1523. LP, Wolsey to Surrey, November 28th, 1523. LP, Surrey to

Wolsey, November 29th, 1523. Thomson, vol.2, pp. 560-561. Tytler, pp. 174-178). (50) (CSPS, vol.1, Queen Margaret to Surrey, Nov 10th, 1523, p.14. LP, Queen Margaret to Surrey, November 24th, 1523. LP, Queen Margaret to the Lords of the Council of Scotland, November 26th, 1523. LP, The Lords of Scotland to Queen Margaret, November 28th, 1523. LP, Wolsey to Surrey, November 28th, 1523. LP, Surrey to Wolsey, November 29th, 1523. Thomson, vol.2, pp. 560-561. Tytler, pp. 174-178). (51) (LP, The Lords of Scotland to Queen Margaret, November 28th, 1523. LP, Surrey to Wolsey, December 2nd,1523. Strickland, vol.1, pp. 172-174). (52) (ALCPA, pp. 191-192. CSPS, Lope Hurtado De Mendoza to te Emperor, February 5th, 1524. CSPV, Marco Foscari, December 27th, 1523. Herkless & Hannay, vol.3, pp. 104-107. LP, Queen Margaret to Surrey, November 23rd, 1523. LP, Surrey to Wolsey December 2nd, 1523. LP, Dacre to Wolsey, December 27th, 1523. LP, Albany to Madame Louise, Countess of Angoulême, January, 22nd, 1523.

Chapter Six

THREADS WROUGHT BY
WOMEN'S FINGERS: 1523-1525

The Lords of Council met with Albany at his home on January 14th,
1524 and agreed that if a comprehension of France into a truce
between Scotland and England could be achieved it should be
accepted. The meeting also decided to reinstate courts to
administer justice on 'great crimes'. Lennox was granted the
position of Warden of the Borders, with authority over Lothian,
the Merse and Teviotdale. He was reported to have the power to
raise Ayrshire, as well as his own feudal possessions of
Dumbarton. Albany also granted him the abbacy of Dryburgh,
which was worth 4,000 Scots marks per year. Lennox was allowed
to take half that amount as a source of revenue, and appointed
James Stewart as Abbot. The Earl of Huntley had passed on, and

his heir was a minor. James Stewart, the Earl of Moray, and illegitimate half-brother of the King was made justicier north of the Forth in place of Huntley. There were suggestions by Dacre that the Earls of Arran and Argyll were not on the best terms with Albany, and that they potentially could be swayed by English offers. [1]

Throughout the winter and spring there were letters written between the English and Albany regarding peace, whilst there were frequent incursions by Scots and English raiders. Although the majority of raids were made by small bands, Dacre and his counterpart Lennox would occasionally lead large forays across the borders. The majority of raids were organised by criminal gangs, and near Berwick on May 21st, 500 Scots captured up to 200 merchants and traders going to the fair and took them to Scotland for ransom. Nevertheless there was no call by either side to muster full-scale armies. The King of England would not allow a peace between Scotland and England which comprehended France, and the English prelates and lords therefore lacked the authority to do so. The English also distrusted Albany's urgings for peace and from letters intercepted to France believed he was playing for time until a more advantageous opportunity arose for France and Scotland to renew hostilities.

Albany however was preparing to leave for France and take David Beaton with him. He entered into an agreement with Queen Margaret in which she agreed to uphold his authority as governor and inform him of any actions against him, and not to agree to a treaty between Scotland and England that failed to comprehend France. In return he promised that the King of France would grant her refuge if she was victimised by Angus, supported by her brother Henry.

As an incentive to buy her loyalty Albany, granted her the wardship of the heir to Alexander Gordon, Earl of Huntley who died at Perth on January 16th 1524. George, the new heir, was eleven or twelve years of age. This arrangement would bring financial rewards, with Margaret being able to administer the vast estates and properties of the heir. She also had the right to marry him off, ensuring marriage bids and bribes from powerful lords to enable their daughters to marry into the powerful Huntley family. When her brother Henry found out about this, Dacre rebuked her for it. [2]

There would also be much annoyance and disapproval of Margaret having been in receipt of English money during the winter, yet Albany's bribes, along with French payments, were apparently winning her over to the cause of France. There were also malicious reports coming from Lord Dacre that she had once more entered into a close relationship with the Governor, and on one occasion had met with him at Holyrood Palace after a visit to the borders, showering him with affection and warmth. The nature of the relationship between Albany and Queen Margaret can only be guessed at; however there was a new man in her life, Henry Stewart, Master of Avondale, a former mercenary and now member of the Royal Household. He would become an important member of the Queen's faction. [3]

On May 20th 1524 Albany set off from Dumbarton along with David Beaton, Abbot of Arbroath. At a Lord Council gathering at Edinburgh during Whitsun week Albany insisted that Queen Margaret should continue to agree to King James remaining at Stirling, and for her to cease correspondence with her brother, the King of England. Margaret made no definite reply except to say that once he had gone 'she must needs do the best she could do for herself', which was a fairly honest way of saying she would be looking after number one. The Lords Council would do what they could within their power to ensure King James remained in Stirling, if he continued to accept the arrangements composed for him. Whilst there were disputes between Albany and the Lords of Council about his leaving, they finally agreed to grant a three-month licence to visit France, and it was also agreed that he should return on August 31st, and failure to do so would result in termination of his governorship.

Albany, upon his return to France, had to contend with

personal issues. His wife Anne died at St Saturnin shortly after making her last will and testament on June 16th 1524. She would make Catherine de Medici, who resided in Rome, her heir, and grant all her personal possessions to her husband. [4]

Once Albany had left for France Dacre quickly wrote to the Chancellor and Archbishop of St Andrews, James Beaton, calling on him to use his influence to broker a meaningful peace between Scotland and England. The Chancellor was recognised by Henry as the most important personage in Scotland adhering to the French interest, and with Albany gone the English sought to find a way of eliminating Beaton from Scottish politics. [5]

During July the violence on the border intensified. An English raiding party of 1,000 raided near Kelso, burning a town called Smallholm. On the way home they fell into battle with a raiding force from Teviotdale and the Merse. The outcome was inconclusive, with both sides taking prisoners. Lord Maxwell led a destructive raid towards Carlisle and fell into hard fighting against an English force. Although the latter captured prisoners, a second party of Scots raiders managed to recover these captives and in turn took 300 English. [6]

The Earl of Angus would arrive in England during the summer. He had apparently enjoyed some freedom of movement within France, despite being exiled there. With the intention of making a pilgrimage to Notre Dame de Pue in Navarre, he instead left Boulogne and on March 21st 1524 he attempted to enter the Empire through Picardy, and then make for English-dominated Calais. This attempt failed, yet he would learn through correspondence with one of his servants, who had been captured on the sea by the English, that Henry VIII would permit Angus to come to England. Angus wrote to Henry from Paris on May 8th, the letter reaching England via Antwerp by May 27th. With an escape route established Angus made his way to Antwerp and then took ship to Berwick. Angus arrived in London by June 28th and was soon joined by his brother William, Prior of Coldingham. Gonzales, Dunbar's French captain, had apparently offered to surrender the castle to Douglas when he learned that he had arrived at Berwick. In return he wanted safe conducts for himself and his troops to return to France. This was probably an attempt to entrap Angus, for Gonzales would have attracted the wraith of Albany and the King of France if he had truly followed this course. [7]

Wolsey and the King would have several meetings with him. Since Angus' exile there is no account of his daughter Lady Margaret Douglas in the Scottish or English records, and it has been assumed that she accompanied him to France, then back to England. She would be eight years of age, and as she was Henry VIII's niece this would have given him a large measure of emotional incentive to support Angus and to try and reconcile him with his sister, Queen Margaret. The prospect of Angus meeting her brother did not make Margaret feel secure as her husband was seen as a dangerously divisive figure in Scotland, and besides that she loathed him. Yet he was fully of the English interest and with Henry's backing could eradicate the French interests north of the border.

First they wanted to deal with Beaton, who was invited to come to a peace conference, or diet, on the borders attended by Angus and Thomas Howard, Earl of Surrey and now 3rd Duke of Norfolk. Whilst the purpose was supposedly to engineer peace, the English were expecting a non-agreement or non-attendance, and in either event Angus would declare that he would support King James to take full regal power and would make a bid to take the government of Scotland, backed by English power. Beaton declined going to the meeting on the borders, and whilst Dacre disbelieved his excuses, the fact that no safe conduct was granted alerted Beaton to the possibility that the English might attempt to capture him. Arran and Lennox were commissioned by the Lords of Council to attend such a border meeting on the 2nd or 3rd of August. [8]

Margaret wrote to her brother and informed him that whilst she was working to further her son's interests by turning 'many lords from the Duke of Albany', Henry's support of Angus endangered this work as he 'will create great jealousies and destroy her authority'. She also threatened that if Henry supported Angus she would find support elsewhere, a hint that she would once more look to Albany and France.

Wolsey and Henry had asked her to reconcile herself to Angus. However she reminded them of the 'false reports' that her husband made, and to which her brother paid heed. She sought peace between Scotland and England and emphasised that the lords were supportive of this. She feared that Henry would squander this opportunity as the lords 'were never better minded than now'. She informed him that she sought to support her son to take full power, and he in reply welcomed this action as it would undermine Albany and the French power. Henry agreed to keep Angus on the borders and not to hamper her efforts, although he still sought to use him during peace negotiations. (9)

Louise, mother of King Francis, spread a rumour through French agents that Angus had been allowed to leave France with the intention of travelling to Scotland and continuing the work carried out by Albany. The claim that Angus was in the employ of the French fed on Henry's suspicious nature. The Earl would vigorously deny the allegations, and the King of France would himself in discussion with the Scottish ambassador claim that Angus left France without permission. (10)

Queen Margaret, perceiving the threat that the meeting, or 'diet', on the borders could pose to her authority, especially with Angus involved, decided to make a bid for power. Throughout the spring and summer, and probably long before Albany had left for France, Margaret had been energetic in making personal agreements or bonds with different lords, seeking their support in challenging the governorship of Albany. In mid-June, under the pretence of going on a pilgrimage to St Ninians in Galloway, she met with supporters who pledged to free King James from Stirling. Her success in these efforts with recruiting a large number of nobles to her cause prompted her to arrange a meeting with Beaton at Alloa, where she showed him letters from those lords to James offering support in bringing him out of Stirling and to Edinburgh, where he would be confirmed as King with full regal powers. The Chancellor would then see that he could not possibly, without risk to himself, challenge Margaret and James.

Margaret also gained the support of Arran, and how this came about is uncertain. Arran was an heir-apparent after Albany and James to the throne of Scotland, and as an enemy of Angus would be a perfect ally for Margaret. He also had considerable landed power. On July 26th James was taken out of Stirling and escorted to Edinburgh by Arran, Lennox, Crawford, Henry Stewart, Master of Avondale, and a large body of the nobility. James was taken to Holyrood Abbey, where a council was called, and at the age of twelve years and three months old he was crowned and proclaimed King of Scotland. He was presented with crown, sceptre and sword of state by the Earl of Arran. [11]

A parliament was called for August 1st in which the Three Estates swore allegiance to the King and to an end of the governorship of the Duke of Albany. The King commanded Beaton to resign the chancellorship and hand over the Great Seal. All crown offices, such as treasurer, chamberlain, lieutenant and others, were resigned to the King so that he could dispose of them as he pleased. Gavin Dunbar, James' former tutor, had been nominated by Albany for the see of Glasgow, and was by papal decree exempted from the Archbishop of St Andrew's jurisdiction. Receiving his pallium in July 8th, 1524, in order to gain the temporalities he would need the support of Queen Margaret, he was prepared to go against his main sponsor, the Duke of Albany. His uncle the Bishop of Aberdeen, also called Gavin Dunbar, would join with the Archbishop of St Andrews and refuse to break their vow to Albany, wanting to wait until September 1st, the day after Albany's appointed return. They also stated that it was wrong to ask a young man to take on the reins of government without having been properly tutored and educated.

Margaret tried to bribe them to join her, and an offer of helping to acquire cardinal's hat with Wolsey's assistance was reportedly made. The Lord Provost of Edinburgh was replaced by Lord

Maxwell at the command of Queen Margaret, and having gained Edinburgh with the support of this resourceful border lord, Margaret would next occupy the castle. (12)

A meeting was agreed by Margaret at the Kirk of Elam on the borders with Norfolk, and Arran was to act as her representative. Arran was to negotiate on matters of common interest if Albany threatened to return, but would not attend the meeting if Angus was present. Margaret emphasised that whilst she had gathered together a great number of lords who had entered into bonds, she did not entirely trust them all, and requested that Norfolk should be able to authorise armed support at short notice if the need arose. The powerful lords she is reported to have entered into bonds with were Arran, Lennox, Moray, Eglinton, Cassilis, Maxwell, Glamis, Avondale, Livingston and others. The actual process of recruiting these individuals must have entailed patient diplomacy and secret negotiations. The fact that she was able to present such a list says much for Margaret's growing political skills. (13)

Margaret wrote to Norfolk and Henry VIII praising the efforts of herself and Arran in bringing about 'a great thing' by electing James to full King. She requested that Arran should be granted the Order of the Garter and given a pension. Henry did show gratitude and sent money - 1,000 nobles to King James, 200 marks to Margaret, and 100 pounds to Arran. Money was also provided to pay for a personal bodyguard of 200 men-at-arms to defend the King. To persuade Margaret to stay loyal to his wishes the payments were to be forwarded once a month. Queen Margaret would later write that the bodyguard had 'hindered much evil to be done', although there were other reports that she used these professionals outside their remit and directly against her enemies.

Many of the bodyguards were sons of noble families, or distant relatives of royalty. Sir David Lindsay, the court poet and valued attendant to James, was a critic of them, and would accuse them of using flattery to win over the King whilst introducing him to cards, dice, horse racing over the sands of Leith and other forms of gambling, as well as loose living and loose morals. Lindsay suggested that the bodyguard would make themselves rich through their position whilst James became poorer. Lindsay and the scholar Bellenden would be dismissed from court in 1524; possibly they made their criticisms too vocal, although James would take an independent stance and continue to pay Lindsay a small pension. Although James' education appears to have been disrupted in 1524, Margaret revealed her higher ambitions for her son. In a letter to Henry supported by the Lords in Council she asked for James to be designated second person of the realm of England after Henry, and if Henry eventually had a son, James was to be compensated by having Berwick restored to Scotland as well as some disputed lands. [14]

Arran's reluctance to attend the conference on the borders was a point of principle in that Angus was still in English favour. Norfolk himself was tasked by the King of England to bring about reconciliation between Margaret and Angus, and also between Angus and Arran. Norfolk would eventually concede, along with Wolsey, that these attempts at turning enemies into friends were too difficult. Margaret and Arran were not prepared to risk losing political position to the power-hungry Douglas. Wolsey would also fear the influence of Angus, and was concerned that if Angus was not able to reach a settlement with Margaret he might look to an alliance with Beaton, which might even entail alliance with France. Wolsey's imaginings appear to have been stretching to all kinds of dangerous possibilities.

The Archbishop of St Andrews was seen by Wolsey as still being a significant threat, despite the powerful coalition around Margaret. He became so fearful of a possible alliance between Beaton and Angus that he and Henry conceived a plan in that Margaret should send Beaton to England as part of an embassy, and the King would then either recruit him to English interests or keep him there. [15]

Margaret and Arran decided to deal with the Archbishop of St Andrews by less subtle means. A parliament was arranged for

August 22nd in Edinburgh. Here the King entered the Tolbooth of Edinburgh with sceptre, crown and sword of honour. At the parliament Beaton was once more asked to recognise the authority of King James and withdraw his oath of obedience to Albany. The Archbishop refused, along with the Bishop of Aberdeen, requesting that they wait until September 1st, the day after which Albany was appointed to return. Beaton apparently rebuked James for turning against Albany and the alliance with France.

After the parliament the Archbishop attempted to find some safe place of haven but was pursued by Margaret's lover Henry Stewart, Master of Avondale, who caught up with him and took the Great Seal. The Archbishop of St Andrews was handed over to the custody of Lord Maxwell and James Hamilton of Finnart to join the Bishop of Aberdeen in the dungeon of Edinburgh Castle. Both were said to have been 'rigorously treated'. For any other supporters of Albany who attempted to escape, the gates of the city were shut and we can assume that many were arrested, or worse. Aware that this act would cause outrage in the Vatican, the Lord of Council sent a supplication to the Pope stating that these actions had been taken because the Archbishop of St Andrews and other churchmen were planning an insurrection, and if failing he would depart to foreign parts and seek help from 'some great party in contrary to the King'. They also asked for a legate to come to Scotland to investigate the case against Beaton. Beaton's clerk M. Instringi would write to the Archbishop's nephew David, Abbot of Arbroath and acting ambassador in Paris, asking him to petition the King of France and the Duke of Albany to write to the Pope demanding the Archbishop of St Andrews' release. [16]

King Henry would later request that Beaton and the Bishop of Aberdeen should be brought to Berwick, where they could be incarcerated in England, as he believed them to be too dangerous to be ever put to liberty. Margaret would write to Norfolk stating that the Lords of Council would not allow the Archbishop and Bishop to go to England, for offences committed in Scotland against the King, which would have also raised questions about England claiming a judicial superiority over Scotland. [17]

The Earl of Arran would not attend a meeting with Norfolk. Instead Gilbert, Earl of Cassilis, Adam Otterburn and Sir Walter Scott agreed with Norfolk and Dacre an abstinence of war from September 4th to December 1st 1524. A later embassy was to be sent to England with further negotiations, and Henry sought to send two ambassadors to Edinburgh, Dr Thomas Magnus and Roger Radcliff. The main stumbling point to his two diplomatic endeavours was that Margaret was still reluctant to send an embassy to England whilst her husband remained a danger to her interests. To further complicate matters, the English did not want to send their ambassadors until the Scottish embassy had been sent. Margaret also stated that Scotland will lose considerably through this embassy, especially in friendship with France. She mentioned that the French were paying up to 50,000 francs per year to various Scots in the form of pensions, and this sum might be lost if Scotland drew too close to England.

Arran himself received a pension from France of 900 francs, besides being honoured with the Order of France. The Duke of Norfolk would later write scathingly of the Earl of Arran and the wearing of his French honours, comparing the buying of Arran's loyalty to like having an 'eel by the tail'. Henry was aware that many Scottish nobles were now receiving money from both France and England. Interfering in Scottish politics involved him in a bidding war, knowing full well that France could easily match his spending. [18]

There were reports from the continent that Albany was preparing to return to Scotland from St Quentin with 4,800 men, and also that agents were in Normandy soliciting ships for the expedition. Gonzales, the Frenchman holding Dunbar Castle, and apparently holding it for Albany in resistance to the King, writes to James that Albany was expected to return to Scotland for 'the good of the kingdom'. He also warned James about the hostile intentions of the council which, he alleged, would deliver James to England if Albany returned. Margaret learned that Angus' brother

William had met up with Gonzales, although she was assured by Norfolk that he had been advised by Dacre and himself to do this in order to learn if Gonzales was planning to leave Scotland. [19]

Margaret and Arran would begin to collect against them new opposition besides the camp of Albany, and friends of Angus. The Earl of Lennox and Glencairn became disillusioned with Queen Margaret's government and left Edinburgh for the purpose of recruiting other lords to mobilise against her. This split seems to have been because the Provost of Edinburgh, Lord Maxwell, had arrested the Laird of Buccleough and the Laird of Cessford, who were involved in a bitter feud on the borders that was threatening further instability. Both were imprisoned in Edinburgh Castle, and Lennox took offence to this as Cessford was one of his dependants. Lord Maxwell had also become one of Margaret's closest followers through her granting of the castles of Threave and Lochmaben as hereditary possessions, as well as making him Steward of Kirkcudbright for a period of nineteen years. [20]

Another source of friction was the fact that Margaret had taken up with Henry Stewart, the Master of Avondale, a young man whom she had appointed to the position of Lord Treasurer. This offended and alienated many of the highest lords and prelates in the land, such as Lennox and Glencairn. Henry Stewart would also hold the Great Seal, the Privy Seal, the Quarter Seal and Signet, allowing him a vast concentration of crown power in his hands, or as the Duke of Norfolk called it, 'a curious accumulation of grave functions for one young guardsman'.

Little is known about Henry Stewart's early years except that he and his brothers were early supporters of Margaret's coup. He seems to have had some prior experience as a diplomat, soldier-of-fortune and financier, and the confidence that Margaret would show suggests he had some competency in these matters. Many of his family, including two brothers, were enriching themselves through membership of the bodyguard financed by Henry VIII. The Duke of Norfolk would hear reports that Stewart practically dominated the court with Queen Margaret's backing. In any argument the Queen would publicly take the side of Stewart. Norfolk was also an early advocate of sending the priest and ambassador Dr Magnus to Scotland, so as to raise a challenge to the way Margaret lived her private life. The political situation in which Margaret was apparently ruled by both Henry Stewart and Arran would make her unpopular, especially as her husband Angus was languishing in England. Many powerful and dangerous people were being cut off from the profits of public office as 'it was grudged she should keep the offices and seals in her own hands'. (21)

Henry VIII was still however proposing to release Angus. The Duke of Norfolk supported this idea, and Wolsey wrote to Margaret that Angus 'might do her good service', which seems a preposterous suggestion considering Angus' past record for mayhem. Margaret would explain in letters to Henry and Wolsey that Arran would 'forsake the good part he has pursued, and take heed to himself' if Angus returned. Under the guidance of Margaret, and whilst residing at Linlithgow, the Earl of Arran would also write to Henry, acknowledging that both held common ancestry in being descended from the Beauforts, as James I's Queen had been Joan Beaufort. Arran would praise Henry's nephew for his manly appearance and countenance, as well as his graces, charms and good behaviour. The Earl also made it clear that if Angus were released then this would threaten the peace between Scotland and England, as well as usurping the will of the Queen. (22)

It was unknown to many that Angus and his brother George had entered into agreements with Wolsey in London on October 4th, where Angus promises that in the event of gaining the government of Scotland, he would reconfirm the raising of James to the kingship. He would also oppose with all his power the return of Albany or the setting up of any French-backed governorship. For any alliance with France or the passing of any act that would affect the authority of James, Angus would consult Henry. Angus would also promise to promote peace between Scotland and England, and friendship between James and Henry, commit himself to reconciling himself to Margaret, and endeavour to end the feud with Arran. He additionally would agree to support Henry militarily against any man except the King of Scotland.

Whilst remaining near the border, one of the Earl of Angus's kinsmen killed Lord Fleming and captured his son Malcolm at St Giles Church, Edinburgh. Fleming was known as the 'best Frenchman in Scotland' and was a close ally of Albany. Whilst Queen Margaret had feared Lord Fleming, especially when he was guardian to her son, she would be very concerned that her husband was now blatantly displaying the reach of his maliciousness into Scotland's capital with a political assassination. [23]

The Bishop of Aberdeen was released by October 20th and would reside in Linlithgow. The Earls of Lennox, Glencairn and others opposed to the present government began to form an opposition and write to Henry demanding the return of Angus. Failing that they would 'seek a new way', which is a suggestion of passing support to the French. The King's half-brother James Stewart, the twenty-four-year-old Earl of Moray, was initially part of this alliance with Lennox and Glencairn, until tempted away by being invited into the King's council. Being in command of vast numbers of men and supplies north of the Firth of Forth, his loyalty was acquired by King James, granting him the lucrative wardship of the minor earldom of Huntley, which had lately been under the authority of Queen Margaret. Moray was also confirmed in his lease of Ross and Ardmanach. He entered into a contract to marry Margaret Douglas, daughter of the Queen, although it appears she was still in England.

Another opponent to the government, the Earl of Argyll, was bought off by being offered a pension of £100 per week. Lennox however was still prepared to act despite these defections and formed a plan to use 500 men in a surprise attack against Arran at his apartments in Holyroodhouse. Once Arran was killed or captured they would use scaling ladders to enter Edinburgh Castle and capture the King and Queen. An individual called James Pringle seems to have informed on this plan, which stopped it in its tracks. [24]

Margaret was keeping her options open, knowing that if her brother allowed Angus to cross the border she might need to find some other kind of accommodation, with a possibility that Margaret and Arran could ally themselves with the Archbishop of St Andrews. Henry Stewart was said to have offered to have the Archbishop of St Andrews release in return for payment, and a rumour was spread that Beaton had already given Margaret 20,000 crowns, possibly to ensure better treatment whilst incarcerated in Edinburgh, and to ensure he was not taken out of bounds, where his fate would be less certain.

Towards the end of October 1524, the Duke of Norfolk received reports that Margaret, Arran and Lord Maxwell were being drawn towards seeking support from France. Henry VIII would be troubled by all these developments, Margaret's relationship with Henry Stewart, her rejection of Angus and the possibility of accommodation with Beaton and possibly Albany. [25]

In a harsh correspondence to Henry through an envoy Appleby, it was indicated that Queen Margaret had been aware of a plot to kill her brother and was being slow to provide details. Robert Cochrane, who called himself the Bishop of Dunkeld, although he had not yet received the papal confirmation, had been lately imprisoned, and had claimed to know of a plot to kill the King of England. James V would explain in a letter to Pope Clement VII dated September 15th, 1524 that Cochrane had granted a pension to James Creichton, a Dominican Friar, despite not having the authority to do so, which seems to have been the basis of his incarceration. There are no details of the plot, although Dunkeld informed the Carlisle herald that there were traitors in the court of King Henry. If Dunkeld had learned of such a plot it must have been during the summer when he had been one of the ambassadors negotiating with the English. It appears his allegations were treated as a ruse by which he hoped to get himself released from prison or gain better treatment.

Wolsey, Norfolk and King Henry were outraged that Margaret had not investigated or even taken the plot seriously, with Wolsey exclaiming that the 'continual delay which the said Queen Margaret hath used in opening and disclosing a matter, as it is said, much to the danger of the King's life and person, so to satisfy her own malice, she would be contented to conceal, and not suffer to be discovered that thing which she might endanger her own brother's life, and consequently, either to destroy her brother, her son, and herself, for revenging her own rancor and malice'.

Margaret was accused of delaying a letter to Henry from Dunkeld. The reason given by Wolsey for Queen Margaret withholding the letter was to get concessions from her brother, possibly in respect of ensuring that Angus remained in England. Possibly it was a false report; nevertheless it caused friction between Queen Margaret and her brother. Despite harsh words, Henry and Wolsey would fear that their policy towards Angus was backfiring and causing Margaret to become hostile and unhelpful to English interests, yet instead of affecting a conciliatory approach Henry resorted to his customary bullying by threatening to withdraw funding for the 200-strong bodyguard. Margaret countered by requesting funding for 300. The Duke of Norfolk, also angered at Margaret, would however advise that kinder words should be used in future correspondence, since England still needed a friendly Scotland. [26]

Magnus and Radcliff finally received a safe conduct to travel to Scotland and both arrived there by October 29th to become ambassadors and residents at King James' court. Arran however was not present at that time as he opposed the English support of Angus. The ambassadors were instructed to continue efforts to reconcile Angus with both Queen Margaret and Arran, and to discuss the prospect of King James marrying Henry's daughter, and the continuance of the pensions. Henry also relented from his previous anger and promised to continue paying for the 200 men of the bodyguard. He gifted James a coat of cloth of gold and a sword, which the ten-year-old King proudly wore the day he received it. The ambassadors would report to Wolsey that young James had all the qualities of a king, and they were impressed by his personality, appearance and social graces. He possessed the knightly skills in jousting, and in swordplay he wore a three-foot rapier which he welded with skill. James also had a talent for singing and dancing. Despite his youth the ambassadors report a king and court that reflected the height of culture and chivalry. James was also seemingly inspired by his uncle Henry VIII, and learning that the proud King wore a buckler, he asked the ambassadors to arrange for Wolsey to send him an ornamental shield suitable for combat. The ambassadors also reported that James had a cruel streak, which they claim was by inspired by his mother. According to them, if a lord or noble angered Margaret, she would encourage James to likewise show his displeasure, whether through withering looks or harsh words. It is clear that James was very devoted to his protective mother and her enemies were also his.

Dr Magnus was tasked with using his priestly training to better censure Queen Margaret's private behaviour, whilst Radcliff, one of King Henry's favourites, was to ingratiate himself with King James through his knowledge and experience of chivalry and martial deeds. [27]

During that time it was reported that Angus had crossed the border into Scotland, and being a popular figure with the commoners due to the heroic and chivalric fame of the Douglas name, he was greeted with great fanfare and celebration. Dr Magnus, the English Ambassador, would try to convince Margaret of the merits of Angus, stating how handsome a man he was, how admired he was in court, and since his time in France how he had gained in manners and courtly behaviour. Margaret however distrusted Angus, and would not allow him to visit the King or go near the workings of government.

Angus wrote to Margaret from his residence at Bonkle on November 1st offering his allegiance to the King and willingness to become his loyal servant. Queen Margaret in turn wrote to Norfolk requesting that Angus should return to Berwick until an agreement could be made between herself, Arran and Angus, and until his return to England Angus was forced under pain of treason to act in a humble manner for such a proud lord, and not travel with more than 40 people in an entourage. Margaret also wrote to Henry chastising him for ignoring her numerous requests and releasing Angus, whom she considered a threat to herself and her son.

Around this period, Katherine, Queen of England, also wrote to Queen Margaret, advising her not to divorce the Earl of Angus as this would affect her daughter Lady Margaret Douglas in regard to legitimacy and legal rights. In reply, Margaret insisted that her daughter's rights would not be undermined, and she would not suffer for the actions of her husband. The whereabouts of Lady Margaret are not recorded, although she may have been at her father's stronghold at Bonkle, or resident in one of her godfather Wolsey's estates in northern England. [28]

About the same time, during late October, the Archbishop of St Andrews had been released and was at court. Margaret explained to Magnus and Radcliff that he had been released because of ill health and said she hoped to bring him to closer friendship with the young King. She also stated that Arran was insistent that Beaton should be freed, and would have set him loose even if she disagreed. Sir George Douglas would disagree with this reasoning, stating that the Queen and Arran had so few friends in Scotland they had released him because he was an ally of Albany, and now 'lean towards France'.

An envoy was sent to France by Queen Margaret and Arran. Francis I, King of France, insisted that he still favoured a marriage between one of his daughters and the King of Scotland, and the continuing of the alliance between Scotland and France. He wrote to the Queen saying that Angus had left France without leave and was obviously a danger to herself and her son. Francis could not offer support as he was occupied with preparing to campaign in Italy and would be taking Albany with him. With no immediate support from Albany, and being frustrated by her brother's support of Angus, Margaret was in a desperate situation. [29]

Margaret decided to call a parliament at the Edinburgh Tolbooth for November 14th which would sit for several days. There would be an attempt to heal the divisions within the nation, consolidate peace between Scotland and England and settle a council on James. Albany was to be removed as Governor of Scotland because he had failed to appear on the designated date of return. Margaret authorised the sending of ambassadors to England, including the recently-released Bishop of Dunkeld, the Earl of Cassilis and Robert Milne, the Abbot of Cambusnethen. There was a hope that a lasting peace treaty through a marriage between King James and Lady Mary, daughter to Henry, could be arranged. Magnus and Radcliff were distrustful of the Archbishop of St Andrews, and had suggested to Margaret that he should be one of the commissioners to be sent to England. They believe that out of malice and out of loyalty to Albany, Beaton would use his freedom in Scotland by building up a pro-French faction to encourage Albany's return. Margaret disagreed and the parliament authorised a secret council around James consisting of the Archbishop of St Andrews, the Bishop of Aberdeen and the earls of Arran and Argyll, with Queen Margaret named head of council. The above council should have done much to bring divergent factions closer together, especially through the favouring of former pro-French rivals such as Beaton and the Bishop of Aberdeen as counsellors of the King.

These apparent efforts to reach a settlement would be preempted on the morning of November 23rd when bells were rung in alarm as armed men swarmed over the walls of Edinburgh city using scaling ladders. They overcame the garrisons guarding the gates before allowing in 400 horsemen. [30] The forces were those of Angus, Lennox, Scott of Buccleough and the Master of Glencairn. With the daylight the invaders advanced to the Market Cross and declared that they were there to free the King from imprisonment by the Queen and advisers. They demanded that they should become custodians of the King and the 'evil-disposed persons' should be dismissed.

The Secret Council of King James quickly assembled, and they were faced with aggressive and dangerous opposition. Angus was joined by the Bishop of Dunblane and met with the Bishop of Aberdeen and several other lords, including the Earl of Argyll. A mob was gathered up by Angus and Lennox and marched towards Holyrood Palace. Queen Margaret was residing at Holyrood, with the forces of her lords and 500 harquebusiers. Margaret ordered that the two cannons on the portal of the Palace should fire and disperse the approaching mob. Whilst the cannonade drove back the invaders, it also killed and wounded citizens and destroyed property. The Bishop of Aberdeen, the Abbot of Cambuskenneth, and the ambassador Magnus were sent by Angus and arrived at the palace for a conference, when they asked for the cannonade to cease. Margaret warned Magnus to leave and 'not presume to meddle in Scottish affairs'. Margaret was obviously distrustful of Magnus, now that Angus, seemingly an English proxy, was attacking the crown and making treasonous demands. [31]

Queen Margaret, on the advice of Moray and Arran, threatened to unleash all the firepower of the guns of Edinburgh Castle upon the city unless Angus retreated. The city burgesses and nobility, including Angus' enemies, concerned about the damage that the war would do to the city, met with Angus and Lennox and ordered that they and their followers should leave in the name of the King.

By 4pm Angus and Lennox had withdrawn to Dalkeith. By nightfall Margaret, her son, Sir Henry Stewart, the Earl of Moray, her bodyguard and her lady attendants had been guided by torchlight to reach the safety of Edinburgh Castle. She took care to ensure all her valuables and jewellery, as well as her clothes, were taken by the nightly procession. All was not fruitless as it would appear to Angus and Lennox, as the Earl of Argyll would join them in opposition to the Queen.

The Earl of Angus did not remain long in Dalkeith and travelled next to his fortress of Tantallon. King James would write a strong letter to Henry VIII, asking him to order Angus back to

England and condemning the Earl for leading 'broken men and rebels' and 'causing great damage to his true subjects'. James would actually accuse Angus of having fooled Henry, saying he was an agent of the King of France and Albany, having been released from exile to cause mayhem in Scotland. [32]

After a visit to Tantallon, Angus went to the west of Scotland with Lennox. The Abbot of Paisley fled when Angus and Lennox invited themselves to spend Christmas in Paisley. The lords took 200 men, and as was the custom of the over-mighty they believed they had the right to quarter their force on any religious place and help themselves to the larder and other resources. The English ambassador would write to Angus, scolding him for behaving in such an oppressive way, which would not reconcile him to the Queen, or please Henry VIII. Many lords would join with Angus, yet not being able to lay siege to Edinburgh Castle for fear of the guns, they crossed the Firth of Forth after Christmas. [33]

Margaret would continue to look for peace with her brother, yet with his strange and unfathomable support for Angus' mischief, she began to look for other more reliable allies. She instructed the commissioners sent to England to negotiate for a marriage between James and Mary, daughter of Henry, yet the English counterparts wanted Scotland to forsake totally the alliance with France. Margaret would state that she could not with honour make a final peace with England 'excluding other realms', as this would give the impression that she was subservient to her brother's will.

In late December two of Albany's ships arrived in Scotland and stopped off at Dunbar. They captured a ship from Flanders and intercepted the papal bulls that were to consecrate a new Bishop of Dunkeld, dated April 27th 1524. The Frenchmen then travelled to St Andrews, where they spent Christmas with the Archbishop. Beaton's nephew David was one of the party, and they were later joined by Gonzales. More ominously for the English ambassador Magnus was that representatives of Angus, Argyll and Lennox were invited to visit St Andrews and confer with the French. The

Queen ordered the French to present themselves to the council and
return the ship, goods and papal bulls.

David Beaton, Gonzales and the French arrived at the court
on January 7th 1525 and presented to the Queen two letters from
Francis I. Fresh offers were made in which Margaret's son James
was offered marriage to Madeleine, a daughter of the King, and
Margaret was offered a pension of 30,000 crowns and a county in
France. Queen Margaret apparently taunted Dr Magnus in respect
to the sum offered as compared to what her brother had given her.

There were also secret negotiations with Gonzales, not just
concerning a marriage proposal between James and Princess
Madeleine but the possibility of a match with Catherine de Medici,
who was the ward of the Duke of Albany and who held vast estates
of the continent including some in France and Italy. Gonzales also
suggested a possible match between Queen Margaret and his
master the Duke of Albany if she could win a divorce from the Earl
of Angus. [34]

Queen Margaret used Sir James Hamilton of Finnart, the Earl
of Arran's illegitimate son, to open negotiations with the Earl of
Angus. In return for accepting divorce, Angus would be reinstated
with full titles and honours, and retain status on the Lord's
Council. Such negotiations were used as delaying tactics for the
faction around Angus. A divorce was not on his agenda, as it would
have lessened his influence with Henry VIII, and would have
deprived his daughter Margaret of any legal right through
illegitimacy as a royal heir to England. [35]

Queen Margaret became ill and confined to her bed during the
month of January. According to English reports, Gonzales rudely
promoted a reconciliation between the Queen and the Archbishop
of St Andrews by invading her bedchamber. He also proceeded to
become overly familiar with the ladies of the bedchamber in a
manner that was offensive to the Queen, a behaviour that
prompted Henry Stewart to threaten to hurl him down the
staircase. Stewart's zealous anger against the Frenchman

continued when he forced his expulsion from an audience with King James in the Privy Chamber.

Dr Magnus witnessed these incidents and would mention them in writing to Henry VIII, commending Henry Stewart. However it is also possible that Stewart was made aware of secret negotiations regarding the possibility of marriage between Queen Margaret and the Duke of Albany, and that his hostility was due to jealousy and fear of losing his influence. Gonzales publicly stated that he feared being killed by the 'the over-officious ruffling lieutenant of the guards'. [36]

The faction which appeared to be gravitating around Beaton became more significant and worrying to Magnus when Angus, Argyll and Lennox themselves showed up at St Andrews in person during January. It was feared that a dangerous pro-French faction was now developing to sweep over English interests. However whilst they were possibly considering the offers of the French, it appears that the faction around Angus, Lennox and Argyll was still supportive of friendship with England. As noted, the French, through Gonzales and David Beaton, were aiming to try and broker a peace between Margaret and the Archbishop, which might pave the way for Albany's return. Margaret decided to take Gonzales' advice and wrote to the Archbishop, the Priory of St Andrews and the Bishop of Aberdeen asking them to come to Edinburgh on January 15th, and discuss the peace negotiations with England brought to Scotland by the Earl of Cassilis, who would arrive on January 8th. Beaton declined, perhaps remembering his last incarceration and distrusting the queen. He also claimed that he was fearful of the Earl of Moray and others. Mutual distrust was the main obstacle to any agreement. [37]

A war of words ensued between the camps of Queen Margaret and the Archbishop. On January 25th an alternative parliament was held at St Andrews which vowed to free the King from the Queen's power and to bring law and order to the country. It ordered that no one must obey a command from the King until that command was considered by their council. Angus, Lennox, Argyll and Beaton were elected guardians of the King, and transferred all public offices to their authority. Having sent articles to the Queen with a list of conditions, Beaton claimed that he and his associates were not given assurances of their safety if they were to meet with Queen Margaret at an Edinburgh parliament. They especially wanted assurances that they would not be shot at by the castle ordinance.

King James replied with a proclamation that assurances had been offered and whilst the nobles and lords had accepted them, the prelates advised by Beaton had refused. Beaton's faction wrote to Henry asking for assistance against his own sister, and stating that they had the welfare of the King in mind. Beaton issued letters ordering a convention to be held at Stirling on February 6th 1525, with the purpose of releasing King James from Margaret and ordering that no one should obey the King's command under the Great Seal until consultation by the Three Estates. The Earl of Rothes would describe the nobles at St Andrews as being 'bound by ropes of sand', unable to be constrained by King's authority or other legal means. Whilst Beaton and his cohorts assured Magnus and King Henry that they were friends to England, Queen Margaret wrote to Henry insisting that Beaton was of the French interest, and was trying to draw James 'to the cast of France'. She asked for the Duke of Norfolk to support her with money and 10,000 men to come to the borders. [38]

Margaret would receive no support from her unreliable brother. The Stirling convention went ahead, and after a short meeting they allocated public offices amongst themselves. Margaret's opponents then marched towards Edinburgh. With Margaret commanding the guns of Edinburgh Castle they dared not risk entering the capital, and instead travelled to Dalkeith. When she tried to persuade the lords on her side to mobilise an army, they replied that they would do so if the King would lead them into battle. Reluctant to risk the life of her son outside the safety of Edinburgh Castle, she agreed to allow her lords to enter into negotiations with those at Dalkeith. The Earls of Arran,

Eglinton, Cassilis, Lord Maxwell and Bishop of Ross would go to Dalkeith, where the talks were apparently amicable. Margaret though was not prepared to back down, and offered the disgruntled lords and prelates the opportunity to hold an audience with her if they would cancel the convention they had called and re-acknowledge her as sovereign and regent of the King. This they refused to do, and Margaret brought her supporters back into Edinburgh. [39]

The magistrates and citizens of the city opened the gates to Angus and Lennox, who entered with 600 men after midnight on February 13th. Another 2,000 horsemen were left at Dalkeith. The Archbishop of St Andrews, the Bishop of Aberdeen and other lords and prelates then entered Edinburgh on the evening of February 14th and threatened that if any castle cannons were fired onto them the culprit's friends, lands and possessions would be targeted and wasted.

Margaret decided to enter into negotiations with Angus and his allies. Her party were given assurance that they could leave the castle and meet with the party of Angus. Both rival lords and prelates joined together for the convention, which began on February 15th and carried on to the 21st. After long and hard negotiations an agreement was finally reached by which Margaret promised that she would make her peace with Angus, although she would still seek a divorce. She would remain the head of a council of peers appointed by the parliament. She would preside over a body of six to eight other individuals for dispensing benefices, whilst she had sole responsibility for dispensing benefices of less than 1,000l. Margaret was also to be principle keeper of her son, and Angus was not to have access to her lands and possessions. The Three Estates would appoint a body of guardians to watch over James day and night, and Margaret would be deemed principle keeper of her son. The nobles who had rebelled against the Queen were absolved from any criminal procedures, as the parliament accepted that they had come to Edinburgh for the 'surety of the King's person and the common good of his realm'. They successfully argued that they had rebelled against the King's authority for his own good. Acts of treasons and forfeiture against Angus, Lennox and others were reversed and deleted out of the register. (40)

On February 24th King James was brought from Edinburgh Castle to the Tolbooth in a solemn procession and there presented with crown, sceptre and sword of state. The Earl of Angus presented the crown and his rival the Earl of Arran presented the sceptre. James was then conveyed to the Holyrood Palace, which would become his Edinburgh residence. A secret council was appointed, comprising the Archbishops of St Andrews and Glasgow, the Bishops of Aberdeen and Dunblane, the Earls of Argyll and Arran, Angus and Lennox. Beaton would later be restored as Chancellor with possession of the Great Seal, the Abbot of Holyrood regained the privy seal, and Master Patrick Hepburn, the Secretary, gained the great and small signets. Symbolic power was once more redistributed out of Margaret's hands. (41)

Despite these compromises, Queen Margaret would keep her options open and sent a letter to the Duke of Albany via John Cantely in which she outlined her fear of Angus, and stated that she would look for support from France if Henry, her brother, sided with Angus. She maintained that during peace negotiations with England she had insisted on comprehending France, which was true. Her thoughts towards Angus were revealed, and although making peace with him she preferred that they stay separate. She also asked Albany to help her procure a divorce, which in turn passed her petition to the Pope via Octavian, his agent in Berne. Magnus however learned of her dealings with Cantely and her intention of seeking to divorce Angus. (42)

Matters on the Continent would remove any possibility of Margaret receiving any help from Albany. Firstly her letters were intercepted at Milan and the contents revealed to Henry VIII and Wolsey. During the autumn of 1524 Francis had pursued the Duke of Bourbon across the Alps, whilst Henry and Charles in Spain failed to cooperate and grasp an opportunity to attack France whilst its King was out of the country. Once in Italy the French appeared to hold the military advantage. All was lost with the battle of Pavia on February 24th, which resulted in the capture of Francis I. Albany had led 6,000 troops on a march to conquer Naples, a failure, as he got entangled in local politics and the march was too slow. He remained at Rome for a while before setting off northwards. Francis was taken a prisoner to Madrid. France would be ruled by a council with Francis' mother Louise as Regent. [43]

With France weakened, Margaret's options for assistance were limited. She now had good reason to fear the influence of Angus, who, disappointed that she refused reconciliation, asked Henry's permission to 'meddle in her property' according to a promise that the English King had made in that he would support Angus against Margaret. The proud Earl also asked why his brother William had not received the benefices of Moray and Melrose, and the Papal Bulls of Coldingham, the support of which had been promised by Henry and Wolsey. Angus had such a sense of his own worth that he did not shirk from making bullish demands of an English King and Cardinal, including requests to victimize the sister of Henry. [44]

When the Lords of Council made Angus lieutenant of the east and middle marches, Margaret decided to escape the presence of her now over-powerful husband. She began to travel more freely around Scotland. Margaret and the King would arrive in Perth during March. Her lover Henry Stewart and his brothers did not feel so secure, and fearing their safety would travel to Margaret's castle at Stirling. Angus now had authority of the upper ward of Clydesdale, Tweeddale and Lauderdale and the sheriffdoms of Edinburgh, Haddington, and the Forest of Ettrick. [45]

Henry himself sent 'right sore and sharp' correspondence to his sister, delivered in private by Dr Magnus at Perth, accusing her of not taking his advice, of not reconciling with Angus, and of suspect correspondence with France and Albany. Magnus reported that the letter drove her to tears, and she complained 'never was such a letter ever written to any noble woman'. She responding defending her actions and claiming that for Henry's part she could 'have been destroyed', and that she had succeeded in getting James to claim the royal authority whilst having Albany ejected from office of governor. It is clear that she considered her brother unreliable, and requested that he should not 'cause Angus to trouble her in her living' and said she had pleaded to the Pope for a divorce from Angus and protection from his aggressive behaviour. Margaret allowed Angus a limited access to James, taking him hunting and hawking. Whilst she would moderate her behaviour and show civility to him, she would not act as his wife. She arranged several private interviews with Angus in which she tried to persuade him to agree to the divorce. Whilst James would act favourably to his stepfather in matters of martial activities, he when alone would ask Angus to grant a divorce in return for promises of royal favours. Angus alleged to Dr Magnus that Queen Margaret was coaching the son to support this position, and it appears that the thirteen-year-old King was attempting to take a leading role in this issue. Many of Angus' allies were also of the opinion that he should grant the divorce and find another favourable match, possibly the Earl of Argyll's daughter. Angus refused, citing his own honour and that of his daughter Lady Margaret Douglas, who would become illegitimate if a divorce was allowed.

During this period the nine-year-old Lady Margaret was sent for by the Earl of Angus and resided at his stronghold of Tantallon. Prior to returning to Scotland she had possibly been residing in England, and although there are no records of her exact whereabouts, Cardinal Wolsey had prior to her birth agreed to act as her godfather, and on many occasions during adulthood Lady Margaret would make use of this relationship. Wolsey also had estates in the north and he may have provided shelter and victuals for her use. [46]

The Lords of Council were also becoming disillusioned with Henry. The Earl of Cassilis, the Abbot of Cambuskenneth and the Bishop of Dunkeld were sent to England as peace commissioners, yet during negotiations, Henry was dissatisfied with Scottish attempts to comprehend France. Henry instead offered a truce until May 15th.

He was also interfering with politics and religion in Scotland in the fashion of an overlord. James V was forced to write to his uncle asking him not to write to the Pope in an act against Gavin Dunbar, Archbishop of Glasgow. Dunbar had been James' preceptor and was now one of his closest advisers, and Henry was siding with James Beaton, the Archbishop of St Andrews, in the matter of the rights of the Archbishop over privileges in Glasgow. Henry would suggest the counsellors that James should appoint. The young King would write conceding that he would consult with his uncle on any future appointees, which was a diplomatic answer at least. [(47)]

The Lords of Council wrote to the Council of France and to Louise, the mother of the captive Francis and acting Regent. It is not clear what members of the council agreed to this correspondence, but it must be assumed it was written by the pro-French sympathisers and done secretly so as not to alert the pro-English sympathisers, such as Angus. The Scots passed their sympathies to the French for the capture of Francis I and their losses in Italy. They justified their rejection of Albany's position as governor as due to him not showing at the appointed time. They also stated that in peace negotiations with England they had always pushed for the comprehension of France. Henry however was making a final peace difficult in that he did not accept a comprehension.

French envoys had arrived with a suggestion that Scotland should make a peace treaty with England to last eight months without needing to comprehend France. Henry, upon hearing of the French defeat at Pavia, decided to reject this and offer a peace treaty until James' minority was at an end, without comprehending France. The Scots asked the French to provide arms and money so that they could prosecute war against England, or alternately they would make a treaty with England until the King reaches his majority. [(48)]

Short-term truces were agreed between Scotland and England, to last until a more long-term treaty could be negotiated. The problem however was the organised criminality on the borders. Parliamentary Acts were raised condemning the clans that were benefiting from this trade; the riders of Annandale, Liddlesdale, the Merse, Teviotdale, Ewesdale and Eskdale were especially singled out, as they were preying on the northern English communities. The English border clans of Tyndale, such as the Charltons and others, had entered into a bloody feud with the English wardens, and were accused of receiving assistance and shelter from the Scottish riders of Ewesdale and Liddlesdale, especially the powerful Armstrongs. There were also fears that the Lords of Council were giving the English rebels assistance, which may not have been wrong as during March Scots borderers and '400 Highlanders' had been reported to have joined together and raided within eight miles of Newcastle. [49]

The Earl of Angus on March 15th was appointed lieutenant of the Middle and Eastern marches, taking an oath that he would suppress 'theft, reif, slaughter, and all other inconveniences' inflicted on the subjects of the King. Lord Hume also pledged to serve Angus in bringing law and order to the middle and east marches. Letters were sent out to lords and barons commanding them to make pledges before the Council to serve Angus in pacifying the borders. The important border lairds such as Walter Scott of Buccleough, Andrew Kerr of Ferniehurst and his namesake Andrew Kerr of Cessford, all bound themselves to serve Angus and to expel from Ettrick Forest and Teviotdale all men, women and children from Liddlesdale, Eskdale and Ewesdale who had sheltered there. Many of these men would be of the Armstrong clan, which would create complications for border co-operation.

Lord Maxwell was appointed warden of the Western Marches, and was said to enjoy a working relationship with the Liddlesdale Armstrongs, the main malefactors on the borders. Maxwell entered into a bond of manrent with a notorious raider called Johnnie of Gilnockie. In return for vowing that he and his heirs would engage in mutual aid and assistance with Maxwell and his heirs, Johnnie was granted the tenancy of lands in Eskdale, near Langholm. Johnnie had two tower houses, Hollows and Gilnockie, the former near Canonbie Parish in the Debatable Land. Johnnie would lead a tough crew to continuously raid the English borders, burning settlements and homes, lifting livestock and extorting blackmail, whilst the English wardens seemed incapable in stopping him. Maxwell did not fulfil his own responsibilities in arresting Johnnie, and it appears that his activities not only infuriated the English but discredited Angus' ability to dispense law on the borders. A prior judicial raid of March/April appears to have been a failure, despite the large numbers that Angus managed to raise in support. [50]

The Earl of Angus and the Bishop of Glasgow would mount a twin police and ecclesial assault on Liddlesdale during May, where during a four-day raid Angus captured several prominent Armstrongs such as Sym the Laird and Davy the Lady. 4,000 livestock were lifted and numerous homes were burned. The Bishop of Glasgow excommunicated the border raiders in an over 1,500 word *Monition of Cursing*, which was proclaimed and published through the borders, and was apparently admired by Cardinal Wolsey when he heard a rendition.

Angus' incursion did little to halt the Liddlesdale raiders from continuing to support their English outlaw allies across the border. However, throughout the summer the English wardens were unhappy with Angus' contribution to negotiations on the borders, with his failures to meet for 'Days of Truce' and his inability to stop the continual raids by Scottish thieves into England. The biggest fear for the English authorities was that in the event of war with Scotland the Tyndale rebels would harbour and assist Scottish raiders. Apart from the above expeditions Angus appears to have been reluctant to leave Edinburgh or be too far from the source of power in Scotland. He made numerous excuses to his English counterparts for non-attendance. During this period he was faced with divorce proceedings from the Queen, who was determined to end their association. [51]

Louise of France would respond favourably to Scottish correspondence from Margaret and the pro-French faction. However, she did concede that at the moment of writing she could not send Albany or any men due to lack of resources. An ambassador, Seigneur de Saignes, was to be sent to Scotland with offers to Queen Margaret of a pension of 4,000 livres if she stayed loyal to the alliance with France, and a safe shelter in France if she found her life and safety threatened. Fully informed by Margaret of the negotiations with England of a possible marriage between James and Henry's daughter, in which James would be named as Henry's heir if he failed to sire a son, the ambassador was to remind Margaret that Henry had previously offered his daughter Mary to the dauphin of France and later to the Emperor, and these were examples of promises that Henry had failed to keep. Louise offered a daughter of Francis to the King of Scotland. [52]

Albany still stayed active as a representative of Scottish interests on the continent, still terming himself Governor of Scotland, and admonishing the Pope for supporting English interests and Henry VIII's recommendations in the dispensing of Scottish benefices. Whilst in Italy he asked the Pope to reverse any acts which were 'to the prejudice of Scotland'. Despite suffering from 'colic and fever', he petitioned the Cardinals of the Holy College and the Cardinal of Ancona to act on his behalf in petitioning the pope. Through communications from Queen Margaret and King James he was aware of the political struggles ensuing in Scotland. He was also endeavouring to get the Pope to agree to Margaret divorcing Angus. [53]

Queen Margaret would stay away from Edinburgh and reside in Stirling, claiming that she stayed away out of fear of Angus. She also left her son in Edinburgh, although the circumstances for this separation of Queen and King are not recorded. If she did believe that Angus intended to do her harm, then she would want to keep some distance between James and herself so that in the event of an attack he would not get hurt. Her absence ensured that she was not able to fulfil her duties as Queen, and thereby the Earl of

Angus and other lords began to dominate the government.

The Scottish parliament with the King present commenced on July 6th. One of the first orders of business was the Queen making divorce proceedings against Angus, and also requesting expenses in respect that Angus had been helping himself to revenue from her lands and possessions. In order to attend the parliament Margaret also expected Angus to make caution in the form of 'great sums' of money, so that she or her household would be free to travel to and from Edinburgh without fear of harm from Angus. The Earl replied that he would provide the caution, although he insisted that he never 'as yet did any harm to her person' and that 'her grace shall be unharmed by me and all that I may let'. Angus though still described himself as her husband and believed he still had legal and spiritual rights over her, acting as if he were the injured party. However, Margaret, with good reason, feared her husband, and did not discount his capability to try and abduct her son or herself. (54)

With the capture of the King of France, prospects for the French nation did not altogether look promising, and Scots of the French faction would have dreaded the loss of a valuable ally, and the domination of the English faction in Scotland. It was Cardinal Wolsey who brightened Scottish prospects, fearing a resurgent empire on the continent; he began to look to France as a counterweight and to open negotiations with the French. This would result in a treaty of peace. The Scots, whilst keeping options open with France, manage to negotiate a treaty of peace with England to last three years, agreed at the Edinburgh Parliament on July 31st. Louise of France, being fearful that Scotland would reject the Treaty of Rouen, offered to James Beaton the Archbishop of St Andrews her influence in acquiring for him a cardinal's hat, whist his nephew David Beaton and the Abbot of Arbroath was offered a lucrative benefice in France. Cardinal Wolsey also tried to win Beaton's alliance with similar offers, and it is clear that the Archbishop would play both sides against each other in this bidding war.

It was through James Beaton's efforts and those of his cohorts in the Scottish parliament that certain pro-French conditions were entered into the treaty proposals. The Scots would seek to comprehend France, yet if that was not possible they were duty bound through previous treaties to assist France by providing men, supplies and ships if requested. Henry VIII was also to use his offices to promote friendship between Scotland and the Empire. The agreement came at an opportune time, as on August 14th France and England would enter into a truce to last until December 1st 1525. The Scots, after some initial resistance from the English ambassadors, were offered the option of comprehending themselves if they wished. (55)

The parliament also settled the issue of appointing secret councils for the King, and came up with a novel idea whereby every three months the council would change its members. In theory this would have allowed James the opportunity to learn more about the nobles and prelates under his kingship. The first member of this council was Angus, which must have been a blow to Margaret and indicates the power and influence Angus had acquired for himself since his return to Scotland. He would join the council along with Gavin Dunbar, Archbishop of Glasgow, James Douglas, Earl of Morton, George Crichton, Abbot of Holyroodhouse, Lord George Seton and David Beaton, Abbot of Arbroath. Their appointments were to last until November 1st and then a new body would take over. Angus and the Bishop of Glasgow were appointed commissioners with special powers to treat for peace with England.

Margaret was demoted of the authority granted to her at the parliament of February 15th, and seemingly all 'gifts, dispositions, donations, acts and statutes' were now the sole responsibility of the council acting in the King's name. King James was present at the parliament and made a speech in her defence. He made a statement which said: 'I trust that the Queen my mother hath not so highly offended, that her Grace should lose, or be put from her authority?' He requested 'that the act be respited, or put to some better train'. After deliberation Queen Margaret was allowed 20 days to come to the parliament and address and challenge these changes, and would for that occasion be allowed full authority. But if she did not show she would be automatically deprived of these powers. Angus also deprived the Earl of Moray of the wardship of Huntley by taken possession of the young Earl of Huntley. He also halted the proposed marriage between his daughter Lady Margaret Douglas and the Earl of Moray. [56]

Margaret did not attend the August parliament, no doubt realising that Angus and her enemies had successfully pushed her from government. Apart from a few loyal allies she could not at that time raise sufficient forces to ensure her safety. She remained in Stirling, and there is correspondence suggesting that the latter turn of events was leaving her despondent. An inquiry had been made to the English King and Council requesting that she should return to England. Henry preferred her to remain in Scotland and stay close to the King. She was evidently distrustful of the ambassador Magnus and the policies of England regarding her. Dr Magnus would through correspondence try to assure Queen Margaret that she would be safe if she returned to Edinburgh. She would not comply, and unfounded rumours would circulate that the true reason she stayed in Stirling was that she was pregnant by Henry Stewart.

Despite assurances from Angus that he would serve Margaret honourably if she was kind to him, Dr Magnus appears to have believed that King James had conveyed a different message and did not believe that his mother would be safe amongst such dangerous people. If true, then James was prepared to subject himself to the ambitions and conspiracies of the nobility, whilst his mother could remain out of danger. Without a mother to guide or advise him, the young King would have to rely on his own youthful judgement amongst a sea of political intriguers. It would be a learning experience that would mould his personality. [57]

Magnus would report that there were divisions within the Council. The Archbishop of Glasgow was accused of being supportive of Albany returning to Scotland. The ambassador from

France, de Saignes, arrived at French-occupied Dunbar in September and paid wages to French soldiers before arriving at Leith. He was rudely attended by the Scots council and nobility, with no one providing adequate lodgings or visiting.

He next went to Fife and met with the Archbishop of St Andrews and the Chancellor of Scotland. It appeared that the King did not wish to meet with the ambassador, and there were suggestions that this was because of Angus, who stayed close to the King and influenced his mind and actions, 'being afraid of being put from him'.

Once Angus had left Edinburgh the ambassador met with the King, on October 10th, gave him letters from the Queen-Regent of France and from Albany and presented the gift of a small dagger from the latter. James was reportedly angry when the ambassador passed on an apology from Albany because he had not returned to Scotland as requested. James denied that he had asked Albany to return and left for Dalkeith to get away from the ambassador. [58]

On September 17th 1525 in London, a treaty of peace was agreed between England and France, with Scotland free to comprehend into the treaty. At Berwick the Scots and English commissioners, who included the Earls of Angus, Arran, Lennox and Morton and the Archbishops of St Andrews and Glasgow, amongst others, agree to a three-year peace, with the Scots insisting on a general comprehension for France. Magnus would warn Beaton in a letter that a comprehension might not be accepted by Henry VIII. [59]

It was reported by English commentators that Angus was using his position as Counsellor and Warden of the Marches to pursue personal feuds. He was unreliable at showing up at Days of Truce and settling redresses, and the Archbishop of St Andrews scolded him for not being vigorous enough in punishing the Liddlesdale Armstrongs, or any other Scots, for raids committed in England. His failure to prosecute significantly against the Armstrongs may be down to the complexities of border politics. The Maxwells had long been fighting the Johnstones over control of the

Western Marches. The actual reason for this feud, which would carry on to be one of the longest in Scottish or British history, is not entirely clear, although it seems to have originated in the early 16th century. The latest round of this contest commenced after the death of an Armstrong at the hands of the Johnstones, and as Lord Maxwell had entered into bonds of friendship with the Armstrongs he was bound to wage war against the Johnstones. Maxwell's support of the Armstrongs was also directly allowing Armstrong raids into England and their armed support of English rebels. This was undermining both Scottish-English border relations and Angus' reputation as a border lieutenant. He in turn would allegedly, although he would later deny it, give support to John Johnstone of that Ilk against Maxwell. [60]

Despite border complications Angus was aiming to acquire more political power and would soon show the extent of his mind and ambition. On November 1st, the date on which the council was expected to hand over King James to a new council, he refused, and took full possession of the King. The next council was made up of the Earl of Arran, Gavin Dunbar, Bishop of Aberdeen, John Hepburn, Bishop of Brechin, Hugh Montgomery, Earl of Eglinton, Robert Shaw, Abbot of Paisley, and John Lord Forbes. Angus took the role of Lieutenant, taking the 'whole rule and government of the King and realm upon him', and bestowed state offices to his family and supporters, his brother George becoming master of the Household and his uncle Archibald becoming once more provost of Edinburgh. Buchanan states that Douglas took the King to the home of the Archbishop of St Andrews and took over the latter's furniture and possessions. He also deprived him of the Great Seal and Chancellorship. It was said that to distract James' mind from his predicament the Douglases would encourage him to indulge in 'every unlawful enjoyment'. James, who would have a reputation in later life for promiscuousness, appears to have begun this behaviour in his early teenage years. Albany, having received reports of the condition of his cousin, would complain to the Pope about the corrupting influence of the Douglases. [61]

The Earl of Arran withdrew to his Clydeside Estates whilst his son, Sir James of Finnart, began to fortify the castle of Cadzow, near Hamilton. Queen Margaret retired from Stirling to the far north, where she would reside over the winter in Elgin with the Earl of Moray. In the next few months, as the Douglases set out to consolidate power, Scotland would once more divide into opposing factions as Arran and Moray began to gather forces south and north of the Firth of Forth.

Chapter Six: References

(1) (Herkless & Hannay, vol.3, pp. 106-107. LP, James Steward, January 22nd, 1524. ODNB, vol.52, pp. 684-685). (2) (Lesley, pp. 127-128. LP, Agreement between Queen Margaret and the Duke of Albany, April 21st, 1524. LP, Dacre to Wolsey, April 25th, 1524. LP, Dacre to Albany, April 24th, 1524. LP, May 27th, Dacre to Queen Margaret, 1524. SP, vol.4, pp. 532-535). (3) (Strickland, vol.1, pp. 173-175). (4) (Herkless & Hannay, vol.3, pp. 107-111. LP, Dacre to the Chancellor of Scotland, June 4th, 1524.ODNB, vol.52, pp. 709-715.Strickland, vol.1, pp. 174-176). (5) (Herkless & Hannay, vol.3, pp. 107-111. LP, Dacre to the Chancellor of Scotland, June 4th, 1524. ODNB, vol.52, pp. 709-715). (6) (Holinshed, pp. 497-500. Lesley, pp. 127-129. LP, Dacre to Wolsey, July 10th, 1524). (7) (Buchanan. p.289. Fraser, pp. 199-200). (8) (ALCPA, p.204. Herkless & Hannay, vol.2, pp. 10-115. LP, Wolsey to Dacre, July 8th, 1524. LP, Dacre to the Chancellor of Scotland, July 16th, 1524) . (9) Herkless & Hannay, vol.3, pp. 113-115. LP, Queen Margaret to Henry VIII, July 13th, 1524.LP, Queen Margaret to Wolsey, July 16th, 1524. LP, Henry VIII to Queen Margaret, July 21st, 1524). (10) (Fraser, pp. 199-201).

(11) (Buchanan, pp. 288-291. Herkless & Hannay, vol.3, pp. 113-116. Lesley, pp. 198-201. LP, Scotland, August 1st, 1524. Tytler, pp. 174-176. LP, Wolsey to Norfolk, September 4th, 1524. ODNB, vol.24, pp. 823-826. Strickland, vol.1, pp. 175-177). (12) (ALCPA, pp. 204-205. Buchanan, pp. 288-291. Herkless & Hannay, vol.3, pp. 113-116. Lesley, pp. 198-201. LP, Scotland, August 1st, 1524.Thomson, vol.2, pp. 560-561. Tytler, pp. 174-176. LP, Wolsey to Norfolk, September 4th, 1524. ODNB, vol.24, pp. 823-826. ODNB, vol.17, pp. 204-207). (13) (LP, Queen Margaret to Norfolk, August, 1524. LP, Wolsey to Norfolk, August 1st, 1524. LP, Queen Margaret to Thomas Hamilton, August 9th, 1524. LP, Wolsey to Norfolk, August 13th, 1524. LP, Scotland,

1524. LP, Margaret to Henry VIII, August 31st, 1524. Tytler, pp. 174-177). (14) (LP, Queen Margaret to Norfolk, August, 1524. LP, Wolsey to Norfolk, August 1st, 1524. LP, Queen Margaret to Thomas Hamilton, August 9th, 1524. LP, Wolsey to Norfolk, August 13th, 1524. LP, Scotland, 1524. LP, Margaret to Henry VIII, August 31st, 1524. Strickland, vol.1, pp. 179-180.Strickland, vol.1, pp. 183-185. Tytler, pp. 174-177). (15) Herkless & Hannay, vol.3, pp. 117-119. LP, Wolsey to Norfolk, August 19th, 1524. LP, Wolsey to Norfolk, August 20th, 1524. LP, Scotland, September 4th, 1524. LP, Scotland, September 5th, 1524). (16) Herkless & Hannay, vol.3, pp. 120-125. LP, Istringi to David Beaton, September 15th, 1524. LP, Scotland, 1524. Strickland, vol.1, pp. 180-181. Thomson, vol.2, pp. 560-561). (17) Herkless & Hannay, vol.3, pp. 121-126. LP, Wolsey to Norfolk, September 4th, 1524. LP, Norfolk to Wolsey, September 19th, 1524. (18) LP, Queen Margaret to Henry VIII, August 31st, 1524. LP, Scotland, September 4th, 1524. LP, Scotland, September 5th, 1524. LP, Queen Margaret to Norfolk, September 14th, 1524 LP, Wolsey to Norfolk, September 15th, 1524. Strickland, vol.1, pp. 191-192. (19) LP, Gonzales to James V, September 5th, 1524. LP, Sir Wm Sandys to Wolsey, September 5th, 1524. LP, Norfolk to Wolsey, September 19th, 1524). (20) LP, Queen Margaret to Norfolk, September 14th, 1524. LP, September 19th, Norfolk to Wolsey, 1524. LP, Magnus and Radcliff to Wolsey, November 2nd, 1524.ODNB, vol.37, pp. 526-528. (21) LP, Queen Margaret to Norfolk, September 14th, 1524. LP, September 19th, Norfolk to Wolsey, 1524. LP, Magnus and Radcliff to Wolsey, November 2nd, 1524. ODNB, vol.52, p.674. SP, vol.VI, pp. 166-168. Strickland, vol.1, pp. 180-182. (22) (Buchanan, p.289. Fraser, pp. 202-204. Herkless & Hannay, vol.3, pp. 126-132. LP, Queen Margaret to Henry VIII, October 6th, 1524. LP, Queen Margaret to Wolsey, October 6th, 1524. LP, Norfolk, Dacre, Magnus and Radcliff to Wolsey, October 23rd, 1524. Strickland, vol.1, pp. 181-182. (23) Buchanan, p.289. Fraser, pp. 202-204. Herkless & Hannay, vol.3, pp. 126-132. LP, Queen Margaret to Henry VIII, October 6th, 1524. LP, Queen Margaret to Wolsey, October 6th, 1524. LP, Norfolk, Dacre, Magnus and Radcliff to Wolsey, October 23rd, 1524. Strickland, vol.1, pp. 182-183. (24) (Buchanan, p.289. LP, Magnus and Radcliff to Wolsey, October 20th, 1524. LP, Norfolk, Dacre, Magnus and Radcliff to Wolsey, October 23rd, 1524.ODNB, vol.52, pp. 709-715. SP, vol.6, pp. 311-312. (26) (Fraser, pp. 200-202. Herkless & Hannay, vol.3, pp. 126-132. LP, Queen Margaret to Henry VIII, October 6th, 1524. LP, Queen Margaret to Wolsey, October 6th, 1524. LP, Norfolk, Dacre, Magnus and Radcliff to Wolsey, October 23rd, 1524. LP, Wolsey to Norfolk, November 5th, 1524. LP, Norfolk to Queen Margaret, November 8th, 1524. Strickland, vol.1, pp. 189-191. (27) (Fraser, pp. 205-206. Lesley, pp. 199-202. LP, Wolsey to Magnus and Radcliff, October 24th, 1524. LP, Magnus and

Radcliff to Wolsey, November 2nd, 1524. LP, Norfolk to Angus, November 7th, 1524. LP, Queen Margaret to Henry VIII, November 7th, 1524. Strickland, vol.1, pp. 182-184. Strickland, vol.1, pp. 202-204. Thomson, vol.2, pp. 562-563. Tytler, pp. 177-180. (28) Buchanan, p.289. Fraser, pp. 205-206. Lesley, pp. 199-202. LP, Wolsey to Magnus and Radcliff, October 24th, 1524. LP, Magnus and Radcliff to Wolsey, November 2nd, 1524. LP, Norfolk to Angus, November 7th, 1524. LP, Queen Margaret to Henry VIII, November 7th, 1524. Strickland, vol.1, pp. 187-190. Strickland, vol.2, pp. 251-252. Tytler, pp. 177-180. (29) LP, Wolsey to Magnus and Radcliff, October 24th, 1524. LP, George Douglas to Norfolk, October 24th, 1524. LP, Magnus and Radcliff to Wolsey, November 2nd, 1524. Tytler, pp. 177-182. (30) (Fraser, pp. 206-207. Herkless & Hannay, vol.3, pp. 139-142. Lesley, pp. 199-202. LP, The Parliament of Scotland, November 27th, 1524. RPS, November 18th, 1524. Thomson, vol.2, pp. 563-564. Tytler, pp. 177-180. (31) (Fraser, pp. 206-207. Strickland, vol.1, pp. 193-195. Thomson, vol.2, pp. 563-564. Tytler, pp. 177-180). (32) (Buchanan, pp. 289-290. Fraser, pp. 206-207. LP, James V to Henry VIII, November 27th, 1524. Strickland, vol.1, pp. 193-195. Thomson, vol.2, pp. 563-564. Tytler, pp. 177-182. (33) (Buchanan, pp. 289-291. CSPS, vol.1, Magnus to the Earl of Angus, Dec 15th, 1524, p.20. Fraser, pp. 208-209. Thompson, vol.3, pp. 16-17.T ytler, pp. 180-183. (34) (Buchanan, pp. 289-290. Dowden, pp. 86-87. Herkless & Hannay, vol.3, pp. 144-149. Lesley, pp. 130-132. LP, Scotland, December, 1524 LP, Magnus to Wolsey, January 9th, 1525. Strickland, vol.1, pp. 198-200. Thomson, vol.3, pp. 38. (35) (Strickland, vol.1, pp. 199-200. (36) Buchanan, pp. 289-290. Dowden, pp. 86-87. Herkless & Hannay, vol.3, pp. 144-149. Lesley, pp. 130-132. LP, Scotland, December, 1524 LP, Magnus to Wolsey, January 9th, 1525. Strickland, vol.1, pp. 199-200. Thomson, vol.3, pp. 38. (37) (Buchanan, pp. 289-290. Herkless & Hannay, vol.3, pp. 146-149. LP, Magnus to Wolsey, January 9th, 1525. Strickland, vol.1, pp. 200-201. (38) Buchanan, pp. 289-290. Herkless & Hannay, vol.3, pp. 147-149. LP, Queen Margaret to Henry VIII, January 24th, 1525. LP, Scotland, January 24th, 1525. LP, Scotland, January 25th, 1525. (39) (Buchanan, pp. 289-290. Fraser, pp. 206-209. Thomson, vol.2, pp. 564-565. (40) (Fraser, pp. 207-210. Herkless & Hannay, vol.3, pp. 147-150. Lesley, pp. 130-133. LP, Magnus to Wolsey, February 22nd, 1525. LP, Queen Margaret and Angus, February 23rd, 1525. ODNB, vol.4, pp. 554-557. RSP, February 18th, 1525. RSP, February 19th, 1525, 1525. Strickland, vol.1, pp. 201-203. Tyler. pp. 179-182). (41) ALCPA, pp. 212-213. Herkless & Hannay, vol.3, pp. 147-150. Lesley, pp. 130-133. LP, Magnus to Wolsey, February 22nd, 1525. LP, Queen Margaret and Angus, February 23rd, 1525. ODNB, vol.4, pp. 554-557. RSP, February 18th, 1525. RSP, February 19th, 1525, 1525. Strickland, vol.1, pp. 201-202.

Tyler. pp. 179-182. (42) LP, Instructions by Queen Margaret to John Cantely, February 22nd, 1525. LP, Magnus to Wolsey, February 22nd, 1525. Thomson, vol.2, pp. 564-565. (43) (Johnson, pp. 172-174. ODNB, vol.52, pp. 709-715. Thomson, vol.2, pp. 564-565. (44) (ALCPA, pp. 218-219. Fraser, pp. 208-210. LP, Angus to Wolsey, March 8th, 1525. LP, Magnus to Wolsey, March 31st, 1525. LP, Queen Margaret to Henry VIII, 1525. LP, Magnus to Wolsey, April 27th, 1525. Strickland, vol.1, pp. 203-204. (45) (ALCPA, pp. 218-219. Fraser, pp. 208-210. LP, Angus to Wolsey, March 8th, 1525. Strickland, vol.1, pp. 202-203. (46) (ALCPA, pp. 218-219. Fraser, pp. 208-210. LP, Angus to Wolsey, March 8th, 1525. LP, Magnus to Wolsey, March 31st, 1525. LP, Queen Margaret to Henry VIII, 1525. LP, Magnus to Wolsey, April 27th, 1525. Strickland, vol.1, pp. 202-204. Strickland, vol.2, pp. 247-248. (47) LP, Bishop of Dunkeld, Earl of Cassilis, Abbot of Cambuskenneth, April 19th, 1525. LP, LP, James V to Henry VIII, May 28th, 1525. LP, James V to Henry VIII, June 8th, 1525. (48) LP, France and Scotland, April 1st, 1525. LP, Magnus to Wolsey, April 27th, 1525. (49) LP, Scotland, March 24th, 1525. LP, William Frankeleyn to Wolsey, April 1st, 1525. (51) LP, Sir William Bulmer and Sir William Eure to Wolsey, May 16th, 1525. LP, Sir William Eure to Wolsey, June 23rd, 1525. LP, Magnus to Wolsey, June 23rd, 1525. LP, Sir William Eure to Wolsey, July 8th, 1525. MacDonald Fraser, pp. 225-227. RSP, February, 1525. (52) LP, France and Scotland, July 1st, 1525. (53) LP, Albany to the pope, June 23rd, 1525. LP, Albany to Cardinals of the Holy College, June 24th, 1525. LP, Albany to Count de Carpy, June 24th, 1525. LP, Albany to the Cardinal of Ancona, June 24th, 1525. (54) RSP, July 1525. (55) Bindoff, pp. 70-73. SP Venice, Cicogna Copy of the Navagero Despatches, Letter no. 383, August 10th, 1525. Herkless & Hannay, vol.3, pp. 150-152. LP, Magnus to Wolsey, May 31st, 1525. LP, England and France, August 14th, 1525. RSP, July 31st 1525. (56) LP, The Parliament of Scotland, August 10th, 1525. ODNB, vol.52, pp. 684-685. RPS, July 1525. Strickland, vol.1, pp. 205-206. (57) LP, Magnus to Queen Margaret, August 30th, 1525. Strickland, vol.1, pp. 205-206. (58) LP, Magnus to Wolsey, September 9th, 1525. LP, Magnus to Wolsey, September 28th, 1525. LP, Magnus to Wolsey, October 28th, 1525. (59) LP, Francis I and Henry VIII, September 17th, 1525. LP, Magnus to Archbishop Beaton, October 16th, 1525. LP, Scotland, October 31st, 1525. (60) LP, Magnus to Archbishop Beaton, October 16th, 1525. ODNB, vol.37,pp. 526-528. (61) Buchanan, pp. 290-292. RSP, July 1525.

Chapter Seven

IF THY BODY SHOULD BE
TORN TO PIECES: 1525-1528

Francis I, a comfortable captive in Spain, signed the Treaty of Madrid on January 14th 1526. He agreed to give up claims to Milan, Naples, Genoa, Flanders, Artois, Tournai and Burgundy. He was released on March 17th, 1526. Despite leaving behind two sons as hostages, Francis upon reaching Paris would immediately repudiate the treaty, claiming he signed under duress. On May 22nd he joined the League of Cognac, a military alliance against the Hapsburg Empire which comprised the Pope, and the City States of Milan, Venice and Florence. England was also invited and although Henry had sympathy for the League, he did not join. [1]

Conflicts would continue on the Scottish-English borders with Angus still seemingly unable to call a halt to them, or control the Scottish raiders. Nevertheless a meeting was arranged at Berwick for January 13th, 1526 in which a peace treaty lasting three years was to be ratified. Further dates of 16th and 17th are allocated for days of truce. The Abbot of Holyroodhouse and Adam Otterburn are the two commissioners who represent the Scots, whilst Angus sent messengers with authority to carry his seals for the ratifications. The Earl of Angus during this period travelled with a strong company as the Douglases were now at feud with the Humes, who were angered at being sidelined out of government by their former partners in robbery and murder.

Besides Angus' own problems with powerful border gangs, rival assemblies were being organised by opponents to his rule and government. The Earl of Arran was mobilising an army in opposition to Angus at Linlithgow, and the Humes and Kerrs of Cessford and Ferniehurst were joining him. The Lords of Council allowed a 'respite to be granted' so that both sides could talk out their differences. However, such a respite would benefit Arran, as the Earl of Moray was coming from the north accompanied by the Queen. Other forces in support were also gathering at Stirling. The Lord Council was 'uncertain' of his intentions although there were fears that he intended to march to the borders and prevent the peace treaty, thereby undermining Angus' government. The forces of the Queen proclaimed that Angus and his two allies Lennox and Argyll intended to send the young King to England whilst they ruled in his stead. [2]

The treaty between Scotland and England was ratified on the appointed day of January 13th. Angus joined with Lennox and Argyll at Edinburgh and proceeded to Linlithgow to confront Arran and the Queen. Angus also brought the King, supposedly against his will, to accompany his force, which he stated was 700 foot and horse. The Queen and Arran was joined by the Earls of Cassilis and Eglinton, the Bishop of Ross, the lords Ross, Semple and Avondale, the Abbot of Jedworth and others. Lesley wrongly states that Argyll and the Archbishop of St Andrews were with the Queen, yet he is correct in stating that Angus approached the Queen's forces with the King's banner displayed, and there was reluctance on the part of opposition to fight against the King.

Arran withdrew to his castle at Hamilton and the Queen retired to Stirling before going further north across the Firth of Forth. The Earl of Moray and the northern lords who had allied with Arran decided to make their peace with Angus, and submitted at Linlithgow before escorting the victors to Edinburgh. Moray was made a member of the secret council and offers were made to Arran, although he would hold out longer. Margaret would also be brought into the peace, and Magnus would write to her, informing that Henry VIII insisted that she was to be comprehended into the peace treaty. As she would not reconcile with Angus she at least should be allowed to live in peace and enjoy her dowry. [3]

Magnus would inform Wolsey 'that the borders have never been better ruled', which possibly reflects the effectiveness of the English wardens and not their Scottish counterparts, as many of the English wardens were not satisfied with Angus' performance as lieutenant. Redresses were often hard to come by as Angus appeared reluctant to go against the riders of Liddlesdale. There were also questions of whether he or Lord Maxwell have authority over that area. Many Days of Truces had been cancelled for various reasons but mainly through Angus' non-attendance. Angus was also hampered by feuding with the Humes and Kerrs of Ferniehurst, who whilst obeying the Lord's Council refused to recognize the authority of Angus. To try and satisfy the complaints of the English, the Council put the blame on Angus for lack of action, and called on the principle clan leaders of Teviotdale, the Merse and Liddlesdale to come to Edinburgh and face questions from the council in respect to the raids and incursions originating from these areas. Lord George Hume and Andrew Kerr of Ferniehurst declined the invitation, which prompted the Council to order them to show or face charges of treason. [4]

Angus would explain to Magnus that many borderers were declining to give redress because news had passed from the continent that Albany was preparing to return to Scotland. Many allies of Albany were emboldened by this news and therefore reluctant to obey Angus. His other enemy, the Earl of Arran, would eventually make his peace with Angus, resulting in being invited to attend parliament, although he is not recorded as taking part in the secret councils. It also appears that the danger of Albany's return compelled Angus to enter into a process by which James, once entering into his fourteenth year, was declared to have now entered his majority and could now rule as an independent sovereign. This occurred at a parliament on June 13th, 1526. [5]

At this parliament there was a judicial attempt to bring some order to the borders. Lord George Hume and Andrew Kerr of Ferniehurst had been threatened with treason and ordered to come before the Three Estates to answer charges. From February 1526 they had refused the summons to Council in Edinburgh, until June 20th, when they both appeared before the Three Estates at Edinburgh. Both were accused of disobeying the Lieutenant and failing to attend Days of Truce, or surrender their attendants, adherents and tenants accused of criminal offences by the English wardens. They were also accused of attempting to undermine the authority of the King and disrupt the peace between Scotland and England, as well as entering leagues with the King's enemy, a reference to the mobilising at Linlithgow along with Queen Margaret and Arran.

Lord Home and the Laird of Ferniehurst would deny the charges against them, and whilst the details are not recorded they would have presented a defence with justifications for their actions. The Three Estates deliberated on the charges and ruled in favour of the accused, absolving them from the points made in the summons of treason and declaring them innocent and free. [6]

This act of absolution ensured that for a short time at least the Hume and Kerrs would work alongside Angus in pacifying the borders. The parliament also settled the issue of the secret council appointing the Archbishops of St Andrews and Glasgow, the bishops of Aberdeen and Galloway and the Earls of Angus, Lennox and Argyll, Glencairn, Morton and Lord Maxwell.

On June 25th William, the son of Cuthbert Cunningham, Earl of Glencairn, was made Lord High Treasurer for a period of four years. Archibald Douglas of Kilspindie, Provost of Edinburgh, was given principle authority to search the port of Leith for attempts to smuggle gold and silver, 'coined or uncoined', out of Scotland. He was also to assign people to search other ports throughout Scotland. One half of that recovered was to go to James and the other half to the searchers. As one can imagine, these searches would be a valuable source of money and funds. Kilspindie would develop a close relationship with James, who in the spirit of a popular poem nicknamed Kilspindie 'Greysteel' after the main character in the work, who was a formidable knight and swordsman.

Buchanan would describe the Earl of Angus' judicial efforts on the borders as 'his many unsuccessful expeditions for checking robberies', yet at the parliament James awarded him a gift of £1,600. A new coin was also produced, contemptuously nicknamed the 'Douglas groat', which was a severely undervalued currency. James was under the control of the Douglases, who were profiting immensely and draining crown finances of much-needed revenue. [7]

The Archbishop of St Andrews was deprived of the office of Chancellor and the Great Seal taken from him by Angus. Although Angus would not be confirmed as Chancellor until August 8th 1527, this technicality did not stop him from using the Great Seal to his profit and advantage, and persuading King James to put his signature to many deeds placed before him. To emphasise his hold on the young King, according to a letter written by Margaret to Wolsey, Angus compelled James to write to the pope claiming that Beaton was the real villain and had usurped royal authority. As a young prince of fourteen years of age it would have been extremely difficult to challenge the restrictive rule of the Douglases, who practically dominated his every waking and sleeping moment. Although his dislike of the Douglases began to grow and to be expressed openly, nevertheless to escape this humiliating imprisonment he needed allies to help them. Once parliament was dismissed he struck up a bond of mutual assistance with the Earl of Lennox, who, like other nobles, was becoming weary of the

Douglases and their continued greed for acquiring state offices, money and position. Lennox was an individual with 'suavity of manners, peculiarly engaging', and the young King could freely confide in his cousin. Lennox would make a commitment to try and organise James' rescue. [8]

A plan would emerge during late July by which James, in the company of Angus and the Humes and Kerrs, would travel to Jedburgh for administering justice, or in the words of a letter from the Council of Scotland to the Earl of Cumberland, to 'pursue the thieves, burn their goods, take their wives and bairns, and ship them to some foreign land'. Such was the nature of royal justice.

Angus was not able to impose order in this wild region and believed that the presence of the King would compel the borderers to submit to his authority. Lennox, who was also in the King's company, would send a message from James to his adherent Walter Scott, Laird of Buccleough, asking him to attempt a rescue of the King. Besides commanding the Scotts, Buccleough could also rely on the Armstrongs and Elliots as allies. James arrived at Jedburgh on July 20th and sent for all the leading lords, ordering them to bring in all the known robbers. Many of those brought in were punished or pardoned depending on the amount of money or goods they could offer as recompense for their crimes. Buccleough had a residence near Jedburgh, and invited James to be his guest. From there he planned to retain the King as his guest until a large enough force could gather and counter that of Angus and the Douglass. Word of the plot came to Angus and he quickly withdrew the King towards Melrose, intending to take him back to Edinburgh. [9]

On July 23rd Buccleough set off in pursuit with 600 riders. According to Pitscottie, Lord Hume and the Kerrs of Ferniehurst and Cessford had left James' company to return home. Buccleough saw his opportunity, and overtaking Angus by rounding the Eldon Hill range he placed his forces on a small hilltop, blocking the route to Melrose. Angus sent a herald asking his intent and got the reply that he intended to rescue the King. Angus threatened treason if he did not desist, but Buccleough and his followers prepared to fight, dismounting and arraying for battle.

Angus sent the King to a small hillock along with his brother George, the Earl of Lennox, Lord Erskine and Lord Maxwell, where they remained on horseback and watched the proceedings. Angus dismounted his forces and advanced towards Buccleough with spears levelled. Many of Buccleough's forces fled during this disciplined onslaught of Angus, with Lesley describing them as 'thieves and broken men'. Yet the Laird and his closest retainers held their ground. The battle was uncertain until Lord Hume and the Kerrs, learning of the battle, returned and attacked the flanks of Buccleough's array. Angus pushed forward as Buccleough's forces began to crumble and disperse. Buccleough was wounded yet managed to escape, having lost 80 of his own men. The Laird of Cessford was lost to the other side. After the victory Angus took the King to Melrose before returning to Edinburgh. [10]

Lennox had been practically an observer, despite having engineered the conflict. It appears that he had been waiting to see the outcome before making a commitment, and with the timely intervention of Lord Hume and the Kerrs he decided to do nothing. Angus would later suspect Lennox of playing games, and came into possession of a letter which he showed to the Lords of Council. Lennox had written to various lords and barons claiming that King James was held in captivity. He would commit himself and friends to 'put our sovereign lord to freedom'. His intrigues discovered, the Earl of Lennox thought it wiser to make himself absent from court. James would not openly express his opposition to Angus, 'but dissembled the matter as best he could'. His movements would be strictly monitored, especially as the Douglases would have strong suspicions, if not proof, regarding his secret communications with Lennox. To keep the control of government, his captives would keep an even tighter grip on the King. [11]

Lennox, with letters obtained from the King, passed them to the strongest nobles in a bid to get them to join him against the Douglases. The Queen and the Archbishop of St Andrews would join with Lennox at Dunfermline. In the company of the Queen and like-minded nobles and prelates, Lennox outlined a plan to ride to Edinburgh and free King James. With 200 horsemen Lennox ventured to the edges of the city at Boroughmuir. Also in this company was William Cunningham, the Lord High Treasurer, son of the Earl of Glencairn and former ally of the Douglases.

Cunningham led eight men and horses towards Holyrood in an attempt to rescue James from Holyrood Palace. The plot was uncovered by Angus, who sent forces to apprehend the raiders, but James is said to have led Cunningham through a route out of Holyrood and to safety. James was then moved to the Edinburgh lodgings of Beaton, which were occupied by the Douglases. James was kept under the watch of George Douglas, the Master of the King's Household, and William Douglas, the prior of Coldingham. They commanded forty men. The Douglases, now making many more enemies, decide to enter into alliance with their old adversary the Earl of Arran. [12]

The Hamiltons could see that there was an obvious profit in making a deal with the Douglases. First they would become once more active in government, and Arran, as grandson of James II, would be able to re-assert his position as heir presumptive after the Duke of Albany. For Arran there had been the danger that his rights in this matter could be undermined through an alliance between the King and Lennox, who was a great grandson of James II. If Arran's own divorce from his first wife was deemed unlawful, this would nullify the rights of the children of his second marriage, who would be deemed illegitimate. There was also the danger that in the event of Arran being killed, Lennox as nephew of Arran, through his mother being Elizabeth Hamilton, would also have a claim to the Earldom of Arran. [13]

After his last effort Lennox, the Queen and the Archbishop of St Andrews moved to Stirling. An army said to number 10,000 was mobilised, drawn from Fife, Angus and Strathearn, and another 2,000 supplied by Beaton. Argyll and Moray were also expected to join Lennox. Upon hearing of this mustering Angus asked Arran to send his forces to Linlithgow and block the progress of Lennox, under the presumption that Lennox would not go to war against his uncle.

With a promise to join with Arran at Linlithgow, Angus marched his forces out of Edinburgh with the King present and Royal banners displayed. Arran positioned his forces to block the bridge across the Avon River, and the rest to command a range of small hills facing the river. As Lennox approached Linlithgow on September 3rd, Arran sent a message asking him to halt his enterprise, and assuring him that despite their kinship he would not 'spare him if he held forward his journey'. Lennox replied that he would reach Edinburgh or die trying. Lennox attempted to cross the river, not at the bridge, but downriver at a difficult ford near a small nunnery at Manual. Whilst his men crossed, their cohesion began to break up in the river, whilst from the hills opposite they endured fire from guns, arrows, and artillery, and any object the enemy could lay hands on and throw. [14]

As the army of Angus marched towards Linlithgow, King James tried to slow the progress in favour of Lennox by feigning illnesses and trying by all possible means to stop Angus aiding Arran. Sir George Douglas, realising that James was obstructing the march, brought the King his horse and forced him to ride. At Corstorphine, the guns at Linlithgow could be heard. Douglas, perceiving that the King hoped Lennox would win and rescue him, made a grave threat, stating that 'before the enemy shall take thee from us, if thy body should be torn to pieces, we shall have a piece'. It was a cruel threat that James would never forget or forgive, and in later years he would forbid anyone mentioning the name of his tormentor George Douglas. [15]

As Lennox's army crossed the Avon they engaged the forces awaiting them. They fought a hard battle, yet Arran's forces used the height of the hills to their advantage and began to push back their opponents. At a crucial point, Angus' forces arrived and entered the fray, shouting their famous cry to arms, 'A Douglas! A Douglas!' The two-pronged attack from Arran and Angus broke the ranks of Lennox's forces, causing a chase from the victors. James would send Andrew Wood of Largo to go forward and in James' name try to end the slaughter, and save the life of the Earl of Lennox and other allies.

Wood managed to rescue Cuthbert Cunningham, the Earl of Glencairn, who was wounded fighting the forces of Angus. Using the King's authority Wood conveyed him to a safe place away from his enemies. Lennox was taken by William Hamilton, the Laird of Pardovan, and disarmed. According to Pitscottie, Sir James Hamilton of Finnart took possession of Lennox and murdered him along with many more captives, thereby eliminating a rival to the succession. Finnart would also brand prisoners with the 'Hamilton Mark', sword slices across the face in the form of an H, so that they would afterwards be identified as the defeated side. Wood found Lennox lying on the field being mourned by the Earl of Arran, seemingly too late to save him. According to chroniclers Arran would call Lennox the 'wisest man, the stoutest man, the hardiest man that ever was bred in Scotland'. Whilst these words were a noble recommendation to a fallen rival, Arran would benefit financial and territorially from Lennox's death. He would also lose an important rival to his position as heir apparent after Albany. Also slain were the Abbots of Melrose and Dunfermline, Stirling of Keir and the Baron of Houston. [16]

Angus and Arran were victorious, and while James could claim that he sought to intervene to stop the slaughter out of humanity, the Douglases would treat these sentiments 'with derision', considering that it was common knowledge that Lennox and his cohorts 'enterprised the matter at the King's command'. Angus could not find legitimate or legal means to punish the King, since Douglas power stemmed from the use of the captive King's authority. Therefore in Pitscottie's words whilst the Douglases 'were covetous and greedy, and oppressors of their neighbours', to the King they acted as if 'they were ever true and kind and serviceable'. Yet James, a mere fourteen years of age, would have to endure terrible humiliation by being forced to witness the drunken celebrations of the Hamiltons and Douglases in Linlithgow town, whilst being forced to suppress his own feelings. As Christopher Dacre would report, the King 'loves not Angus or Arran'. [17]

The victors, with the King in tow, next marched to Stirling. They failed to capture the Queen, who dismissed her staff and along with the Archbishop of St Andrews escaped to the north. The army chased after them, but the Queen and Archbishop were hidden by friends. They were forced to move from one hiding place to the next as Angus and Arran vigorously searched for them. Beaton is said to have dressed himself as a shepherd, and Queen Margaret is said to have also learned to put on disguises, becoming a vagrant whilst attempting to move amongst her subjects undetected. We know little of her adventures during this time, although they say much about her ability to adapt to this dangerous situation.

Angus and his forces captured Dunfermline and looted the abbey, and upon reaching St Andrews they razed the castle to the ground. All of Beaton's goods and movables were plundered before the army returned to Edinburgh. [18]

On November 12th a parliament at Edinburgh was called which conveyed on November 27th. The victors would benefit from the forfeitures of the fugitive and deceased nobles who had supported Lennox. Trials were formed against those nobles that had supported Lennox, although they could escape prosecution if they compounded money towards the Hamiltons or Douglases. Gilbert Kennedy, Earl of Cassilis, would be put on trial for not joining Angus and Arran. His relative Hugh defended him successfully by producing a letter from the King asking Gilbert to support Lennox, although because of lack of men he was unable to join him. Seemingly the King had sent many such letters out prior to the battle.

Cassilis was discharged of the charge of treason. The following year he would be murdered by Hugh Campbell, Sheriff of Ayr, on the sands near Prestwick. Supposedly this was instigated by

Hamilton of Finnart, although at the time both Cassillis and Campbell were involved in a bitter legal dispute over rights to Turnberry and lands in Carrick. [19]

The Stewart family of Henry, consort of Margaret, were deprived of their public offices, and the Lordship of Avondale would pass to Arran. Wardship of Lennox's heir Matthew was split between Angus and Arran, and both effectively split the profits and revenue of the Earldom. Angus was made keeper of Falkland town and palace, and had himself appointed Chancellor and Steward of the Lordship of Fife. Angus received the lands of Lord Lindsay and those of other lords and nobles to the north and east. Sir George Douglas received the property of the slain Keir of Stirling. William, master of Glencairn, was deprived of the post of Lord High Treasurer because of joining his father Cuthbert, Earl of Glencairn at Linlithgow against Angus. This post was granted to Archibald Douglas of Kilspindie, provost of Edinburgh. His good wife would satirically become known as 'Lady Treasurer', to indicate how crown revenue was being used to finance and benefit the Douglas family and dependents. [20]

The Archbishop of St Andrews was given an opportunity to return to court. In return for resigning the Abbey of Kilwinning to Arran, paying £2,000 to Angus and £1,000 each to Sir James Hamilton, Archibald Douglas of Kilspindie, and George Douglas, besides further distribution of gifts and money, he was permitted to come out of hiding and was welcomed back to Edinburgh. Queen Margaret was also invited to return to Edinburgh, by Angus himself, out of consideration for her brother Henry VIII. She was met at Corstorphine on November 20th by her son King James with a small retinue and escorted through the streets of Edinburgh to Holyrood Palace. It was reported that they stayed in quarters close to each other, and that apart from when he was hunting or enjoying sports, he stayed close to her. In the world he lived in, where treachery and betrayal were common, his mother was possibly the only person he could truly trust. [21]

Despite Angus' dominance the French continued to occupy

Dunbar and had a strong influence in that region, although disbarred from the councils of government. Now that the French were allied with England, there would be little help for those opposed to the Douglases and Hamiltons. Still, there was a psychological aspect of this French occupation in that Dunbar could provide a launch pad for Albany's return, a matter that troubled not just Angus but also the English government. [22]

A sum of money passed to Angus had bought Margaret and Beaton the right to spend the Christmas festivities at Holyrood Palace with James. The amicable relationship between mother and son would change when the latter refused Margaret's request for her lover Henry Stewart to attend court. She then left Edinburgh and returned to her castle at Stirling, of which Angus had allowed her possession in return for ridding herself of the company of Henry Stewart and his brother. Margaret was soon joined by the Archbishop of St Andrew. She would later be accused of seeking to travel to France, no doubt sickened by the lack of support from her brother and the dominance of her husband Angus. She would be motivated in personally seeking some kind of support from France, and continued to push for divorce with Albany's compliance. [23]

Albany, when receiving reports of the battle of Linlithgow, was desperate to return to Scotland and asked Francis to give him leave. He wanted to reinstate Queen Margaret and topple Angus and Arran and the 'murderers, thieves, and men of evil life' who followed them. Francis would not be inclined to offer too much support to a Scottish intervention and would be minded to discourage it, due to the peace of 1525, and not wanting to antagonise Henry VIII. Although the English King at that time was not a member of the League of Cognac formed against the Empire, he was, along with Wolsey, supportive in its aim to counter the growing power of the Empire. Francis would eventually enter into an alliance with England, the Westminster Treaty of April 30th. Henry's motivation was to rescue Pope Clement VII from the imperial power that was steadily encroaching into Italy, and win a divorce from Catherine of

Aragon, the aunt of Charles V, so that he could marry Ann Boleyn. Although not providing military support, he did grant Francis I funds of 100,000 crowns to fund war in Italy. He would also renounce English claims to the French throne in return for a pension, and his daughter Mary was to marry the second son of Francis. He would also grant to the Duke of Milan 50,000 ducats, which helped him reclaim his duchy from the Imperialists. [24]

In May 6th, 1527 the Imperialists, led by the Duke of Bourbon, sacked Rome. The Duke died whilst fighting on the walls, and in retaliation the Spanish and German troops would run rampage through the streets, slaughtering men, women and children; even orphans and hospital patients were killed. Churches, monasteries and convents were pillaged and destroyed, and priests, monks and nuns received no mercy. 10,000 bodies were buried on the north bank of the Tiber, and 2,000 thrown into the river. The Pope surrendered and became a virtual prisoner. He paid 200,000 ducats and gave to the Imperialists the cities of Ostia, Civitavecchia, Piacenza and Modena. Wolsey travelled to France, seeking support from cardinals to petition the Pope to favour Henry's divorce in return for military help. The April 30th Westminster Treaty between England and France would be ratified on May 29th 1527. [25]

This new understanding between England and France would not bode well for any intentions that Margaret had for travelling to France, as Francis in his new friendship with Henry would assure him he would not welcome her against his wishes. In this period of Anglo-French détente Henry, through Albany's ambassador Turenne, would even praise Albany's governing of Scotland, calling him a 'good and wise prince'. He would describe his sister as being 'incompetent to exercise' power in Scotland; another example of Henry's brutal and treacherous attitude to his sibling that he would even spit poisonous opinions against her to a former enemy. [26]

Angus did his utmost to ensure peace on the borders, yet his hold on law and order was tenacious. There were still organised criminal gangs such as the Armstrongs, Nixons, Elliots and Crossers, who originating from Liddlesdale and the Debatable Lands, encroaching into the English middle march. During the spring Douglas would launch a number of judicial raids into Liddlesdale, one in April resulting in some hangings and the taking of hostages. Such actions brought a temporary respite, but were largely ineffective in curbing the frequent incursions across the border, and Angus would end up hanging his hostages. [27]

By the advice of Angus and Arran, King James led an expedition of 5,000 to Jedburgh, where a Justice Ayre was called. James entered into bonds with the headmen of the border families. He would discover something of the workings of justice, and learn the state of affairs on the borders through the level of civil actions raised. He would have addressed pleas to the crown, which involved charges of murder, rape, theft and arson. He would also be aware that Justice Ayres could be a source of finance, through fines and immurements. James could get an idea of how effective his crown officials and sheriffs were in countering the violence and crime on the borders. [28]

Before this judicial expedition had set off from Edinburgh a convention was held on June 27th at Holyrood Palace, where outside in the courts and gardens were gathered 2,000 Douglases and Hamiltons. It was during this convention that a former groom of Lennox called John Stewart attacked and stabbed Sir James Hamilton of Finnart, the alleged murderer of Lennox. Hamilton lived, but the incident threatened to turn Hamiltons against Douglases because the former were suspicious of the latter as instigators of the attack. The attacker had managed to slip into the crowd but was uncovered as he still had blood on his person, or caught with 'red hand'. He was tortured for nearly a month, and if anyone else was involved in the plot to kill Finnart, John Stewart said nothing except expressing regret that he had not done a better job. 'Fye on the feeble hand that could not effect what the heart thought, and was determined to do!' he said. He was finally executed by being led naked through the streets of Edinburgh with his skin being pierced with red-hot instruments. His hand was chopped off before he was executed. [30]

As summer approached and the nights grew lighter, Angus and the wardens were failing to effectively challenge the organized criminal families on the borders, either through compliance, corruption or inability. Lord Maxwell for example was said to enjoy a bond of friendship with the Armstrongs and would side with them in their feud with the Johnstones. Lord Bothwell did not make any notable effort to prosecute the rider families in the East Marches. Despite Angus' recent raid against the Armstrongs and others, he would refuse to enter the Debatable Grounds, which the gangs and 'broken men' would use as a platform to raid into England, with the excuse that this area, neither Scottish or English was beyond his authority, a somewhat feeble excuse considering Angus' history of aggressive expansionism and opportunism. That he would bar himself from raiding into the Debatable Ground due to a technicality does not sound sincere. There would be later accusations against Angus that the lawlessness of the Armstrongs suited him, that the judicial raids against them and others were used to fill his own pockets with plunder, and that he also used them as cover to intimidate and coerce rival powers on the borders into signing bonds of friendship or manrent. In this context he had a fierce rival in Robert Maxwell, who was siding with the Armstrongs. [31]

The Scots raiders on the borders would ally themselves with English raiders, the Lisles led by Sir William Lisle of Tyndale. Described as a traitor by the English authorities, he was the leader of a confederacy of outlaws who were terrorising northern England. The Armstrongs would join with the English gangs and help to free Sir William and his son Humphrey from a prison in Newcastle, and then bring them to sanctuary in Scotland. The failure of Angus or the border wardens to find and apprehend the Lisles brought a censure from King James, who was in turn receiving letters from King Henry and the English authorities complaining of the English outlaws receiving shelter in Scotland, with Lisle calling himself 'captain of all thieves'.

The English and Scots reivers invaded Northumberland and burned the town of Holmeshaugh. Whilst Angus would claim that it was in the Debatable Ground that Lisle lay, as already noted, he would lamely claim that this area was not within the bounds of his office. [32]

A parliament was held in August and on the 8th of that month Angus was officially appointed Chancellor, to be assisted by the Bishop of Aberdeen. By September some on the Duke of Richmond council had suggested that Angus was not as vigorous as he should be in administering the borders. There were also suggestions that the two wardens, Lord Bothwell and Lord Maxwell, were becoming less punctual in keeping days of truce on respectively Liddlesdale and the western marches.

Sir William Eure accused Angus of giving wrong information about the Lisle's whereabouts, asserting that they were in the middle marches and especially in Liddlesdale, and were supported by the Armstrongs and Crosers. He complained that pleas for redress committed by the Liddlesdale gangs were met by 'no answers but delays'. By December the Duke of Richmond was more diplomatic in his criticism of the Scots in respect of their apparent inability to apprehend Lisle, informing Wolsey that despite many pleas to the King and Angus he had received 'pleasant' replies but little else. Henry VIII's solution to the problem in a letter to King James was to allow his own wardens to enter into Scotland, especially Ewesdale, which he learned the Lisles also used as a refuge, asking also that such an incursion should not be considered a 'violation of the treaty' between Scotland and England. [33]

The Earl of Northumberland was appointed warden of the borders in late December, and set out to suppress the raiders. Whilst Angus offered to meet with Northumberland and discuss how to address the issue of the lawlessness, he was also concerned with stories that Albany was seeking to return to Scotland, whilst claiming that King James had invited him. He wrote to Henry VIII and Wolsey in respect of the dangers that would ensue if Albany were to set foot on Scottish soil again. Albany was also said to be requesting a safe conduct from Henry VIII, and considering that there was peace between England and France then this had become a possibility. Whilst Angus was not succeeding in taming the frontier, Henry in previous correspondence had complimented Albany in stating that he would prefer Scotland 'should be governed as if you remained there', which if a genuine opinion would have brought the possibility that Henry might allow Albany a safe passage to Scotland in order to bring stability to the borders. James would deny that he had invited Albany to Scotland and would ask Henry in correspondence not to allow him to return. He also wrote to Francis I and to Albany himself, and detailed reports that the late Earl of Lennox's uncle, Robert, Lord of Aubigny, was engaged in hiring ships to sail over the waters. The combination of a determined Albany and a vengeful Aubigny coming to Scotland could only, as James stated, bring 'trouble amongst the people'. [34]

There was also trouble north of the Firth of Forth, where the Earl of Moray had taken the castle of Spynie. Archibald Douglas of Spindie had been granted by the crown the temporality of Moray, where the castle stood. Moray was threatened with treason if his incursions were not reversed. Letters had also been sent to the Earls of Argyll and Atholl charging them not to ride with companies larger than their usual household and guards, under 'pain of treason'. Without doubt the Douglas government was feeling less and less secure, and incapable of stemming the power of the lords of the north. [35]

In February 1528 Northumberland managed to capture and execute many of the Lisles, after an English threat to invade Liddlesdale had lost them sanctuary in Scotland. One of the Lisles would claim that in their raids into England they were given some support not just by Angus but by Lord Maxwell and Lord Bothwell. A raid by Dacre involving 2,000 men was ambushed by Armstrongs, and when artillery provided by Northumberland allowed Dacre to reinvade and destroy Johnnie Armstrong's tower at Hollows on the Esk, the Armstrongs retaliated and burned the town of Netherby. In this latter raid they were assisted by Lord Maxwell.

It has been suggested that Queen Margaret was sanctioning Maxwell's aggression. She was seeking a breach in the treaty between Scotland and England, and a further undermining of Angus' ability to administer law and order on the borders. Throughout the year the spiral of raids and ambushes continued. (36)

Whilst the ideas of religious reformation had taken root in Germany and was spreading through Europe, the Scots had introduced an act in 1525 prohibiting the works of Martin Luther or other reformers, which were reaching the eastern coastal towns and cities through merchants and ships returning from the Baltic Sea region. The first major Scottish figure in this religious movement was Patrick Hamilton, who has been described as the son of Hamilton of Kincavel and nephew of the Earl of Arran. Through his mother he was also said to be related to the Duke of Albany.

Patrick Hamilton studied at Paris as a student. He attended lectures by Eramus and Reuchlin and his curiosity took him to Wittenburg and Marburg University to become influenced by the works of Luther, Melanchthon and Lambert. He returned to Scotland and began to spread his catechism, called Patricks' Place, based on the doctrine of justification by faith. His preaching was openly defiant of church authority and doctrine.

In 1528 Hamilton was captured by the Archbishop of St Andrews' men and taken to the castle. After a hurried trial he was convicted of being an 'obstinate heretic' and burned at the stake outside St Salvador's College. Archbishop James Beaton was advised that burning Hamilton had been counter-productive, since now people were curious as to why he had been burned, and were actively seeking out his works, reflecting how 'the reek of Master Patrick Hamilton has infected as many as it blew upon!' Within a few years individuals belonging to the grey or black friars began to question the teachings of the church. [37]

Religious upheavals would be a concern of the future, but for the present the conspiracies and intrigues for acquiring civil power were continuing. Whilst Albany was not invited by James to return to Scotland, Queen Margaret was in contact with the Duke through her agent John Cantely. Through Cantely's mediation Albany would write to the Pope about the activities of Angus in Scotland, whether imprisoning the King, slaying nobles or stealing the crown revenues. Also through his own agent, Octavian at Borne, he would petition the Pope to allow Margaret to divorce Angus. The grounds are not mentioned, although Lesley believes that Angus had previously been married to a sister of Lord Hume, and had not been properly divorced. Whatever reasons or even incentives Margaret offered can only be speculated. However Albany's efforts were successful and on March 11th, 1528 the divorce proceedings were proclaimed by the Cardinal of Ancona in favour of Queen Margaret and at the cost of 100 ducats. It appears that Albany covered this cost as well as a previous 250 ducats in bribes. Having lost legal rights to Margaret's lands, and being no longer the legal consort to the Queen or stepson to the King, the Earl of Angus' political power had been sharply diminished.

Queen Margaret would receive official notification of the divorce later in March, and once the news spread to England the repercussions were deeply felt. Wolsey called the divorce 'unlawful' and warned her to avoid the 'inevitable damnation' by reconciling herself to Angus, whom Wolsey still considered her 'true husband'. Wolsey's comments are ironic considering he had been petitioning Pope Clement VII to grant the divorce of Henry VIII from Katherine of Aragon. Whilst these efforts failed, with the Pope having escaped Rome in December 1527 to arrive at Orvieto, he would not give a definite answer to the requests of English envoys who visited him. Overall Wolsey would see his schemes and plans unravel, to the displeasure of King Henry VIII. [38]

The friendship between England and France would offer fresh

opportunities for James when both declared war on the Empire in January 1528. Threatened with a possible invasion of the continent by English armies, on February 7th 1528 at Bruges the Emperor Charles V authorised Peter Cornellis to travel to Scotland and ask King James to declare war against England. If he refused Cornellis would then ask the Archbishop of St Andrews, and failing in this he would turn to the Earl of Angus. The Emperor would have been aware that Angus was an adherent of Henry VIII, yet he may have been confident that the proud Earl was susceptible to bribes and gifts, and that he could turn him against the English King. Cornellis would approach other nobles and lords. If alliance was not feasible the King was to be requested to allow imperial troops to use Scotland to launch an invasion into England. Cornellis would also approach other lords and ask James to allow them to support an imperial army. There is no record of this envoy meeting with the King, the Archbishop or the Earl, however negotiations did occur; they were suspended in May 1528 due to the conclusion that English forces were not preparing to pass over to the continent. It is possible to view James' actions during the spring months in the context of these negotiations, in that here was the potential for a profitable friendship with the Empire. First James would need to take power and rid himself of the Earl of Angus, who was Henry VIII's chief agent. [39]

Buchanan states that the Douglases controlled the behaviour of King James by 'allurements and improper pleasures'. Whilst these were distractions that allowed the Douglases to administer government as they pleased, the King was waiting for an opportunity to liberate himself from their grip and from the strict watch imposed by the household guards. As there was no individual powerful enough to challenge the Douglases they began loosen their vigilance over the King, and James would be allowed more freedoms. It was also said that he was allowed out into the towns in disguise, when he would pretend that he was an ordinary commoner and thereby learn the habits and aspirations of his subjects. He would acquire a political education from witnessing the machinations of the Douglases and the other nobles he had grown up with, whether Albany, Arran, or his own mother. Being devious was an important quality of nobility, and he would need to convince the Douglases that he was a friend and not a captive enemy. [40]

After confirmation of her divorce Margaret would marry Henry Stewart, without the permission of king or council. On March 27th James is said to have laid siege to Edinburgh, although in fact Angus gathered an army, with James as the figurehead, to advance towards Stirling. Queen Margaret, seeing her son at the head of the army, opened the gates and rushed down to meet him in the company of her new husband Henry and his brother James. On bended knee she handed the keys to the King and asked mercy of her husband. With a grim-faced Angus looking on, James ordered Lord Erskine to ward Queen Margaret, her husband and his brother in the castle. In many respects this act ensured that they would be out of the power of the Earl of Angus and under an incarceration which was also a form of protection. Appointing Lord Erskine as custodian was also a clever move by James, as it guaranteed a loyal subject to guard his mother.

At Stirling Castle the King would manage to have an audience with his mother away from the watchful eyes of the Douglases, and a plot developed to engineer an escape from Angus. In return for custody of Stirling Castle he would grant the lands and lordship of Methven to her husband. For Queen Margaret this was an important moment, in that her son was preparing to take the kingship by his own hands, and he would also recognise Henry Stewart as his stepfather whilst elevating him to the peerage with the grant of Methven. The servants of his mother were instructed to bring adequate stores, provisions and munitions into Stirling Castle to prepare against the Douglases. Meanwhile the unsuspecting Earl of Angus had plans for James to lead a judicial raid on the borders in co-ordination with the English wardens. James and Angus were at Edinburgh on May 27th and called for an armed muster for June 22nd. [41]

Before his planned expedition to the borders, James decided

to take in some leisure pursuits, and travelled to Falkland Palace with his Douglas escort. It appears that whilst at Falkland Archbishop Beaton invited Sir George Douglas to nearby St Andrews to discuss some lands and other business. Angus would go to Castle Tantallon, possibly to prepare for the raid towards to the borders. Archibald of Kilspindie had also left to go to Dundee on business, which left James with James Douglas of Parkhead, captain of the Royal Guard. Falkland was an attractive place for James as he used its park for hounds and hunting.

During the night, before a planned hunt in the Forest, James slipped out of his quarters. Disguised as a yeoman, he went to the stables and took a horse along with two attendants to Stirling. If Pitscottie's account is accurate it was a daring escape, and it was only the next morning that Sir George Douglas, having returned to Falkland the previous night, discovered the King missing from his bedroom.

When James arrived at Stirling Castle after a hard night's journey, he was greeted enthusiastically by the captain and garrison. The regal standard was raised above the ramparts. Exhausted after his journey, he entered the castle and collapsed into sleep. The escape seemed to have occurred in late May or early June. [42]

Argyll, Moray, Eglinton, the Lord Maxwell and the Archbishop of St Andrews would soon join the King and Queen Margaret at Stirling. Significantly Arran would also offer his support, a sign that the Hamilton alliance with the Douglases was over. The price of this would be that James would need to forgive Sir James of Finnart for his slaying of the Earl of Lennox. This James did and Finnart would become his companion in the bedchamber, the equivalent of personal bodyguard and confidant. James was being forced to be coldly pragmatic, and forming a close relationship with Finnart was likely a better option that having such a dangerous individual as an enemy. He also needed the support of the Hamiltons.

The sixteen-year-old James' first acts as a freed monarch were decisive and determined. He sent out letters ordering a council meeting for June 29th, whilst proclaiming on June 19th that no one of the faction of Douglas should come within six miles of the council under pain of treason. They were also ordered to resign all public and state appointments. James also wrote to the Earl of Northumberland stating that he would not be able to keep his appointment on the borders. When the Douglases discovered that the King was gone word was sent out to Angus, Archibald of Kilspindie and other Douglases. Once they had gathered together, which must have taken a couple of weeks, they made their way to Stirling in an attempt to disrupt the council meeting. They were stopped by a herald who read out a threat of treason if they ventured further. Whilst many of the force wanted to proceed, Angus and George Douglas decided to withdraw to Linlithgow before travelling to Edinburgh. By July 2nd, the Earls of Menteith, Glencairn and Rothes had arrived at Stirling, along with the Lords Drummond, Ruthven, Maxwell, Lindsay, Graham, Avondale, Montgomery and Sinclair. [43]

The King next ordered a convention for Edinburgh to take place on July 10th.The Douglases would leave the city early in July and the King and his army entered the city. During the parliament the Douglases were officially deprived of their state positions, the Chancellorship going to Gavin Dunbar and the Treasurer going to Robert Cairncross. Lord Maxwell replaced Douglas of Kilspindie as Provost of Edinburgh, and would become chief carver for the royal household, a position which assured him a close association with the King. Allies of the Douglases would seek to mediate on their behalf and gain a pardon. After some consultation and discussion proposition was made to the Douglases that Angus was to exile himself beyond the Spey, while George and Archibald of Kilspindie surrendered themselves to imprisonment in Edinburgh Castle. In return for this, after a period of time felt sufficient, the King might allow them clemency. This offer was refused, and the Douglases decided to resort to open resistance. During this period of uncertainty, James was guarded day and night in Holyrood

Palace by the nobles clad in armour. The King himself would take part in the guard duty. [44]

James wrote to Henry VIII and Wolsey outlining his reasons for acting against Angus. He made it clear that he blamed his uncle for many of Scotland's recent problems. He reminded him that despite Angus being exiled to 'France by advice of the Scotch Estates', he 'was invited thence by Henry VIII to England', and then Henry allowed Angus to cross into Scotland despite the pleas from James and his mother. He asked Henry not to afford Angus his protection. James also stated that Angus had been exploiting the resources of chancellor and warden for his own means. The Treasury accounts produced by the treasurer, Archibald Douglas of Kilspindie, for the period October 1526 to August 1527 would show a debt of £3,654.8s. [45]

The troubles on the borders were thought to have been a result of Angus' machinations, as judicial raids against criminals and raiders were covers for attacks on other barons, to force them to enter bonds of mutual aid and protection. When at a later date English commissioners were asked by Scottish counterparts whether Angus had in his two to three years as warden of the borders ever successfully concluded any redresses, they 'could make no good answer' and it was admitted that they' could not praise his administration'. [46]

A parliament was settled for September 2nd with the main business being the charges of treason against the Douglases. James retired to Stirling and stayed there with his mother until August 29th. As the day of the parliament beckoned the Douglases were offered protections to attend so as to plead their case. They had no intention of risking their necks by attending parliament and were more inclined to use force and intimidation to make their defence. Kilspindie and George and William Douglas, possibly as a sign of contempt, entered Edinburgh and occupied one of their homes. Their arrogance was such that they did not expect any armed attack, and their troops were positioned across the city.

Lord Maxwell, Provost of Edinburgh, with a small force came

close to capturing the Douglases when he surrounded their house. They managed to escape and joined the Earl of Angus, who was fortified within Tantallon Castle. Angus sent William, Abbot of Coldingham, to Roger Lasselles, Captain of Alwich, and asked if they could receive shelter. Lasselles offered him temporary quarters in Norham Castle until a decision was received from the Earl of Northumberland. In Angus' charge were his daughter Margaret and George Gordon, the young fifteen or sixteen-year-old Earl of Huntley, who appears to have attached himself to the Douglas cause. Angus would later ask for shelter for those two as well as the wife of Kilspindie. [47]

When the parliament met on September 2nd the main business was the trial of the Douglases. However the issue of the forfeitures had already been addressed by the Lords of Council; the lands of the Douglases would be parcelled out and distributed to the King's loyal supporters.

The trial began on the third day of the parliament. James had appointed six bishops and five earls, each believed to be enemies of the accused, to oversee the trial. The Douglases sent John Bannatyne, the secretary of Angus, to defend against the charges. The charges laid out were that the Douglases had controlled crown policy through possession of the King for two years against his will, and without the command of the council, and that through this control of the King they had forced him to be present at the battles at Melrose and Linlithgow, although Walter Scott of Buccleough was absolved for his participation as he had been secretly instructed by the King to be present. They were also accused of assembling forces to deny James entry into Edinburgh in July, and of supporting the Johnstones in their feud against the Maxwells, which although denied by Bannatyne, may explain Maxwell's support of the Armstrongs.

They were also accused of treasonably storing munitions and weapons in Tantallon, Douglas, Newark and Colbrandspeth for use against the King. Bannatyne would make a vigorous defence, but the evidence was stacked against his employer and his family, and they were found guilty and forfeited of all lands and possessions in Scotland. These were distributed to the Lords Bothwell, Maxwell, the Sheriff of Ayr and the laird of Buccleough. The Humes would refuse any Douglas lands on the east march, a refusal that would anger James as that area could still offer the Douglases opportunities to hurt the King.

James' new stepfather, Henry Stewart, was officially made Lord Methven and appointed Master of the King's Artillery. He bore as a badge a motif of a dragon in honour of Margaret's Welsh father Henry VII, and a crest of a standing crowned Queen holding a sword in her right hand and leaning on a wheel with her left. It possibly represented his wife. Methven and the Queen would become two of James' principle advisers. [48]

The King ordered a muster for September 8th at Haddington for the express purpose of chasing the Douglases off their lands, and allowing the new beneficiaries of Douglas property to earn what they had been granted. Unfortunately this expedition broke up through disagreements amongst the lords. There were also concerns that since it was the harvest season an expedition would cause damage to the agricultural economy. With the armies' dispersal James withdrew to Edinburgh.

Angus wrote to Wolsey and Henry VIII requesting refuge in England if James drove him out. This was granted and the Earl of Northumberland was instructed to assist Angus in this matter. Angus would also request that the English borderers offer their services. [49]

To annoy the King as he resided in Edinburgh, Angus led a force of eighty horsemen and wasted the lands and possessions of his enemies. Angus would mock that he had burned the villages of Cranston and Cousland so that 'the King might have light to see to rise with upon Friday in the morning'. As Angus withdrew to one of his several castles, James was quick to act, raising a force from Edinburgh and venturing to the town of Lanark, which he overcame, then laying siege to the castle of Douglas several miles distant. He remained there a few days before returning to

Edinburgh. He left a covering force to capture Douglas Castle.

James next made an attempt at Coldingham, supported by the Humes and with a force of five hundred horsemen. Angus' brother William had died a few days before, and Lord Hume's brother the Abbot of Jedburgh was installed as prior of Coldingham. Angus had withdrawn from Coldingham as James approached, and lay a few miles distant, watching the royal convoy and awaiting fresh troops to augment his own company, many of whom were English borderers who 'secretly assisted' him, having been given permission by the English authorities to do so.

When Angus felt confident enough to advance towards James on October 3rd, the latter decided to withdraw speedily to Dunbar whilst hotly pursued. At Dunbar he would have been greeted by the French troops left there by Albany. Angus returned to Coldingham and drove out the Humes. [50]

Despite this reverse James was determined to win this contest. His next target was Tantallon, the impressive castle overlooking the Bass Rock on the Lothian coast, and he called a muster for October 18th. James led a recorded 10,000 to Tantallon, although that number appears too high. He also brought ordinance and powder from Edinburgh and borrowed the French cannon from Dunbar, still held by the garrison of the Duke of Albany. To ensure the safe return of the guns James left three noble hostages. During the advance to Tantallon a regimental band played 'ding dong Tantallon'. The Earl of Angus remained outside the castle walls, waiting for an opportunity to attack the King's army as the siege ensued and earthworks were thrown up.

For sixteen days the guns bombarded the castle, but to little effect. The worst casualties were on the side of the besiegers when a magazine ignited. The siege failed; Pitscottie would wonder whether it was because the walls were too strong or else Angus had bribed the gunners.

James returned to Edinburgh, but the artillery train was attacked in a moonlight raid by Angus with 160 horsemen at Dirleton. The captain, David Falconer, was taken and said to have been 'cruelly murdered' by Angus. [51]

Upon capturing the artillery, Angus decided to return the bulk of it to the King supposedly as a sign of good faith, and with an insistence that he was a loyal servant and it was the advisers around the King who were the real enemy. James may have been doubly insulted, firstly with the loss of his guns and now a message from Angus claiming he was an innocent victim wrongly persecuted by his enemies. Yet Angus would soon be receiving funds from England, with Wolsey authorising 100l to be given to him through his brother Sir George. Despite his protestations, Angus was very much being sponsored by England to cause mischief in Scotland. James would say as much when Northumberland complained about lack of redress due to raids by Crossers, Nixons and Elwoods, and would counter with the fact that England 'resets Scotch traitors'. In his opinion the Scots wardens could not be expected to meet with English counterparts until the 'old and accustomed pride' of the Douglases was 'repressed'. [52]

The Douglases were further weakened when Angus' Lordship of Bothwell and its impressive castle was granted by James to the Earl of Arran on November 16th. James was also determined to get Tantallon into his hands, and had in his favour the approaching end of the three-year truce, which Henry would want to extend due to his own intentions of leading an army to the continent. Angus was concerned about such a treaty in that a continued peace between Scotland and England would give James the opportunity to destroy the Douglases. He therefore needed to have his family comprehended into such a peace.

James commissioned Sir James Hamilton of Finnart and Hugh Campbell, the Sheriff of Ayr, to meet with Kilspindie and George Douglas at Colburnspath to negotiate terms with the Douglases. Finnart would present himself as a friend seeking to arbitrate a favourable settlement for the Douglases, yet at the same time he would advise James to be as ruthless against them as possible. The Douglases could not accept the terms offered, although there is no record of the terms. [53]

Adam Otterburn and the Abbot of Kelso were the Scots commissioners appointed to negotiate peace with England, and would meet their English counterparts at Berwick on November 7th, 1528. Whilst one sticking point was the comprehension of Angus and the Douglases into a peace treaty, the Scots commissioners refused this condition. Nothing was concluded at this meeting; appeals for redress were not met, and whilst the English Commissioners sought up to five years the Scots had been mandated to offer three years at most. The meeting was to be extended from December 9th to January 15th, and James informed Magnus, the ambassador to Scotland, that the Scots Commissioners would have more powers and be allowed to negotiate up to five years. [54]

Henry would seek peace with Scotland, since he apparently feared that James might ally himself with Charles V, a distinct possibility now that England and France were allied against the Empire. It is not clear if Henry was aware that the Emperor had made approaches to the Scots earlier in the year, but in his continental ambitions he was forever frustrated with having to factor in the foreign policy of the Scots. Henry however continued to favour Angus in a comprehension, an insistence that upset and confused King James, and he reportedly started to weep with frustration. Eventually he would compose himself and once more articulate his reasons for refusing to accept Angus or restore him to his lands. He reminded Henry of the treasons that Angus had committed, and added a few more details for the record.

Instead of being a friend to England, Angus supported those thieves on the borders that threatened the peace. James alleged that Angus had conspired to have him killed, and that the Douglases had put to death several of his servants through participation in a pretend raid. From James' point of view it would be difficult to comprehend how Henry could ask his nephew to forgive individuals as dangerous and destructive as the Red Douglas. From Henry's point of view the Douglases were valued tools to create tensions inside and outside Scotland. [55]

Tantallon Castle was still a problem for the King. The captain, Simon Penning, would complain that although the castle had enough food and drink it was lacking ammunition, bullets and powder. There were attempts to buy him away from loyalty to Angus with certain nobles and gentlemen commissioned by James to negotiate with him, to offer gifts and grants of land and most importantly offer him and his family and friends, except Douglases, remission for their crimes in return for surrendering the castle.

In consideration of this offer Simon Penning sent word to Angus and George Douglas that he had no powder, bullets or ammunition to resist a siege, requesting that on a given date they should bring these items to Tantallon, or he would be forced to surrender. Angus acknowledged that he could not bring those items into Tantallon as he did not have them, and bringing them by sea would be difficult as the King's ships blocked the harbour to Tantallon. With that answer Penning surrendered Tantallon to the King. [56]

On December 14th the Treaty of Berwick was signed, agreeing to a treaty between Scotland and England to last five years. Angus was not comprehended into it, but he and his family were given refuge in England allowing them to raid across the border. James would on November 28th 1528 appoint the Earl of Argyll Lieutenant of Lothian, the Merse and Teviotdale, and through his efforts working alongside Lord George Hume, Angus and his adherents would by May 1529 be expelled from Scotland. Most of the Angus lands would fall to the crown, but Argyll would be rewarded with the barony of Abernethy. [57]

The Lady Margaret Douglas had escaped Tantallon long before the siege. An athletic red-headed thirteen-year-old, she and her attendants would either accompany the Earl of Angus on his travels along the borders of Scotland or find shelter and sanctuary with friends and allies, or in barns or caves.

At the castle of Norham during early September Angus, the

Lady Margaret, the wife of Archibald of Kilspindie and attendants were granted permission by Henry to take refuge. King James at that time had sent scouts to the border regions to find his sister so he could bring her to court and welcome her as a royal sister. There would also be reports that Queen Margaret was going to marry her daughter to John Stewart, a brother of her husband Henry, who governed Doune Castle. Lady Margaret would have known of these plans, as her father is quoted as fearing that she would be 'stolen and withdrawn into Scotland'. Strickland suggests that she was poisoned against her mother by her Douglas kin, and being brought up by her father she would display a powerful loyalty towards him. She was also said to have an adventurous and independent spirit, and was possibly less inclined to enter into a formal royal life as opposed to the adventures and excitement of being a hunted princess. She would accompany her father around the border country whenever safety allowed, but during those periods when the battles and skirmishing became dangerous, she would be returned to Norham. The castle itself was run down and in need of repairs, a result of decades of border warfare and economic hardship.

Lady Margaret would move to Berwick during the summer of 1529, and whilst her clothes were in rags she was reportedly in good spirits. Thomas Strangeways, the governor of Berwick and an adherent of Cardinal Wolsey, Margaret's godfather, sent the Carlisle herald to the Cardinal requesting orders. Wolsey instructed Strangeways to provide adequate comfort and protection, and whilst the governor showed great kindness to the royal princess and her entourage, he would complain that he had received no money from the Earl of Angus for the upkeep. [58]

King Henry during this time had not invited her to court; possibly he had considered using her as a bargaining lever with his sister Queen Margaret. It was his other sister Mary, the widow of the French King Louis, who on hearing of Margaret's hardships compelled Henry to bring her south. Henry relented and the Lady Margaret would visit Queen Mary and her new husband the Duke of Suffolk before the New Year 1530. She would then be moved to Beaulieu, where she would be housed along with Henry's daughter Mary, and would be in frequent contact with Queen Katherine of Aragon. The princess was now a part of Henry VIII's royal establishment. [59]

Chapter Seven: References.

(1) (Johnson, pp. 183-185). (2) (ALCPA, pp. 235-236. LP, Magnus to Wolsey, January 1st, 1526. LP, Magnus to Wolsey, January 12th, 1526. Strickland, vol.1, pp. 206-208). (3) (ALCPA, pp. 236-237. Fraser, pp. 223-225. Lesley, pp,133-134. LP, Angus to Magnus, January 22nd, 1526. LP, Magnus to Queen Margaret, February 11th, 1526. Strickland, vol.1, pp. 206-208. Tytler, pp. 181-183). (4) (LP, Scotland, February 12th, 1526. LP, The Lords of the Secret Council to Magnus, February 16th, 1526. LP, Magnus to Wolsey, March 7th, 1526). (5) (LP, Scotland, March 20th, 1526. Tytler, pp. 182-184). (6) (RSP, June 13th, 1526). (7) (Buchanan, pp. 291-294. ODNB, vol.16, pp. 620-621. RSP, June 13th, 1526. SP, vol.4, pp. 235-236). (8) (Buchanan, pp. 291-292. Fraser, pp. 225-227. Herkless & Hannay, vol.3, pp. 159-161. RSP, June 13th, 1526. Tytler, pp. 187-189). (9) (Buchanan, pp. 291-294. Fraser, pp. 226-227. Lesley, pp. 133-136. LP, The Council of Scotland to the Earl of Cumberland, July 4th, 1526. Pitscottie, pp. 313-316. Thomson, vol.2, pp. 566-567. Tytler, pp. 182-185). (10) (Buchanan, pp. 292-293. Lesley, pp. 133-136. Pitscottie, pp. 313-316. Thomson, vol.2, pp. 566-567. Tytler, pp. 182-185). (11) (ALCPA, pp. 250-251. Buchanan, pp. 292-293. Fraser, pp. 226-228. Holinshed, pp. 499-503. ODNB, vol.24, pp. 823-826. Thomson, vol.2, pp. 567-568). (12) (Buchanan, p.293. Fraser, pp. 226-228. ODNB, vol.24, pp. 823-826. ODNB, vol.52, pp. 707-708. SP, vol.4, pp. 235-236. Strickland, vol.1, pp. 207-209). (13) (Buchanan, p.293. ODNB, vol.24, pp. 823-826. ODNB, vol.52, pp. 707-708. Thomson, vol.2, pp. 566-568). (14) (Buchanan, pp. 293-294. CSP Milan, Augustino Scarpinello, Milanese Ambassador in England, to Francesco Sforza, Duke of Milan, September 1526. Fraser, pp. 229-231. Holinshed, pp. 500-504. Lesley, pp. 135-137. Thomson, vol.2, pp. 567-568. Tytler, pp. 184-186). (15) (Buchanan, pp. 293-294. CSP Milan, Augustino Scarpinello, Milanese Ambassador in England, to Francesco Sforza, Duke of Milan, September 1526. Fraser, pp. 229-231. Lesley, pp. 135-137. Thomson, vol.2, pp. 567-568. Tytler, pp. 184-186). (16) (Buchanan, pp. 293-294. CSP Milan, Augustino Scarpinello, Milanese Ambassador in England, to Francesco Sforza, Duke of Milan,

September 1526. Fraser, pp. 229-231. Holinshed, pp. 502-504. Lesley, pp. 135-137. Pitscottie, pp. 318-321. ODNB, vol.24, pp. 823-826. ODNB, vol.52, pp. 707-708. ODNB, vol.4, pp. 235-237. Thomson, vol.2, pp. 567-568. Tytler, pp. 184-186). (17) (LP, Sir Christopher Dacre to Lord Dacre, December 2nd, 1526. Pitscottie, pp. 321-323. Thomson, vol.2, p.568. Tytler, pp. 184-186). (18) (Buchanan, pp. 295-296. Lesley, pp. 136-137.Pitscottie, pp. 322-324. Strickland, vol.1, pp. 213-215. Tytler, pp. 184-186). (19) (Buchanan, pp. 294-296. Fraser, pp. 230-231. LP, Sir Christopher Dacre to Lord Dacre, December 2nd, 1526. ODNB, vol.31, pp. 241-242. ODNB, vol.52, p.674. Tytler, pp. 184-186). (20) (Fraser, pp. 230-231. LP, Sir Christopher Dacre to Lord Dacre, December 2nd, 1526. ODNB, vol.31, pp. 241-242. ODNB, vol.52, p.674. SP, vol.4, pp. 235-236. Thomson, vol.2, pp. 568-569. Tytler, pp. 184-186). (21) (Fraser, pp. 231-232. LP, Sir Christopher Dacre to Lord Dacre, December 2nd, 1526. Tytler, pp. 184-186). (22) (LP, James V to Henry VIII, January 7th, 1527). (23) (Fraser, pp. 231-232. Herkless & Hannay, vol.3, pp. 167-170. LP, Magnus to Wolsey, March 26th, 1527. LP, May 1st, Turenne to Albany, 1527). (24) (Johnson, pp. 187-188. LP, Scotland, October 1526. LP, Italian News, February 19th, 1527. LP, May 1st, Turenne to Albany, 1527). (25) (Bindoff, pp. 84-86. Norwich, pp. 292-294). (26) (LP, Scotland, October 1526. LP, May 1st, Turenne to Albany, 1527). (27) (Fraser, pp. 232-234. LP, Magnus to Wolsey, February 14th, 1527. LP, Henry Duke of Richmond, March 3rd, 1527). (28) (Buchanan, pp. 296-297. Fraser, pp. 231-233. Lesley, pp. 139-141). (30) (Buchanan, pp. 297-299. Lesley, pp. 139-141. LP, Magnus to Wolsey, February 14th, 1527. LP, Henry Duke of Richmond, March 3rd, 1527.Thomson, vol.2, pp. 569-570. Tytler, pp. 184-186). (31) (Macdonald-Fraser, pp. 229-233). (32) (LP, Magnus to Wolsey, July 4th, 1527. LP, Archibald Earl of Angus to Henry VIII, August 10th, 1527. LP, The Lisles, August 12th, 1527. LP, Angus to the Duke of Richmond, August 18th, 1527). (33) (LP, Magnus to Henry VIII, August 22nd, 1527. LP, The Duke of Richmond's Council to Henry VIII, September 7th, 1527. LP, Henry VIII to James V, September 10th, 1527. LP, Sir Wm Eure to the Duke of Richmond, September 12th, 1527. LP, Sir William Eure to Wolsey, October 27th, 1527. LP, The Duke of Richmond to Wolsey, December 2nd, 1527). (34) (LP, Henry, Earl of Northumberland, December 27th, 1527. LP, Angus to Henry VIII, December 29th,1527. LP, Angus to Wolsey, December 29th, 1527. LP, James V to Henry VIII, January 7th, 1528. LP, James V to Albany, January 8th, 1528. LP, James V to Francis I, January 10th, 1528). (35) (ALCPA, p. 262. p.271). (36) (LP, Earl of Northumberland to Wolsey, February 11th, 1528. LP, Border Correspondence, March 6th, 1528. LP, William Lord Dacre to Wolsey, March 6th, 1528. MacDonald-Fraser, pp. 229-233. Thomson, vol.2, pp. 570-571). (37) (Buchanan, pp. 297-298. Knox, pp. 3-6.

Thomson, vol.2, pp. 569-570). (38) (Fraser, pp. 216-218. Lesley, Lesley, pp. 139-142. LP, Albany to Clement VII, December 31st, 1527. LP, Queen Margaret to Albany, March 23rd, 1528. LP, John Duncan to Albany, March 29th, 1528. LP, Wolsey to Queen Margaret, April 2nd 1528. Norfolk, pp. 294-296. Strickland, vol.1, pp. 211-213). (39) (CSPS, 326. Instructions to the Same about what he is to say to James, King of Scotland, February 7th, 1528. CSPS, Cornelius Duplicius Scepperus to Alfonso Valdes, the Emperor's Secretary, May 21st, 1528). (40) (Buchanan, pp. 297-299. Hume-Brown, vol.1, pp. 317. LP, Scotland, July 1528). (41) (Buchanan, pp. 297-299. Fraser, pp. 237-238. Hume-Brown, vol.1, pp. 317.Lesley, pp. 140-142. LP, Will Lord Dacre to Wolsey, April 2nd, 1528. Strickland, vol.1, pp. 214-216. Tytler, pp. 188-190). (42) (Buchanan, pp. 297-299. Fraser, pp. 237-239. Hume-Brown, vol.1, pp. 317.Lesley, pp. 140-142. Pitscottie, pp. 325-327. Strickland, vol.1, pp. 214-216. Thomson, vol.2, p.571. Tytler, pp. 188-190). (43) (Buchanan, pp. 299-301. LP, the Earl of Northumberland to Wolsey, July 2nd, 1528. ODNB, vol.37, pp. 526-528. Thomson, vol.2, pp. 571-573. Tytler, pp. 188-190). (44) (Buchanan, pp. 299-301. Fraser, pp. 238-239. LP, the Earl of Northumberland to Wolsey, July 2nd, 1528. Strickland, vol.1, pp. 217-218). (45) (LP, James V, July 14th, 1528. LP, Magnus to Wolsey, November 14th, 1528. ODNB, vol.16, pp. 620-621). (46) (LP, James V, July 14th, 1528. LP, Magnus to Wolsey, November 14th, 1528). (47) (Fraser, pp. 238-240. LP. Roger Lasselles to the Earl of Northumberland, September 4th, 1528. LP. Roger Lasselles to the Earl of Northumberland, September 10th, 1528. Thomson, vol.2, p.573. SP, vol4, pp. 533-536). (48) (Buchanan, pp. 299-300. Fraser, pp. 239-241. Lesley, pp. 140-142. LP. Roger Lasselles to the Earl of Northumberland, September 4th, 1528. LP, The Parliament of Scotland, September 8th, 1528. LP. Roger Lasselles to the Earl of Northumberland, September 10th, 1528. ODNB, vol.52, p.674.SP, vol.6, pp. 166-168). (49) (LP, Angus to Henry VIII, September 10th, 1528. LP, Northumberland to Wolsey, September 17th, 1528). (50) (Fraser, pp. 243-245. LP, Lassels to the Earl of Northumberland, September 11th, 1528. LP, Angus to Northumberland, October 4th, 1528. LP, Northumberland to Wolsey, October 9th, 1528. LP, Magnus to Wolsey, November 14th, 1528. Thomson, vol.2, pp. 573-574). (51) (Buchanan, pp. 301-302. Fraser, pp. 245-246. LP, Angus to Northumberland, November, 13th, 1528. McGrigor, pp. 32-33. Pitscottie, pp. 331-333. Thomson, vol.2, p.574). (52) (Fraser, pp. 245-246. P, Wolsey to Magnus, October 17th, 1528. LP, Angus to Northumberland, November, 13th, 1528. Pitscottie, pp. 331-333). (53) (LP, Magnus to Wolsey, November 14th, 1528. ODNB, vol.24, pp. 826-827). (54) (LP, Henry, Earl of Northumberland to Wolsey, November 16th, 1528. LP, Magnus to James V, November 18th, 1528. LP, James V to Magnus, November 24th, 1528. LP,

Magnus to the Lords of Scotland, November 24th, 1528). (55) (LP, Magnus to Wolsey, November 30th, 1528. LP, James V to Magnus, December 2nd, 1528. Thomson, vol.2, pp. 574-575). (56) (Pitscottie, pp. 331-334). (57) (Buchanan, pp. 301-302. Fraser, pp. 251-253. ODNB, vol.9, pp. 748-749). (58) (McGrigor, pp. 32-36. Strickland, vol.2, pp. 253-254). (59) (McGrigor, pp. 32-36. Strickland, vol.2, pp. 253-254).

Chapter Eight

THAT THE KING MIGHT HAVE
LIGHT TO SEE: 1528-1541

Angus was supposed to have boasted that by burning villages
outside Edinburgh he would provide James with enough light to
see the coming morning. The Douglases did provide James with
illumination in respect to human nature. The young king had
received a hard education; treated as a commodity, he had been
conspired and fought over since the death of his father at Flodden.
Many nobles and prelates during his minority had shown
themselves to be self-serving. James though would quickly display
a learned brutality when on November 10th, 1528 at Edinburgh, he
produced *Letters of Fire and Sword* for his illegitimate half-brother
John, Earl of Moray, lieutenant of the North, given him permission
to raise an army and suppress the criminality of the northern
distracts. The Act passed is chilling to read as he ordered the 'utter
extermination and destruction' of the criminals and their 'kin, their

assistants and partakers'. He allowed Moray's army to use whatever methods available to execute the criminals, whether 'slaughter, burning, drowning and other ways', and only to spare the lives of priests, women and bairns. Whilst refusing to 'put hands in the blood of women and bairns', James ordered that they should be gathered up, taken to the sea coasts, and taken out of the realm by ships at crown expense. They were to be transported to Zeeland and Norway, their futures to be determined by whatever fate and circumstance awaited them. [1]

James had shown himself a decisive and brave individual when he needed to be, and with the expelling of the Douglases, he would vigorously set out to impose royal law and order on the borders. In June 1529 he presided over Justice Ayres and collected pledges from the strongest families. In the following November he passed to Dumfries, Galloway and Ayrshire, imposing his authority and punishing lawbreakers. These efforts did not altogether stop the reivers, and in 1530 James would be forced to make several expeditions to the borders. During May 1530, instead of having his judgement clouded by the politics and personal arrangements of the border magnates, he had sixteen of them warded for a short time, including Lord Maxwell. In addition fifty lairds were compelled to give pledges to ensure they would uphold justice.

James set out to impose his own authority and executed several notorious criminals. The biggest criminals were the Armstrongs, although they may have claimed that in raiding England they were patriots. Nevertheless Scotland was at peace with England and on July 5th 1530 James summoned Johnnie Armstrong and his company to meet at Caerlanrig. Despite safe conducts James had the Armstrongs arrested and immediately hanged on the nearest trees, along with his companions. Johnnie would protest after being refused mercy that he 'asked grace of a graceless face'. The border ballad 'Johnnie Armstrong' was written by Sir Walter Scott and largely romanticised him as a hero in the style of Robin Hood.

The Warden of the Western Marches, Robert Maxwell,

although warded in Edinburgh, is said to have betrayed Armstrong. Whilst treachery was the mode of capture that James used, he would have learned this from Albany, who in 1516 similarly offered Alexander and William Hume friendship and safe conducts before having his French cohorts arrest them in the Church of St Giles. The difference with the Humes was that they at least went through the semblance of a trial before being executed. [2]

Despite this example of arbitrary border justice, James would attempt to enforce royal authority and establish a structured system of rule and law. In 1532 he established a Court of Justice with one president and 14 senators. Salaries and funding were to be provided by clerical taxation and confirmed by papal bull. The college which was set up to hear civil cases still stands today. He also re-established the office of advocate for the poor, and he appears to have been popular with the populace in general. There is recorded evidence of James issuing letters of protection to poor tenants threatened by eviction from landowners, and of proposals to introduce reductions in teinds and mortuary payments. There is also the famous story of 'the Gudeman of Ballengeich' travelling the country in disguise to learn the opinions and attitudes of the people he ruled over. He also had a reputation for promiscuous behaviour which he supposedly picked up in his early youth during the enforced guardianship of the Douglases.

Blaming the Douglases for such an education would be somewhat unfair as it was well attested, as noted in the opening chapter, that the Scottish aristocratic courts had a reputation for open sexual attitudes. According to Sir David Lindsay in his 'Flyting', James had an interest in crude and lewd couplings. He is said to have had at least seven, or nine, mistresses and fathered a large number of illegitimate children, all of which were provided for one way or the other.

Marriage was an important consideration and James would receive several offers from the continent. Charles V had proposed his widowed sister the Queen of Hungary, but she declined.

Charles next put forward his niece Christiern, daughter of the King of Denmark, who had been ousted by Frederick from his throne. The nation of Norway was offered as her dowry, although this would have meant Scotland having to conquer that vast overseas land whilst contending with Frederick. James decided against this potentially dangerous marriage. Whilst James considered marriage alliances with the Empire, he needed to balance this with an alliance with France, which had been important to Scotland throughout the centuries. He did however send envoys to the Netherlands to negotiate a continuance of a hundred years' commercial treaty in which the Queen of Hungary, the regent of the Netherlands, and Charles V were present. Sir David Lindsay of the Mount was one of the envoys, which would allow him an insight into the cultural fashions and styles of the Imperial Court. [3]

James was also interested in introducing cultural innovations from the Continent, and sponsored projects at Linlithgow Palace, Stirling Castle, Holyrood Palace, Falkland Palace and other buildings where latest Renaissance ideas and styles were employed in designing the courts and outer structures. He also promoted musical and literary works. An accomplished musician, he could play most string instruments, and French, English, Flemish and Italian music would be encouraged and would influence Scottish compositions. Robert Carver, John Fethy, David Peebles and Robert Johnson were court composers during James' reign. Scottish poets like David Lindsay enjoyed royal patronage, and he may have performed a prototype of the satirical play *Ane Satyre of the Thrie Estaitis* at Linlithgow Palace in 1540. The literary stalwarts at court were the likes of the historians Hector Boece, who wrote a Latin History of Scotland, and John Mair who translated Livy's History of Rome into Scots. John Bellenden under royal commission began in 1531 to translate Boece's History into Scots vernacular, a work that was finished in 1533. James obviously saw the value of using history to give a sense of national identity.

James would be an advocate of the chivalric ideal, and enjoyed martial tournaments and jousting; during his marriage trip to France he jousted with the dauphin. James was also given a number of important orders of chivalry such as the Imperial Golden Fleece (1532), the English Garter (1535) and the French St Michael (1536), and in 1537 whilst in France he received the blessed cap and sword of the papacy, denoting him a defender of the church against heretics. This would have been galling for Henry VIII, who had imposed the reformation in England through the 1534 *Act of Supremacy*, and was now deemed a heretic by the Pope. Henry would throughout the years try to entice his nephew away from the Roman Church by pointing out how much wealth he could acquire by dissolving the church and monasteries. James would stay loyal to the church. Although James would toy with marriage proposals and alliances with different nations other than France, he eventually stayed loyal to the alliance with Catholic France, an important mainstay of foreign and domestic policies.

James' cousin Albany would not return to Scotland, although he kept up a correspondence, offering advice and support when possible, a friendship for which the young King would express gratitude. The Duke's main role for France was diplomatic, and between 1530 and 1533 he arduously and successfully negotiated a marriage contract between his niece Catherine de Medici and Henry, Duke of Orleans, the future King of France. He escorted Catherine, the Pope and several cardinals from Italy to France via a fleet of ships that he organised.

Catherine and Henry were married by Pope Clement VII on October 28th 1533. It was an impressive diplomatic coup by Albany, and had displayed his immense political skills, as well as organisational skills, especially by providing transport and escorts for the journey. During the wedding ceremonies at Marseilles Albany's half-brother Philippe de la Chambre was made a cardinal. [4]

The Duke also saw to Scottish interests when he attempted to ensure that the terms of the Treaty of Rouen were fulfilled and that James would be provided with a daughter of the King of

France as his bride. Francis was not keen to provide a royal bride and instead offered Marie de Bourbon, the daughter of the Duke of Vendôme. The contract was signed by Francis and Albany at Cremieu on March 6th 1536, and the confirmation on the 29th. Suffering from an illness, Albany retired to his estates at Chateau Mirefleur soon after the marriage negotiations and died on June 2nd, 1536. He was buried next to his wife at Sainte Chapelle, Château de Vic le-Comte. As already noted James would visit France in 1537 and refuse the match with Marie de Bourbon, instead marrying as his first wife Francis' eldest daughter Madeleine.

During his career as Governor of Scotland Albany had successfully balanced the interests of those of France with those of Scotland. During his first period in Scotland he had ensured that Scotland and England did not go to war, allowing France to concentrate its attention towards Italy and the Empire. He had also brought a measure of stability to Scotland, temporarily ending the factious fighting and displaying a talent for organising armies and putting down dissent. The lessons that Albany would teach James were about the appropriate use of force, an understanding of the rule of law and how financial rewards and bribes were necessary to keep the rebellious in check.

Albany had been successful in administering the factious environment of Scotland through his considered experience of law, war and statecraft on the continent. During his second visit to Scotland he won no victory against the English, yet showed organisational skills in expelling the pro-English faction of Angus and then raising a large enough army to counter English aggression in the borders. His military aim during the 1522 expedition was either to defeat an English army or capture an English city like Carlisle, and thereby divert forces from the continent. His actions were successful in reminding the English government of the dangers of a Scottish-French alliance to English interests on the borders. Similarly, Albany on the third visit sought to capture Wark in 1523 and push a foothold into England. Severe weather and the time of year spoiled this plan, but once again England was made aware of the potential dangers on her northern borders. He also showed diplomatic skills in pursuing Scottish interests whilst on the continent, negotiating the Treaty of Rouen, ensuring royal rights to nominate benefices to the Pope, winning economic concessions for Scots merchants and organising the divorce of Margaret to the Earl of Angus, which helped destroy the latter's credibility as a legal authority over the King.

Albany's enemy Angus on the other hand was a successful magnate in acquiring power yet did not know how to keep it. He alienated many powerful personages with widespread corruption, criminality, murders, and through promoting the interests of his family. Once Angus had eventually been expelled from Scotland, Henry VIII granted him a pension of £100 per year, which would be increased to £1,000 in later years. His brother George would also receive a pension. Their uncle, Archibald of Kilspindie, tried to make peace with James and regain his possessions, but he was refused, and would travel to France, where he would die.

Henry would continue to annoy James through his support of Angus, and James would continue to reject all efforts at reconciliation. James had nothing but hatred for the Douglases, and no more brutal example of this could be shown than the sentence of witchcraft against Angus' sister Lady Glamis, who in 1537 was also accused of attempting to poison James. She and her husband Lord Forbes were burned at the stake. The Earl of Angus and his brother George bided their time until James' death, when they would once again become important players in Scottish politics. [5]

After her son claimed power by his own rights in 1528, Margaret had her dower lands restored to her. With her new husband accepted by King James and elevated to the peerage, she would often use Castle Methven as a residence, along with her apartments in Edinburgh and Stirling. One act by James would anger her, when her possession of Doune was separated from the crown and granted to Lord Methven's brother James. Apart from that disagreement she enjoyed a generally good relationship with her son during the early years of his reign. She still worked for a stronger alliance between Scotland and England.

In 1531 Henry VIII sent Lord William Howard, the son of the Earl of Surrey who won victory at Flodden, to lead an embassy to St Andrews. By all accounts Margaret bore him no ill will for Flodden, and they became friends. The reason for the embassy was for James to marry Princess Mary.

A competition arose between English and Scots with regard to which was better at sports. From a sense of fun, Margaret would bet on the English against her son's champions.

Henry VIII was seeking to divorce Queen Katherine of Aragon, which would make Mary illegitimate with no claim to the crown succession of England. In this event Queen Margaret had hopes that Henry would formally recognise her son as an heir to the crown of England in the event of him not producing male heirs. However her relationship with her brother would continue to be acrimonious and she would never understand his support for her ex-husband Angus. Henry VIII in turn would not acknowledge Lord Methvin, or 'Muffin' as he called him, as an acceptable husband to his royal sister. [6]

With Angus out of Scotland, Queen Margaret set out to claim her dower lands. On June 1532 she travelled to attend a Justice Ayre at Ettrick Forest, leading 60 men-at-arms and 24 foot-runners. At the Castle of Newark, occupied by the Laird of Buccleough, she demanded the keys. They were surrendered to her after some reluctance, which melted when word was sent to the Laird from King James. Lord Methven's brother James was given the task of administrating the lands and revenues of Ettrick Forest with the assistance of 200 men. [7]

Queen Margaret appeared comfortable leading companies of soldiers on the field, and also enjoyed the pursuits of hunting. This sport was often used in diplomacy to introduce important foreign visitors to Scottish life as well as an excuse for drinking and feasting. In 1534 she accompanied James to a hunting holiday in the Highlands to entertain an envoy from the Pope. James had the previous year committed himself to the Holy See. Margaret's friend and ally the Earl of Atholl organised the activities as well as preparing a great palace in the Highlands so that the Queen, King and guests could lose themselves away from urban life for three days and nights. Atholl provided a wide variety of food and drink for the royal party and guests to feast on, and the King and his mother would often throw themselves into leading hunts through the forests and hills. After these excursions the party would return homeward, stopping at various estates to enjoy further hunting and socialising. [8]

Whilst James and his mother entertained papal envoys, his uncle Henry VIII had been excommunicated by the church for divorcing Katherine of Aragon, leading to the establishment of the English Reformation and the end of papal sovereignty. Henry needed better relations with his northern neighbour. He sent his ambassador Lord William Howard to Scotland to report on his 'dearest sister, the Queen-mother of Scotland'. Queen Margaret would respond favourably to Henry's overtures of peace and reconciliation and stated that despite the controversies of the divorce and the English religious settlement, 'brotherly and sisterly love ever to endure', saying 'trust no less in me than in yourself in all and sindry things at our whole power'. It was a declaration of loyalty to her brother, surprisingly forgiving in respect to his years of interference in her affairs. She would follow up by sending loving greetings to her 'sister' Anne Boleyn, Henry's new Queen. [9]

Whilst the clergy of Scotland in secret condemned the marriage of Henry to Anne Boleyn, Queen Margaret would work to bring a concord between the royal houses of Scotland and England. Lord Howard in 1534 was tasked to arrange a conference between James and Henry. York was proposed. There were ideas being floated that in return for James not becoming a focal point for Catholic resistance against the English Reformation, and possibly adopting Reformation himself, there was a possibility that

James would be recognised as heir-apparent, with Princess Mary being asked to step aside in the succession. He would also be granted the Dukedom of York. Queen Margaret obviously supported the prospect of her son becoming King of Scotland, England and Ireland, and she began to act as a spy, in return for English money, to report on conversations she had with her son. In one dialogue James revealed that he was going to send his ambassador south to inform Henry that he would not accept the Reformed religion. James though hinted to his mother that he was aware of her correspondence with Henry her brother, and was reportedly angry. However the York conference did not happen. It was alleged that James received a £3,000 annuity from the church to reject Henry's proposals. [10]

By 1536 the fickle and suspicious Henry would decide to divorce Anne Boleyn, which caused consternation to Lord Howard, who was a close relative. It also hampered further opportunities for Queen Margaret. Her daughter had climbed to a stronger position in the English succession by becoming betrothed to Lord Thomas Howard, half-brother of the ambassador Lord William and uncle to Anne Boleyn. Initially King Henry and Queen Anne had been supportive of the match, but when Henry had Anne Boleyn executed and married Jane Seymour, Lord Thomas was charged with treason by the parliament of June 8th, 1536. The charge was that he intended to marry Lady Margaret Douglas, and in the event that Henry would die without heirs then Thomas would pursue the crown of England through the claim of his wife. Queen Margaret was at Perth in 1536 when she learned that her daughter Lady Margaret Douglas had also been thrown into the Tower of London.

Queen Margaret at the same time had been considering reconciling with Angus if she could win a divorce from Methven, on the grounds that Methven was within four degrees of consanguinity with the Earl of Angus. Methven was also accused of reportedly using up her financial resources to such an extent that she was 8,000 merks in debt. He also had a mistress, Janet

Stewart, who had borne him four children. Margaret's attitude to her husband's mistress is unknown, although it could not have been a secret. James refused her request for a divorce.

Whilst this reconciliation with Angus is viewed as yet another example of Margaret's inconsistency, there was logic at work. This step was to insure against challenges against her daughter's legitimacy in the event that Lord Howard forwarded Margaret's claims to the succession. The Howards were powerful magnates in England. As Queen Margaret had been friends with Lord Thomas' brother William, she would have supported the marriage, and any efforts to strengthen her daughter's place in the English succession.

She considered remarrying the Earl of Angus so as to help the cause of her daughter in the event that Henry died without legal heirs. Whilst there is much circumstantial evidence to accuse the above parties of conspiracy, it should be remembered that Henry had supported the match of Lady Margaret and Lord Howard, and had also long supported reconciliation between his sister and Angus. It appears that Henry was good at creating conspiracies against himself.

The royal impeachment clearly speaks of conspiracy, and Queen Margaret's name is drawn into it: 'and for the more likelihood and vehement suspicion of the same traitorous intent, the Queen of Scots [his sister Margaret Tudor], as it hath lately been hinted and spoken, and come to the King's knowledge, hath coveted to come into this realm, to be restored and reconciled to the Earl Douglas [Angus] her late husband, father to the said Lady Margaret [Douglas], from whom she hath been long divorced by the laws of the Church, minding by the same by all vehement presumption and likelihood to advance the said Lord Thomas Howard and the said Lady Margaret into the favour of this realm, by reason whereof the traitorous intent of the said Lord Thomas might be the sooner brought to pass.'

Queen Margaret wrote to her brother expressing surprise at his inconsistency and in the first few lines outlined the contradiction of Henry supporting the union between Lady Margaret Douglas and Lord Howard, and then turning against Lady Margaret for agreeing to the marriage: 'Please you understand we are informed lately that our daughter, Margaret Douglas, should, by your Grace's advice, promise to marry Lord Thomas Howard; and that your Grace is displeased that she should promise or desire sic [such] thing ; and that your Grace has delivered to punish my said daughter, and your near cousin, to extreme rigor; which we can no way believe, considering that she is our natural daughter, your nepotess, and sister-natural to the King our dearest son, your nephew, who will not belief that your Grace will do sic extremity upon your own, ours, and his, being so tender to all three as our natural daughter is.'

Margaret further requested the release of her daughter and her return to Scotland. Henry would not reply, but due to illness he allowed the Lady Margaret to reside in the more comfortable Sion Abbey. Later in renouncing the marriage and claiming that it was not consummated, Margaret would be allowed back to the Royal Court. Lord Howard would later die of illness in the Tower. [11]

This was another example of the inconsistent behaviour of Henry VIII, which often drove him to despotic acts. It also reveals the often ignored qualities and strengths of Queen Margaret that she continued to work, often in the shadows, for the advancement of her family. The impeachment against Lord Howard and the accusations against Queen Margaret show how seriously the so-called plot was considered by parliament. The stakes were high for the Queen of Scotland; if it had been successful then Margaret would have been mother to two sovereigns. Whatever the historians say about Queen Margaret, they could not fault her ambition.

King James would no longer confide in his mother. She had continued a secret correspondence with her brother, whilst later being part of an alleged conspiracy against him. James possibly decided that he could not allow Queen Margaret access to his councils whilst she followed independent agendas which could undermine his own policies. Even when he travelled to France to wed Princess Madeleine, she was no longer privy to the plans for the journey. The correspondence with her brother is often viewed as a betrayal, yet it could be argued she was using such communications to give her brother an advantage in negotiations for a purpose that would have united Scotland and England in an early union of the royal crowns. (12)

When James married Mary of Guise as his second Queen, Margaret was once more given the respect of a Queen Mother. Possibly recognising similar qualities in the determined Margaret, Queen Mary invited her mother-in-law to court, where she was treated graciously.

Whilst no longer admitted into political councils, Queen Margaret took a great interest in the design and structuring of royal castles and palaces, and she would collaborate with her son in supporting the import of European ideas and innovations to be adopted into Scottish architecture and interior design. The architecture of court was a mix of high Gothic in the Burgundian Netherlands style and Italian classicism. The Holyrood New Tower and the Gateway of Linlithgow Palace and the front tower and south ends of Falkland Palace were influenced by the high Gothic, with distinctive gun-loops, armorials, gilded weather-vanes, crenellations and gargoyles. She made a significant contribution to the architectural structures of Scotland. (13)

She remained a figure at court until her death at Methven Castle on October 18th 1541. According to English sources she asked her confessor to implore James to heal the rift with the Earl of Angus. It was a strange request considering the bitterness, and the only explanation is that Margaret was concerned for the rights of her daughter Lady Margaret Douglas, who was still residing in England. If the forfeitures against Angus were to be reversed, then Lady Margaret would have a claim as heiress to his vast estates in the event that he died without male heirs. James did not reinstate Angus during his lifetime, and he failed to arrive in time to see his mother pass on, yet he did not fulfil the terms of

Margaret's will, which wanted her possessions and valuables to go to her daughter. James decided to claim them for the crown.

Chapter Eight: References

(1) (SHD, pp. 103-105). (2) (ODNB, vol.29, pp. 619-627. Thomson, vol.2, pp. 575-576). (3) (Thomson, vol.2, pp. 576-577). (4) (MacCulloch, pp. 199-201. ODNB, vol.52, pp. 709-715). (5) (Fraser, pp. 252-256). (6) (Strickland, vol.1, pp. 221-223). (7) (Strickland, vol.1, pp. 221-222). (8) (Strickland, vol.1, pp. 216-221. Thomson, vol.2, pp. 578-579). (9) (Strickland, vol.1, pp. 222-225). (10) (ODNB, vol.28, pp. 450-452. Strickland, vol.1, pp. 226-227. Thomson, vol.2, pp. 580-581). (11) (McGrigor, pp. 49-61. Strickland, vol.2, pp. 261-270). (12) (Buchanan, pp. 312-315). (13) (ODNB, vol.29, pp. 619-627. ODNB, vol.24, pp826- 827. ODNB, vol.36, pp. 651-652).

EPILOGUE

Queen Margaret had proved herself a strong-willed fighter during the minority of her son, especially against the considerable odds raged against her. With her main priority being the royal rights of her son, she had been forced to battle or negotiate through dangerous waters where she would often be forced to change political direction in order to survive. Her ultimate ambition was for a meaningful peace between Scotland and England, and a place in the English crown succession for her son James. In this ambition she would also show determination to halt hostilities between Scotland and England. Remembering the slaughter at Flodden, she would use whatever agencies at hand to find a peaceful solution. Sometimes she was successful in her contributions, such as in late 1522 where the French and English give her credit for helping to stop a bloody battle on the borders. And even in late 1523 she played her part by making a proclamation on November 10th calling for an end to hostilities and the start of talks (pp. 119).

Not always able to command an army, she played one power against the other with varying levels of success, whether France and England, or Scottish nobles and prelates. Margaret had no choice but to act in this fashion, being often badly supported by her brother. In 1524 Henry and Wolsey dropped their disguise of diplomatic competence by sabotaging Margaret's successful and clever ousting of Albany in favour of the divisive and dangerous Earl of Angus. Margaret had no choice but to retrace her steps and seek alliance with Albany. In this she was better served, being able to gain a divorce from the Earl of Angus, which gave momentum to her son's campaign to oust his stepfather.

After James took control of government, during the period 1528 to 1534, he still sought the advice of his mother. In respect of foreign policy they had differences. Whilst Margaret looked to her country of birth, James was intrigued by the complicities of international politics and preferred to compete in that political arena.

Queen Margaret's son James V was very much a creature of the minority government of 1513-1528, from whence emerged a king who was a complex character, with many flaws yet much strength. He had been dominated by several contrasting individuals - Queen Margaret, Albany, and Angus - and he learned lessons from each of them. Yet he learned the lessons well and quickly, establishing himself as a strong king with drive and ambition. His uncle Henry sought to establish a relationship with James, not based on mutual respect but on domination, and during the course of James' life there would be sporadic wars on the borders between Scotland and England with no clear winners. In late 1542 a Scottish invasion of England resulted in a decisive defeat at Solway Moss. James had been intending to lead another army, but instead he became ill and retired to Falkland Palace. Although the cause of the illness is uncertain, King James would soon die there.

A few days before James' death a daughter was born at Linlithgow to his wife Mary of Guise, the future Mary, Queen of

Scots. Scotland would be once more tormented by a period of minority government.

Queen Margaret was buried in the Carthusian Monastery of Perth. She left a legacy that would live on in the form of her daughter Margaret Douglas, born in the ruined castle of Harbottle after a dangerous journey through battle-ravaged lands. Lady Margaret Douglas would marry Matthew, Earl of Lennox, and produce the future Henry, Lord Darnley. Henry would marry Mary, Queen of Scots, and daughter of Mary of Guise, who would be the parents of James VI of Scotland. In 1603 James VI would become James I of England and unite the realms of Scotland, England and Ireland under the Union of the Crowns.

BIBLIOGRAPHY

PRIMARY SOURCES

(ALCPA) Acts of the Lords of Council in Public Affairs, Scotland 1501-1554, Hannay, R.K. (ed.) (1932) H.M. General Register House. Edinburgh.

(ALHTS) Accounts of the Lord High Treasurer of Scotland, 13 volumes, Paul, J.B. (ed.) (1904) H.M. General Register House, Edinburgh.

Buchanan, George, The History of Scotland. Aikman, J. (ed.) (1827) Glasgow.

(CP) Calendar of the Cecil Papers in Hatfield House, Vol.1, 1306-1571.

(CSPS) Calendar of State Papers, Spain, volumes 1-13.

(CSPSS) Calendar of State Papers, Spain (Simancas).

(CSPV) Calendar of State Papers relating to English affairs in the Archives of Venice.

(CSPVA) Calendar of State Papers relating to English affairs in the Vatican Archives.

(ER) The Exchequer Rolls of Scotland, M'Neil, G.P. (ed.) (1898) H.M. General Register House, Edinburgh.

(HP) Hamilton Papers, vol.1, vol.2. Bain, J. (ed.) (1890) H.M. General Register House. Edinburgh.

Holinshed, Ralph. Holinshed's Chronicles of England, Scotland and Ireland, Vernon, F. Dnow. (ed.) (1965) New York, AMS.

Lesley, John. Bishop of Ross, The History of Scotland, (1829) The Bannatyne Club. Edinburgh.

(LP) Letters and Papers, Foreign and Domestic, Henry VIII.

Pitscottie, Robert Lindsay of, The History and Chronicles of Scotland, (1814) G Ramsay and Company.

(RPCS) Register of the Privy Council of Scotland, Burton, J.H. (ed.) (1877), H.M. General Register House. Edinburgh.

(RPS) The Records of the Parliaments of Scotland to 1707 (RPS) www.rps.ac.uk/

(RGSS) Register of the Great Seal of Scotland, Thomson, J.M. (ed.) (1814, revised 1912).

(SBSH) The Source Book of Scottish History, Dickinson, W.C. (ed.) & Donaldson, G. (ed.) & Milne, I.A. (ed.) (1958) Thomas Nelson & Sons.

(SHD) Scottish Historical Documents, Donaldson, Prof. G. (ed.) (1974 edition with corrections), Neil Wilson Publishing. Glasgow.

SECONDARY SOURCES

Bellesheim, Alphons, History of the Catholic Church of Scotland, William Blackwood & Sons. Edinburgh & London.

Bindoff, S.T. (1950) Tudor England, Penguin Books, Middlesex.

Bingham, C. (1971) James V, King of Scots, Collins. London.

Buchanan, P. (1985) Margaret Tudor, Queen of Scotland, Scottish Academic Press Ltd.

Byrne, K. (1997) Colkitta, House of Lochar, Argyll.

Calderwood, D. History of the Kirk of Scotland, Rev. Thompson, Thomas. (ed.) Woodrow Society. Edinburgh.

Cameron, J. (1998) James V: The Personal Rule, 1528-1542, Tuckwell Press. East Linton.

David, M. 'Henry VIII's Scottish Policy', in Scottish Historical Review, vol. 61 no. 171 (April 1982).

Donaldson, G. (1965) Scotland: James V to James VIII.

Dowden, J. (1912) Bishops of Scotland, (ed.) Thomson, J.M. James Maclehose & Sons. Glasgow.

Eddington, Alexander. (1926) Castles and Historic Homes of the Border, Oliver and Boyd. Edinburgh.

Fraser, W. (1885) The Douglas Book. Edinburgh.

Gordon, Rev J.F.S. Monasticon, vol.3, Gordon John Tweed, Glasgow.

Grant, A. (1984) Independence and Nationhood: Scotland 1306-1469, Edinburgh.

Gregory, Donald (1881) History of the Western Highlands and Islands of Scotland from A.D. 1493 to A.D. 1625, T.D. Morison Publisher.

Grub, G. (1861) Ecclesiastical History of Scotland. Edinburgh.

Herkless, J. Cardinal Beaton, William Blackwood & Sons. Edinburgh & London.

Herkless, J. & Hannay, R. Kerr. The Archbishops of St Andrews, (1915) William Blackwood & Sons. Edinburgh & London.

Hume-Brown, P. (1911) History of Scotland, Cambridge at the University Press.

Johnson, A.H. (1932) Europe in the Sixteenth Century: 1494-1598, Rivingtons, London.

Luckoch, D.D. The Church in Scotland, Herbert Mortimer, Dean of Lichfield (ed.) (1893) Wells, Gardner, Darton & Co. London.

Mackie, J.D. 'The English Army at Flodden', in Miscellany of The Scottish History Society, vol.8. (1951) Edinburgh.

McCulloch, D. (2003) Reformation: Europe's House Divided 1490-1700, Penguin Books. London.

MacDougall, N. (2001) An Antidote to the English: The Auld Alliance, 1295-1560, Tuckwell Press, East Lothian.

MacDonald-Fraser, G. The Steel Bonnets, (1971) Harper Collins.

MacFarlane, Angus. (2001) Clan MacFarlane, A History, House of Lochar, Argyll.

McGrigor, M. (2015) The Other Tudor Princess, Margaret Douglas, Henry VIII's niece, Stroud, The History Press.

MacLean-Bristol, N. Warriors and Priests: The History of the Clan MacLean, 1300-1570, Tuckwell Press, East Linton.

Maxwell, Sir H. (1902) A History of the House of Douglas, Freemantle.

Merriman, M. (2000), The Rough Wooings: Mary Queen of Scots, 1542-1551. Tuckwell Press, East Linton.

Moffat, A. (2008) The Border Rievers. Birlinn, Edinburgh.

Nicholson, R. (1974) Scotland: The Later Middle Ages.

Paterson, R.C. (1997) My Wound is Deep: A History of the Later Anglo-Scots Wars 1380-1560, John MacDonald Publishers Ltd, Edinburgh.

Reid, David. (ed.) David Hume of Godscroft's History of the House of Angus.

(ODNB) Oxford Dictionary of National Biography (2004) Oxford University Press, Oxford.

Scott, W. (1830) History of Scotland, Longman, Rees, Orme, Brown & Green, London.

Somerset Fry, P. & F. (1982) The History of Scotland, Routledge, London & New York.

Small, J. (1874) The life of Gavin Douglas. Edinburgh.

(SP) Scots Peerage, vols 1-9, (1904) (ed.) Paul. J, B. David Douglas, Edinburgh.

Spottiswood, J. History of the Church of Scotland, (1851) (ed.) Russell, M. & Napier, M. Spottiswood Society.

Stuart, M.W. (1940) The Scot who was a Frenchman: being the life of John Stewart, Duke of Albany, in Scotland, France and Italy, London.

Strickland, A. (1851) Lives of the Queens of Scotland, Harper & Brothers Publishers, New York.

Thomson, Rev T. A History of the Scottish People, vol 3, Blackie & Son, Limited, London, Glasgow, Edinburgh and Dublin.

Tytler, Patrick, Fraser. (1828) History of Scotland, William Tait, Edinburgh.

Williams, R. (1997 edition) The Lord of the Isles, House of Lochar, Argyll.

INDEX

C

D